Death on the Western Frontier

Kansas 1875-1879

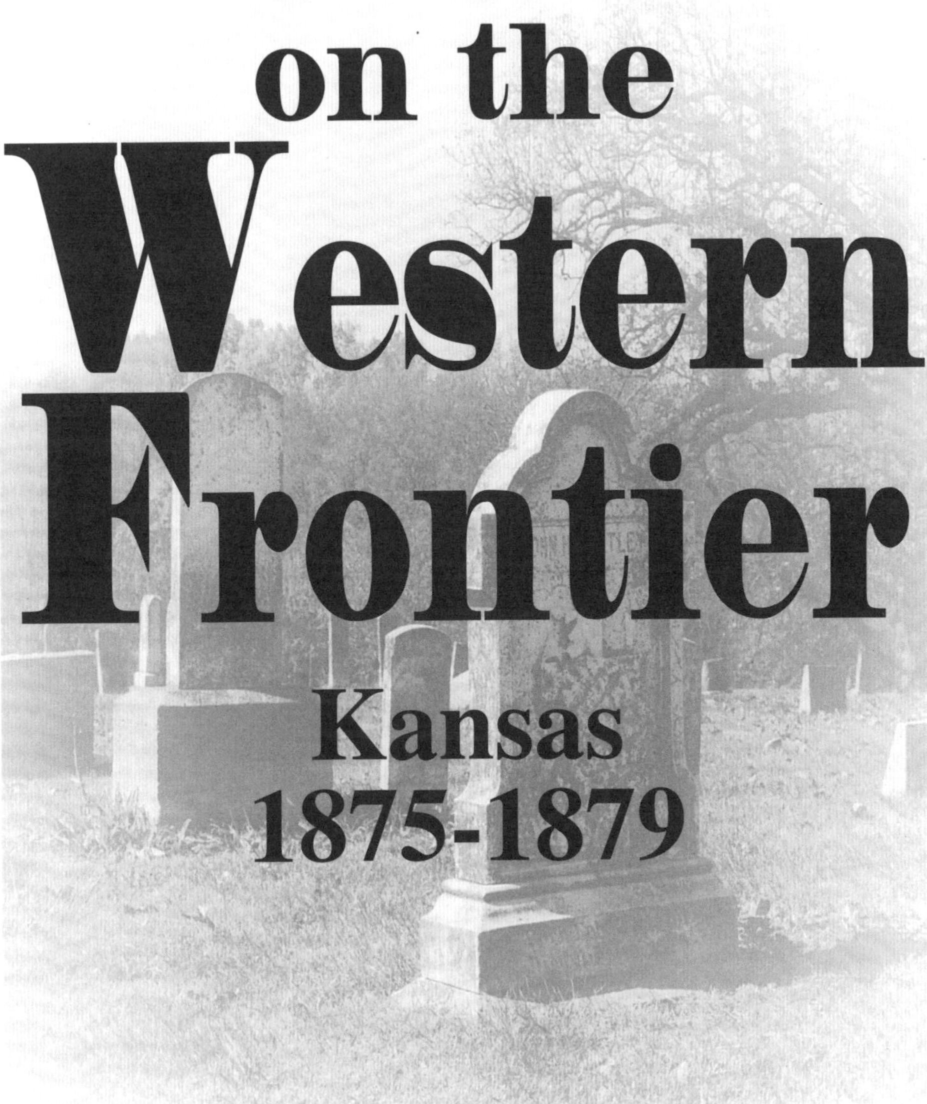

Death on the Western Frontier

Kansas 1875-1879

by **Eugene D. Fleharty**
and **Gary K. Hulett**

Sunflower University Press®
1531 Yuma • P.O. Box 1009 • Manhattan, Kansas 66505-1009 USA

Printed in the United States of America on acid-free paper.

Cover photo by Angela L. Dawdy

Layout by Lori L. Daniel

ISBN 0-89745-244-5

Sunflower University Press is a wholly-owned subsidiary
of the non-profit 501(c)3 Journal of the West, Inc.

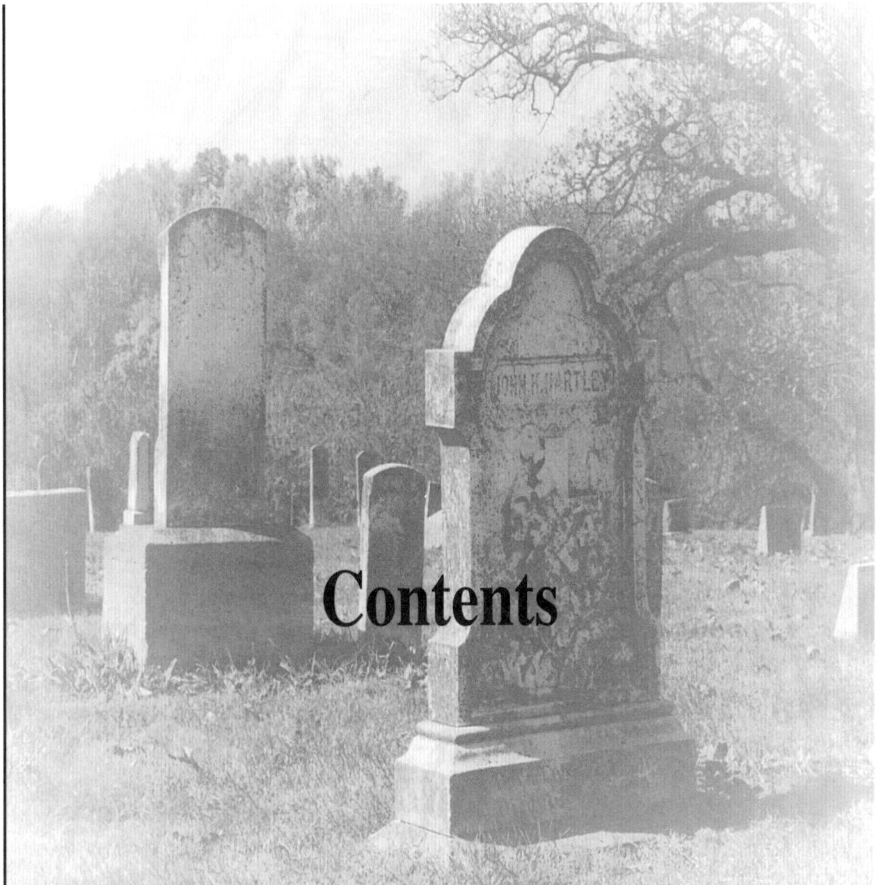

Contents

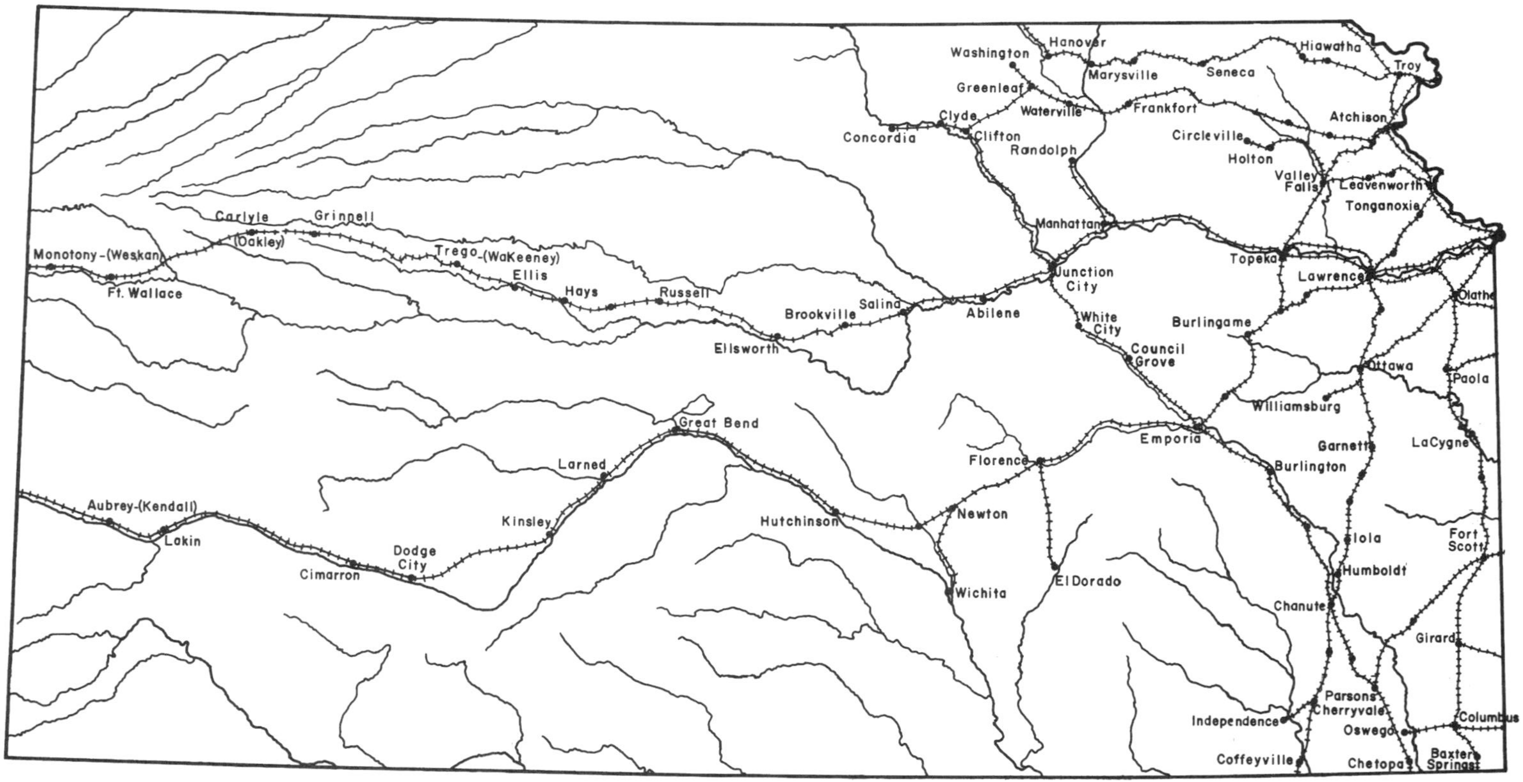

Major Kansas towns and rail lines in 1878. From *Historical Atlas of Kansas*, 2nd ed., by Homer E. Socolofsy and Huber Self (Norman: University of Oklahoma Press, 1972, 1988).

Introduction

DEATH, ESPECIALLY UNEXPECTED OR violent death, evokes a mixed response of emotion and curiosity in most people. We want to know more. We have an interest in mortality, and the fascination is heightened if the death is premature or violent. We avidly read the articles beneath glaring headlines that attempt to explain why some murder their children, lovers kill themselves in a suicide pact, innocent bystanders are gunned down by an unknown assailant in a speeding car, or a defenseless convenience store clerk is shot by robbers — the accounts continue day after day, week after week.

But what of the people who lived in years gone by and now occupy silent graves? Who were these pioneers? What sort of lives did they lead? What caused their deaths?

In 1877, on the bottomland near the Pawnee River west of Larned, Kansas, Mr. Atkinson harbored many of those same questions when he discovered a depression in the ground that resembled an old grave. A *Larned Press* article of May 18, 1877, noted:

> **After digging a couple feet below the surface Mr. Atkinson came across several stones on one of which were found the words, "Washington" and "J. Hildreth" carved, also a line separating them and underneath, the date: "Dec. 10," and "J. M. 1850." On another stone was carved the name of "J. H. Shell" and other characters that could not be deciphered. On a third stone found engraved "H. R., 1847," and underneath there was plainly cut the name of "J. R. Boyd" and still below this the name of "J. R. Pring."**
>
> **At the bottom of the excavation were found a part of the skull; one or two of the ribs and one of the lower bones of the leg of a human being. That part belonging to the skull was very near the center of the grave — for such it evidently was.**
>
> **Who were the parties whose names were handed down on those? Who was the person buried there? Was he one of those whose names have curiously came to light? Was it a person who was crossing the plains with an emigrant train and was stricken down by death, and buried there by his companions? Or, was he a hunter, and in combat with red man, slain?**

In small family plots and in well maintained cemeteries, old tombstones with worn engravings, often barely legible, disclose that many frontier people died in their early 20s or 30s. Why did they die so young? Did some lingering disease strike them down? Were they murdered — perhaps took their own lives? Maybe they were trapped in fires, killed by marauding Indian war parties, bitten by rattlesnakes, or perished in tragic accidents.

The stark, weathered gravestones sometimes cry out for an explanation — a grave of a mother next to a small one for an infant, both with the same date of death. And beside these interments, that of the father who died three days later. What tragedy befell this family?

Or perhaps the family plot — father, mother, and four children — all of whom died years before their parents, but within a week of each other. What calamity killed them? An infectious disease? A natural catastrophe?

The Kansas prairie region was selected for a bird's-eye view because even though rich in resources, it presented a unique, more harsh living environment to the settlers than that to which they were accustomed. This austere, and in many ways, forbidding land taxed the immigrants to their limits.

The period of 1875-1879 was chosen because settlements and homesteads were beginning to dot the prairies of Kansas. And to accommodate the expanding population, two great railroads, the Atchison, Topeka, & Santa Fe, and the Kansas Pacific had been completed across the state. In addition, land was cheap by today's standards, and the U.S. government's Homestead Act of 1862 provided 160 acres free to anyone who would live upon it and improve it. Railroads also had been given government land to sell to immigrants, to help pay for the railway construction.

With these incentives, many settlers came West to secure their fortunes on the open prairies, and by using the abundant resources, they created a new social milieu. It was truly a time of active settlement, where dreams were fulfilled for some but shattered for others, by early and often terrible demises.

Deaths as reported in over 70 archival newspapers published in the small prairie towns of Kansas between 1875 and 1879 have been examined. These "unofficial diaries" provided a rich source of information about the lives — and deaths — of those who emigrated to the American West to settle the Great Plains.

As Craig Miner has stated regarding his work *The Wichita Reader* (1992), newspaper accounts from 1875-1879

> [*offer*] all kinds of writing, fiction and non-fiction, poetry and prose, from all sorts of people, though, understandably and appropriately, there is a lot of journalism in it. The one exception is scholarship: none of the pieces was written originally to be purposefully analytical in an academic way, or to use collected research materials, as contrasted with direct and immediate observation, as a source. Scholarly work . . . is appropriate, . . . but straight contact with the raw materials of our past should not be a privilege limited to an elite. These readings may not provide the careful student . . . with a great deal of new

> information, but . . . should provide flavor and nuance galore. To one who has casually looked at the local past it should be a feast and a revelation, consumable in independent bites at any spare moment.

Newspaper editors during 1875-1879 wrote in a style that imparted the color of those times far more effectively than if we were to retell the stories. And, thus, we have opted to let the newspapers impart those stories of death as it occurred on the Kansas frontier, with three or four that had taken place in adjacent states. In the accounts, an editor would occasionally print a person's name with two or three spellings. We treated the initial spelling as correct. When more than one newspaper carried the same story, we chose the one that was most colorful and provided the greatest detail.

Information regarding an individual's death was found in one or two different locations within the early newspapers. Formal obituaries commonly listed personal statistics, including where the deceased were born, where they lived, who they married, who survived them, who officiated at the funerals, and where the dead were buried — not particularly interesting unless one knew the individual. But if the death was unexpected or, especially, if violent, it was also reported in a more detailed account. In contrast to newspaper reports today, the circumstances surrounding the death or the events that led to, or followed, the death were detailed and frequently contained graphic, vivid descriptions. Contemporary newspapers are more "sanitized" so as to not offend readers.

Some early newspapers had a wide variety of obituary styles. Brief obituaries that provided little detailed information were commonplace.

> **A little son of Mr. John Griffin, of Salt creek, died Tuesday night and was buried Thursday, at the Fairview Cemetery. It was nearly two years old.** — ***Hutchinson News*, December 12, 1878**

Other obituaries presented a more elaborate chronicle of life events and were usually about individuals who had attained some stature within the community — the owner of a local business, a politician, a judge, or frequently a member of the clergy.

If the deceased was a member of a service or fraternal organization, the obituary frequently contained a formal resolution that expressed the feelings of that group. The obituary below was prepared by the Independent Order of Odd Fellows, of which the deceased was a member.

> **. . . A committee was appointed to draft resolutions expressive of the feelings of members upon the death of their bereaved Brother. The committee reported the following which was unanimously adopted.**
>
> **Whereas, It has pleased an all wise Providence, in his wisdom to take from us one of o[*u*]r number — one who was respected and beloved by us all — teaching us that man's life is short and full of sorrow, and that we know not at what hour the hand that gave shall take away; and**
>
> **Whereas, It is but just that a fitting recognition of his many virtues should be had; Therefore, Be it Resolved by Corona Lodge No. 137, I. O. O. F. First, That while we deeply feel the loss of our brother we bow in humble submission to our loss, and do mourn for him who has been so early, and while yet in the prime of life, taken from us.**
>
> **Second, That in the death of Brother Wolfe this Lodge has lost a valuable member, society a good citizen, his family a kind husband, companion and protector.**
>
> **Third, That our heartfelt sympathy be extended to his family in their affliction, sorrow and bereavement.**
>
> **Fourth, That, in further respect for the deceased, the members of this Lodge will wear the usual badge of mourning for the space of thirty days, and that our charter and implements be draped in mourning.**
>
> **Fifth, That a copy of these resolulions [*sic*] and preamble, under the seal of the Lodge, be sent to the family of the deceased, snd [*sic*] published in the Ford County GLOBE and Dodge City Times.** **— *Ford County Globe*, July 22, 1879**

Such elaborate obituaries were far less common than the brief reports and often were not published gratuitously (Eakle and Cerney, 1984), which might explain the fewer number published. Paid obituaries may have been more prevalent in the larger, metropolitan newspapers than in the four-page weekly papers, which were so common in the frontier villages. In larger cities, the chances of the deceased being known by large numbers of people would have been relatively small, whereas in the early settlements, individuals were widely acquainted with most of the readership. Consequently, the accounts in small-town weeklies were often personal and emotional.

DIED: At his residence in New Cambria, Saline County, Kansas, Nov. 18, 1878, Jacob Donmeyer. The deceased was born in Cambria County Pennsylvania, Sept. 27, 1830, and has been a resident of this county nearly 7 years. His age was forty-eight years one month and twenty-one days. His mother, one brother and two sisters preceded him to the grave. His aged father, four brothers and five sisters are still living. He leaves a wife, seven sons and three daughters, a son-in-law and one grand-daughter, besides many friends and acquaintances to mourn his loss. At the age of 21 he united with the Lutheran church, and remained an active member until death, at which time he was an office bearer in the New Cambria congregation. May his mantle fall on a worthy successor, and by his unexpected removal may we be admonished to prepare for death, judgment, and eternity. The funeral was the largest ever witnessed in this part of the county. The sermon was preached by Rev. Kirtland, the present pastor of the Lutheran church at this place, from a text selected from the 7th verse, of the 12th chapter of 1st Samuel: "Now therefore stand still, that I may reason with you before the Lord." His bereaved widow and family have the sympathy of the whole community.

"Let storms of woe in whirlwinds rise,
Each cord on earth to sever.
There — bright and joyous in the skies —
There is our home forever."

— *Saline County Journal*, November 28, 1878

Obituaries were commonly closed with a brief poem. Less frequently, poems that memorialized the death of a loved one were more elaborate.

Dear Sister! O, can it be,
That tiny loved face no more we'll see
On this side of eternity!

That God has called thee home in love,
To join thy little ones above.
In the long unbroken chain,
So rudely snapped in twain;
We did not, could not think,
Ever there be a missing link;
Yet if it is God's will divine,
We will not murmur or repine.
Our cup is filled with grief and pain,
Yet we would not call thee back again;
For well we know God's will is best,
And thou hast found sweet quiet rest.
Thy few short years of life, while here,
Was frought with many a bitter tear;
Of was thy heart in sorrow bowed
O'er thy loved babe's return to God.
And as reason left its throne,
Bitterly did their loss bemoan,
Calling in accents deep and wild,
For thy "beautiful baby child!"
Me thinks these little angels bright,
In shining garments pure and white,
Hovered o'er thee as thy spirit took its flight
To the realms of endless light;
Singing sweet songs of joyous love,
While wafting thee to thy home above.
Be still ! O throbbing heart!
Tis' but for a little while we part;
These few short days will soon be o'er
Then may we meet on that bright shore,
Where tears and partings are no more.

G. A. C.

— *Saline Valley Register*, September 18, 1878

Many deaths were likely not reported at all, or if so, it was a week or two after the fact. No rapid means of communication was available between the settler who lived miles from the nearest towns and the newspaper office. Information was passed almost exclusively by word of mouth or perhaps by a hand-written note to be delivered to the editor when opportunity permitted.

And such communications received from outlying townships were not always accurate, especially when local editors had to rely on verbal reports, often second or third hand. In a few cases, this unreliable and unconfirmed information resulted in the printing of premature obituaries.

A "Dead" Man Sends His Respects.

To the Editor of the Gazette:

Having read my own obituary notice, as kindly published in your lively little paper, and after having mourned my own death for the customary length of time, I now beg leave to inform you that I am again able to tramp the broad prairies of Kansas, and I ask you to inform the public in general of that fact. Wishing the people in general may not lose any sleep over this important fact, I am very respectfully, TEXAS FRANK.

— *Rice County Gazette*, September 11, 1879

The inability of the editor to corroborate facts also permitted an occasional prank to be perpetrated on the local editor.

Died.

At the residence of T.H. Jackson, North Main street, Hutchinson, Kansas, December 9th, at 6 o'clock p.m., Bessie Turner Jackson. Funeral ervicies [*sic*] took place at 10 o'clock Tuesday morning, December 10th.

During Bessie's sickness she clearly exhibited all the traits of a cristain [*sic*] and passed away after a short illness without a murmur. In recording the depth of this interesting and promising lady, we are peculiarly impressed with the solemn truth that neither worth nor merit can avail against the insatiate demands of death. When death calls, neither our fondest hopes or friendship['s] dearest ties can interpose with skill to stay his uplifted arm and arrest the lovely victim from the grave. By this dispensation of Providence an interesting lady is cut down in the morn of life, and numerous friends are called to weep over the last

remains of her whose memory will be retained to future years solemn and mournful to the soul.

The above was thought to be the expression of a parent's grief and the death of a daughter. When we learn that it was only a dog that had died, our pity is changed to contempt for the author. All who read it, of course thought it the last tribute that over burdened and grief stricken parents play to a lovely child, shrouded for the grave. When people, in whose bosoms the tenderest sympathies were aroused, have gone to condole [*sic*] with Jacksom [*sic*] the playful creature has led them to the carcass of a dead pup. There is something in this so unkind, so cruel, and so withering to every human instinct that it could only be characterized properly by the bitterest Fort Dodge profanity. Perhaps no one to whom the joke is revealed will tell him what they feel. He will have no means of seeing himself as others see him. At the expense (to use the language of Lord somebody) he has written, himself, to outrage a community.

— *Hutchinson Herald*, December 28, 1878

But regardless of the stories' sources, the age of the victims, or the causes of their departure from this world, tales of death ultimately create speculation and reflection on life. The editor of the *Ellis County Star* wrote on the life and death of people buried at a "Boot Hill" cemetery. The occupants of Boot Hill graveyards were primarily individuals who had met a violent death, often a result of gunshot, and buried with their boots on.

On the northern limits of our city rises a prairie mound, and capping it's [*sic*] summit may be seen a few stone and wooden crosses, marking the last resting place of a class of men, now fast disappearing, before civilization, law and order.

The eminence refered [*sic*] to, is pointed out to a stranger, as a relic of the ancient, *regime* of Hays, and bears the euphonious and characteristic title of "Boot Hill." On the eminence and it's [*sic*] slopes, lie thirty seven victims of the pistol and the knife — men whose lives were full of wild adventure, whose delight and animus were to carry terrorism in their presence and spread it on their approach and who, like all such desparadoes [*sic*], at last

died, to use a border phrase, "With their Boots on." In other words, their summons to Eternity came to them as unexpected and sudden as lightning's flash — came, perhaps, as they had meted death to others, and without mercy or shrift hurled them suddenly into the "vale of shadows."

"Boot Hill" encompasseth these victims of a mistaken life as a mother enfolds her little ones, hiding as it were, from curious eyes in sorrow, the offspring that disgraced the fullness of her love. It is, but earth recreated, and the God of Nature may not register their lives a wreck — existence, a loss? "Boot Hill" has it's [*sic*] victims; may it not too, have its romance.

There, side by side, quietly sleeping the last long sleep, that knows no waking but in eternity lie these victims of a wild career. For all, they were men — not cowards; they are not ALL "bad," and there was something in the very quality of the daring courage that led them into the wild revelry, where life for life, was game — that under other circumstances, would have led them into scenes where as leaders of a storming party or a forlorn hope, laurel wreaths would have been their tribute. As it is, they lie unhonored and unsung.

No, they were not *Always* bad.

Who knows of their childhood, and from what tender influencs [*sic*] they may have strayed? Who of us all, dare question the innocence of their childhood? Mothers' have watched over their baby-foot-steps, joyed in their joy and grieved with their grief. Mothers' may have, in the long ago, parted from them, and in prayer and tears sent them forth into the world's tempest of temptation, pure in thought, pure in purpose, holding high and noble aspirations, alas! only to fall. No mother's tears have fallen o'er their last resting place, but the great mother of all has gathered them to herself — and Earth hides from sight her erring children.

There is one more, a little child, sleeping on "Boot Hill," a victim, to the lawless society in which it existed. Innocent of any crime and fleeing from safety from a drunken street brawl — the little one had but scarce crossed the thresh-hold of the building on the corner of Main & Ft streets, ere it fell; shot through the brain, by a stray bullet from a pistol in the hands of one of

the "roughs" fighting on the street. We give it as one, and the most pittiful [*sic*], of the hundred bloody scenes that marked the early history of this locality in which some of the most noted desparadoes [*sic*] of the Western border engaged.

But all this is past and gone, and like the thirty seven and the little one who lies beside them, they and their deeds live only in memory. **— *Ellis County Star*, March 22, 1877**

Frontier deaths — all causes, other than disease — were categorized, in 1866 in William Aitken's *The Science and Practice of Medicine*, as "lesions." Aitken's *Lesions from Violence tending to Sudden Death* (p. 190), included "lesions [*that*] are the evident and direct results of physical or chemical forces, acting either by the will of the sufferer, of other persons, or accidentally."

We have, subsequently, divided this category into five classes:

- death as a result of a natural phenomenon — fire, freezing, drowning, weather phenomena, encounters with dangerous animals, and so forth (Chapter 2);
- accidental deaths that might involve another person or an inanimate object such as a firearm (Chapter 3);
- deaths as a result of homicide — first and second degree murder, self-defense, infanticide, and child abuse (Chapter 4);
- deaths as a result of white-Indian conflict (Chapter 5);
- and deaths from one's own hand (Chapter 6).

The final chapter is devoted to the funerals that were conducted on the frontier and early cemeteries.

From a thorough reading of those unofficial prairie-frontier diaries, we have discovered that the causes of death on the Great Plains from 1875 to 1879 parallel those of modern America. The degree to which the causes of death have remained unchanged over 100 years is truly remarkable!

Chapter 1

The Good Die Young

THE QUESTION "How long could a person be expected to live?" was asked in frontier times, just as it is today. The table in the following article, from 1879, presented life expectancies for the settlers on the Great Plains.

It is not every one who asks himself this question, because, strangely enough, it is the belief of most persons that their lives will be exceptionally lengthy. However, life assurance companies are aware of the credulous weakness of those whose lives they assure, have therefore, complied [*sic*] numerous tables of expectancy of life for their own guidance, which are carefully referred to before a policy is granted.

The following is one of those well authenticated tables in use among assurance companies, showing the average length of life at various ages. In the first column we have the present ages of persons of average health, and in the

second column we are enabled to peep, as it were, behind the scenes of an assurance office and gather from their table the number of years they will give us to live. This table has been the result of careful calculation, and seldom proves misleading. Of course sudden and premature deaths, as well as lives unusually extended, occasionally occur, but this is a table of the average expectancy of life of an ordinary man or woman:

Age.	Years to live.	Age.	Years to live.
1	80	50	21
10	51	60	14
20	41	70	9
30	34	80	4
40	28		

Our readers will easily gather from the above tabulated statement the number of years to which their lives, according to the law of averages, may reasonably be expected to extend.

— *Ellsworth Reporter*, October 30, 1879.

State documents declare that "no legal provisions for the reporting of deaths, other than a few isolated cases of city ordinances, existed in Kansas prior to 1885" (*Guide to Public Vital Statistic Records in Kansas*, 1942, p. 137). However, based on the obituaries studied, disease was probably the most common cause of death.

In newspaper reports of death by illness, however, usually no elaboration was offered and the specific disease was not always reported. Either the editors were not informed, had a policy of not printing the causes, or possibly the attending physician, if there was one, could not diagnose the disease. Instead, newspaper accounts used phrases noting someone died after a "long and tedious illness," or "suffered with great patience for nearly a year," or "after a short illness." Approximately one-third of the examined newspaper accounts of death failed to list any cause. And when determinations were given, they were frequently in general terms (*e.g.*, "died of a fever"). In addition, many different names were used for the same disease — *cholera-infantum*, also called "summer complaint."

The following diseases that resulted in death were found in various obituaries. The most common were consumption, sometimes called "quick consumption" or "scrofulas consumption," diphtheria or putrid sore throat, typhoid fever, membranous croup, pneumonia, heart disease, scarlet fever or scarletina, and dropsy or general dropsy, cancer, chicken pox, spinal meningitis — sometimes referred to as "cerebro-spinal meningitis" or "cerebro-spinal fever." Less commonly mentioned were prolapsis of the brain, quinsy and rush of hot blood to the heart, congestion of the lungs, inflammation of the bowels (appendicitis), affection of the stomach, erysipelas, rush of blood to the brain, congestion of the brain, measles, convulsions, hemorrhage of the lungs, and white-swelling and bronchitis.

Communicable diseases sometimes reached epidemic proportions, resulting in many deaths within a brief period of time. Diseases probably were responsible for most of the deaths to children on the Kansas frontier and notations to that effect were common.

Sixteen children have died here during the past month, with diptheria [*sic*]. **— *Saline Valley Register*, September 4, 1878.**

On the frontier it was not unusual for a family to suffer the death of more than one child due to scarlet fever or diphtheria.

Since the last issue of the TRIBUNE, we have been called upon to mourn the loss of our youngest child, George Leopold, an infant five months and twenty days old. This is the fourth time that the swift winged messenger of death has crossed the threshold, and snatched one of our darling little ones from the family circle. Bitter as are the pangs of grief at parting with these little treasures, without whose gentle influences life would be a dreary waste, yet, we strive to bear these afflictions with patience, trusting in the dispensations of an all wise Providence.

— *Inland Tribune*, August 11, 1877.

The loss of a child often inspired the most heartfelt obituaries.

Many of the little ones have died in Larned and vicinity recently, and those who have never lost a child are unable to

understand how great a void the death of one darling baby can make. There is, we think, nothing on earth that can cast so long and so black a shadow as a small coffin. It is emphatically the shade of death that freezes a parent's heart. Small as is an infant's tomb, it is sometimes capacious enough to hold the brightest and dearest joys of a whole family circle. The little child is often the brightest focus where all the rays of gladness in the household center, and from which they are again reflected over happy hearts- and when this central light is eclipsed, great darkness falls over all. How many of these must be in Heaven gathered up from all climes, even from heathen shores, who have died so young as to retain no memory of earth, and to whom the world of glory seems as their native land; whose souls were washed and regenerated so early that no stain of this world was ever visible there. Whatever wound of sin there may have been, healed without a scar; there every thought has been moulded by the scenery and society of heaven, and they stand continually before the Father. In how large a sense may we say "of such is the kingdom of Heaven!" Truly the little hillocks in our prairie cemeteries represent an angel above! **— *Chronoscope*, January 1, 1879.**

Within the past week many of the little children of this city have narrowly escaped the dark valley of death, while several have passed from the sorrows of earth to gain the bright land of angels. It is painful to parents to have their bright little babes so suddenly snatched from their family circles. The joys of this life would count but little pleasure, were it not for the innocent prattle of these precious little ones, who seem to have been sent into the world to smooth the rugged walks of life, soften our harder natures, inspire us with bright hopes for the future, and teach us lessons of love, purity and goodness. It is hard for parents to yield up their little treasures into death's cold and icy embrace, and the strong man becomes a weak child when called upon to submit to this sad affliction. The mother, whose very being seems entwined within and around these little pledges of love and affection, is often unable to bear up under the severe

ordeal, and her grief at parting with the jewel of her soul, is indeed the most intense that she finds in this fleeting life. But after all, we are taught to bow to the will of Him who gave us being, who gives us what of pleasure this life affords, and to realize that these afflictions are intended for our special benefit, which suggest themselves in a thousands ways to our consciences, when once we are called upon to suffer this loss.

The families who have been called in the last few days to look for the last time on the faces of their little treasures, as they lay with folded hands and placid brow, will realize that the little ones have been saved from many trials of a life beset with cares and troubles, and taken to Him who remembered "little children" when he trod the thorny paths of life.

Our citizens deeply sympathise [*sic*] with these bereaved parents, in their trying hours of affliction, and we all trust that our city may be spared any further visitations from death's cold hand. **— *Inland Tribune*, July 14, 1877.**

Some parents felt moved to eulogize their own beloved child, sharing and perhaps ameliorating their grief.

TURPEN — On July 17th, 1877, Thomas Victor, infant son of Mattie H. and William J. Turpen. Aged, two years and five months.

"Seest thou that dead child." — {Shakespeare}

It is not until those little ones we have held on a parent's knee and taught to lisp Papa — whose innocent prattle was to our ear the sweetest music, are wrenched from us that we realize how priceless were heaven's gifts. The room in which I write is pervaded by the awful solitude of death. That cold clay which but yesterday sparkled with baby life, was dearer to me than words can tell, and only he who has felt the rapturous emotions of early fatherhood ever can know. My fair-haired, bright-eyed boy! I was so proud of him; what father is not acquainted with the ecstacy of such affection. Often have I blushed for my weakness that I could so ill conceal what every parent must feel. A mother in the delirium of anguish, a sister whose sorrow cannot all find expression in tears, and father whose heart is sorely bruised,

completes this stricken family. But we would rather remember, even with such grief, this withered flower than to forget that it ever bloomed. We dreamed no day-dream where he was not, we built no air castle with which this cherub boy was not associated. He glided like a wavelet of sunshine into all our bright anticipations. To us, he was as a dewy mist gathered from a meadow of flowers and woven into a rainbow of promise. But remorseless death has struck him with its wing. He will awake no more with us, but in the glorious summer land of eternity. Angel Victor! Thank heaven for the thought, that, what we can but regard as our irreparable loss, is his gain; that when the purple was gathering about his mouth; when the dew of death was settling upon his infant brow, his Day was breaking in the east and his Morning was being born upon the mountains. But the hues of paradise caught in no picture fancy can paint, consoles this mother, this sister and this father, over the loss of what to them was more than a jewel of devotion. Sainted friends, receive him:

Through our tears human nature seems to partake less of earth and more of heaven. Those friends and neighbors who come at this hour to solace us with the balm of sympathy will be remembered with gratitude until these hearts cease to beat forever. **W.J.T. — *Hutchinson Herald*, July 21, 1877.**

Children were, of course, not the only victims of disease. Many children were orphaned by the death of both parents.

Very sad indeed is the death of Isaac G. and Elizabeth Johnson, who died in this city last Thursday evening of typhoid fever — their deaths occurring one hour and twenty minutes apart. The family came to Salina a few weeks ago and the father soon found employment and they were quite contented in their new home. About the 15th the father and mother were taken with typhoid fever. Neighbors attended them during their sickness and did everything that could be done to comfort them during their sickness. Three little orphans are left without relative to care for them, and without friends to supply their wants. It is to be hoped their lot may fall among kind hearted ones.

— *Saline County Journal*, August 29, 1878.

Many of the diseases that resulted in premature death in the late 19th century are now better understood and result in relatively low mortality. Few in the United States die from cholera, diphtheria, scarlet fever, chicken pox, measles, or appendicitis. And although conditions such as pneumonia and tuberculosis remain problematic, they do not kill as many young people today. Deaths from stroke and liver failure have not been entirely overcome by modern medicine, however. And still other ailments of 1875-1879, such as cancers and heart diseases, remain as the primary causes of death today.

Sharing their sorrows and their joys, neighbors on the frontier frequently became close friends amidst their difficult life. When death claimed a friend, it could be especially troublesome, and in this following instance caused a neighbor to eloquently reflect on his friend's life and the emptiness and sorrow that remained.

I sit alone in the homestead of the Cole family, over whose threshold the father of the household has just passed for the last time; for the Angel of Death entered this dwelling last night, closing the weary journey and opening the gate of eternal life and rest. For long and weary years the frail body has been racked with pain, till moan after moan escaped the white lips, but not a murmur or complaint, only songs of praise and thanksgiving to the Loving Father, "who afflicts not willingly nor grieves the children of men." And now he is gone. We shall see his loved form no more on earth. His voice, whose tones were so precious to those he loved, is hushed forever on earth, and they will miss him. The faithful wife who for many years has shared with him life's brightest joys and deepest sorrows, will feel for lonely days as if the shadows were left to her to bear alone, And yet I should not say just that for in the devotion and love of her noble, manly sons and precious daughters. She has a comfort that relieves this afflictions of much of its gloom and gives her strong arms, and loving hearts on which to lean in her lonely widowhood. The children are fatherless, 'tis hard to say or think that in all this broad earth we have no father. How hard, only those who have lost a father know. And in this home where every tree and every

improvement, every effort towards comfort is associated with him at the expense of ceaseless toil and self denying effort many will be the heartaches at the thought that he is not here to enjoy the fruit of his labors. But he is not. Thank God he is now enjoying the rest that remaineth. Yes, even now, while those who loved him, kind neighbors and interested friends, are laying his emaciated form in its last resting place, to await the resurrection morning, his voice is raised in glad songs of triumph to the "Lamb who was slain," who hath redeemed us by His blood. For he said, "My trust is in Jesus," and with him we know in whom he believed, and that HE is able to keep that which is committed to His care until that great day.

With much sympathy,

Your Friend.

— *Ellsworth Reporter*, May 8, 1879.

But not everyone who died on the frontier was well known to the local community. Immigrants continually passed through the villages on the prairie en route to more distant locales. In some cases, they traveled in groups that knew one another before moving Westward, but frequently, single families passed through who were hardly noticed by the resident settlers. And when difficulties arose that were beyond the capabilities of the individual families to solve, they had to seek help from the residents. Sometimes they encountered settlers who were willing to assist, but unfortunately at other times some would not.

An Emigrant family on their way from Iowa to Great Bend Kans, stopped here last Friday having a very sick infant whose mother had recently died, the father asked one of our business men for permissiom [*sic*] to occupy an empty house for two or three days that the little one might have better care than they could give it in their wagon. The noble man said they could have the house by paying a months rent in advance, the man was too poor to do this, the little one died Monday morning on the prairie. Two of our young ladies dressed the little one very prettily. Chancy Taft made it a neat little Coffin; a few of us gatherful [*sic*] with the family in the school house and sang a sweet Hymn or two, and Rev. Wright offered the mourners consolation

from the Bible, and in fervant [*sic*] prayer, and then the little group went up to our hillside burying ground and laid the little one away. — ***Ellsworth Reporter*, August 15, 1878.**

Many people traveled to (and through) the Great Plains in search of a climate that might alleviate some debilitating illness. This was particularly true of consumption (tuberculosis). Occasionally, these people died before a more benevolent climate was found.

George Westerfield, a young man, aged 26 years, an invalid, on his way to the Pacific coast for his health arrived here from Greenwood county, in this state, on the 13th, and stopped with S.E. Dwyre, near this place, for a few days to gather strength. While he was here he was taken worse and after a few days of suffering died, crossing the "cold river" on the 23rd, as the day began to dawn.

Mr.Westerfield had been an invalid for four years and was persueing [*sic*] the phantom of life, after the elixir of health, hope, like an ignis fatuus, constantly luring him on, but the bands of death were continually tightening, until at las[*t*] the hereafter claimed him as its own and he departed for the everlasting shores, with the realizing hope that there is a better land where mortals put on immortality and when death is swollowed [*sic*] up in victory. — ***Larned Press*, August 31, 1877.**

Although many pioneers died prematurely, a few fortunate individuals were able to withstand the vicissitudes of the open prairie and died of old age.

Mr. Benajah Martin, near Offerle, is in good health, though past ninety-nine years of age, and praises this country as being the finest and healthiest in which he has ever yet lived. After a few years' stay, however, he may conclude to move farther, and grow up with the country, for this will hardly give the young man a chance. But let us hear some of his reasons for liking this upper Valley best. The climate, with its bracing breezes and rare atmosphere, makes him feel almost like a boy again, and it is with great difficulty that his son-in law, McCreary, keeps him from taking

a claim and going to house-keeping or "baching" as other[*s*] do. The rains fall so seldom, and the winters are so mild and suited to stock raising, that he wishes most of all to have a herd of cattle to graze and corral along the streams south of the river, winter and summer, without feed, except the grass and the hay, sun dried as it stands on the plains. He likes the roads and trails, solid as turnpikes the whole year round, and slippery only for a few hours after the heaviest rains. He likes above all the intelligence and thrift, the morality and religous character of a large proportion of those coming in and making homes around him. It gives promise of a grand future to all this beautiful country, stretching for a hundred miles every way.

[Since the above interview, Mr. Martin died and was buried at Offerle a week ago last Friday. — Ed.]

— *Kinsley Graphic*, December 28, 1878.

Chapter 2

An Unforgiving Environment

FROM TIME IMMEMORIAL HEAT, winds, lightning, flood, fire, blizzards, earthquakes, and animal attacks have threatened lives — every geographic region and era has a distinctive array of natural phenomena that have claimed a toll on life and property. This was certainly true in pioneer times on the Great Plains, where an often uncharitable and unforgiving environment was coupled with the arrival of new inhabitants who were unacquainted with the climate. Thus the stage was set for a drama that often included danger and death.

The Weather

Cold

Although no accounts of blizzards were found during the period examined, one sorrowful story was discovered of an itinerant freezing to death in an early March storm.

A tramp was buried in Ellis or in the Ellis cemetery, if you will, last Monday. The poor fellow (a man of about thirty-five years of age) was going west, and had reached a point about eight miles this side of Buffalo [*Park, KS*], Saturday night, where he laid him down to sleep, by the side of the railroad track, and never woke. He froze to death. The body was prepared for burial and buried at the expense of the Kansas Pacific. Nothing was found upon his person denoting from whence he came, or where he was going, or who he was; and probably, it will never be known.

— *Hays City Sentinel*, March 9, 1877.

Heat

One of the most distinctive features of life on the Great Plains is the intense summer heat. Hot, dry, and windy days are common on the prairie during June, July, and August and are a perilous threat to people who are exposed out-of-doors. Sunstroke and heat exhaustion are life-threatening medical problems that can occur on such days, particularly if no water is available to cool a feverish body. Although deaths from such dreadful heat undoubtably occurred on the frontier, only three incidents were found between 1875 and 1879. The following report epitomizes the merciless temperature of the summer weather on the Colorado plains.

A party of 16 surveyors in the employ of the Government, under command of Maj. Medary, left this city a short time ago . . . for a tour eastward to the Indian Territory line.

After leaving Trinidad the company proceeded eastward, and were soon at work locating townships. On the morning of Thursday, the 5th inst. [*present month*], a squad of five men was sent out from a point on Willow Creek to run a transit due north 18 miles, with orders to join the camp at nightfall. The men performed the work assigned them and at dusk set out for camp, which had also been traveling northward during the day. The surveyors started east from their objective point and after walking six miles, made camp. In going in this direction they made a great mistake; for they should have gone due west after finishing their work in order to find the camp wagons. Comprehending their mistake, and being very thirsty and out of provisions, it was proposed to travel south in hopes of striking a creek. Two of the

party refused to do this, preferring to remain where they were, hoping that the camping outfit would come up to them in a few hours. Friday morning the three, headed by Mr. Sheets, started for Cariso Springs. They lost their way, and would have perished but for the timely arrival on Monday of men from the camp, who were in search of them.

The search for the other two (whose names were S. M. Winchester and William Johnson) was continued with an interest bordering on frenzy. Not until Monday, the 9th, did the searchers get any clew [*sic*] of the missing men. About 2 o'clock p.m. on that day they came upon poor Winchester out upon the open plains; but he was too far gone to be saved. A few drops of water were given him, but in five minutes he was a corpse, dying in the arms of a companion, who had arrived too late.

Further search was made for Johnson. A large rock, which towered up grandly on the boundless plain, was visited and there, in a crevice, was found a note from Winchester, dated the 7th, saying that Johnson and he were lost, but had made up their minds to go south in the hope of striking the Willow. The note was written in a firm hand and showed that the writer was in his right mind. The diligent searchers started south, and after traveling six miles were rewarded by finding a canteen belonging to Johnson. For three days more they scoured the prairie on horseback in every direction, and on Thursday, the 12th, gave up the search, unsuccessful in finding the unfortunate man. The coyote has probably found him, and ere this has devoured all that remained of a once bright and promising young man. Winchester was taken up to camp and buried beside a spring of cool water and his grave marked. — ***Garden City Paper*, July 10, 1879.**

Tornadoes

A common saying in Kansas is "if you don't like the weather wait a few minutes, it'll change!" This popular adage reflects the fact that Kansas and the entire Great Plains is infamous for rapid and turbulent weather reversals, a tendency that is common in a region where warm moist air from the Gulf of Mexico collides with cold air from the Arctic. These air-mass clashes frequently produce a churning weather front that sweeps across the flatlands, causing intense precipitation, high winds, and, unfortunately, property damage and loss of life. On hot, sultry summer days, thunderstorms with torrential rain, lightning, hail, and winds are common.

One of the most deadly aspects of severe thunderstorms is the tornado, which can leave a path of death and destruction for miles across the prairie. Such occurrences were often referred to as "hurricanes," though today this term is reserved for serious tropical storms.

Yesterday morning the weather was cool and the sky cloudy, with a slight wind from the west. Toward noon the clouds became heavier and darker, and the wind changed to perfect gale from the northwest. About three o'clock the wind began to be changeable, shifting to every point of the compass, and large heavy green-colored clouds began rolling and flying through the sky. The hurricane struck our town from the northwest, and was ushered in by a blinding rain storm with the hurricane behind it, blowing at the probable rate of 70 miles per hour. . . . During the progress of the storm a long dark cloud revolved from the northwest to the southeast, presenting a view not soon to be forgotten. After the main wind had passed over, it was followed by a rain that closely resembled a water spout, accompanied by hail. We measured one hail stone, and it was 8 inches in circumference around the long way, and 5 inches around the short way. Taking it all in all, it has been the most destructive storm our people have ever experienced. — ***Cawker City Free Press*, May 31, 1879.**

In spite of extensive and elaborate early warning weather systems presently in place, seasonal storms still cause widespread destruction throughout the Great Plains. Newspaper accounts reveal the ferocity with which tornadic storms struck the early settlements.

Yesterday afternoon, about three o'clock, the attention of the citizens of Salina was directed to heavy black clouds covering the sky at the Northwest, and in an hour's time the clouds covered nearly half of the horizon — sending forth thunder, lightning, rain and hail. A little before four a funnel-shaped cloud hung down in the southwest, and below it could be seen what seemed like smoke arising from the ground to meet it, which was in

reality dust, pieces of timber, grass, grain, etc., sucked up by its mighty power. Off on the hill the lower part of the cloud whirled and moved, contracted and expanded — all the world like an elephant's trunk. Following this engine of destruction, others were formed — some six or more — moving in contra directions. It was a fearful display of the power of the elements. At the time these were first seen, they were taken by some for water-spouts, and very little was thought of them until reports of the disasters they bred came in from the country.

The first report was from a neighborhood three and a half miles west of town, on Mulberry creek. . . . The whirlwind . . . struck Mr. Charles Whitney's house, and there was never a more terrible exhibition of destruction than there. His house was a large one, and well constructed. It was literally chopped into kindling wood, and the furniture was broken in pieces and scattered to the four winds. Stoves and such ware were broken up as if a sledge hammer had been vigorously used. After the storm Mr. Whitney was found lying some ten rods from the house, and his wife still further on — both horrible [*sic*] mangled and insensible. It is possible that Mrs. Whitney may recover, but the doctors consider it doubtful with regard to the recovery of Mr. Whitney. His skull is badly fractured. His son, a boy of fifteen years, suffered no injuries. . . .

The severest cyclone passed through the southern part of the county, striking Falun about 4 o'clock. In that locality considerable damage was done on its route, and sad hovoc [*sic*] it made. Mr. Peter Peterson; living near Major Forsse, lost his wife and daughter aged six years, and had his house and all his personal effects blown to the four winds. Mr. Peterson was in the field breaking when it struck his place, and he was thrown to the ground and blinded by the dust. When he regained his feet and was able to see he could not realize for a time where he was, so completely was everything swept away. But such a sad revelation as awaited him! When he began search after his family the first discovered was the lifeless form of his wife, badly brusied [*sic*] and mangled. At a distance from her lay his daughter, dead, her limbs having been broken below the knees and her body bruised. Added to the crushing blow came the realization that he had not

a home nor anything pertaining thereto — everything gone. It was a sad tale he related to us. . . .

— *Saline County Journal*, June 8, 1876.

Sometimes the full extent of tornado damage was not known until later. Subsequent reports usually revealed much greater destruction than originally presumed.

The hurricane did not originate at this place as some believe, but was first seen seventy-five miles west of here, at near two o'clock, p.m. The storm divided when near Stockton, one part traveling down the North and the other down the South Fork of the Solomon river. The surface of the ground gives evidence that each of the storm-paths were on an average a mile in width, and traveling at the rate of about seventy miles an hour. When the storms reached this place they united, and swept down the valley, rising before it reached Beloit. The first calamity we heard of was at Delphos, where 15 were reported killed and larger number wounded. At Frankfort, on the Central Branch Road, 5 were killed outright and over 18 seriously wounded. At Irving 13 were killed outright and over 32 were very dangerously wounded. In the vicinity of Frankfort there were 8 killed outright and 15 seriously injured. Making a total at the present writing of 41 killed and 65 wounded that are known. At Concordia and Clyde and along the path of the storm, reports of killed and wounded reach us, which will beyond doubt make the total deaths by the storm number at 55, and the wounded at 80 persons. . . . We hope we shall never witness a similar visitation during the remainder of our residence in Kansas.

— *Cawker City Free Press*, June 7, 1879.

Lightning

When storm warnings are given on radio or television today, the announcements commonly advise people of the potential dangers. These warnings are particularly appropriate, because lightning causes unexpected deaths in the open, treeless spaces of the Great Plains.

Reports about people who were hit by lightning were often exceedingly graphic and must have caused great anguish among the loved ones who read the gruesome particulars.

On Friday afternoon, at about four o' clock in the afternoon, as George Going, son of Sheriff Going of this city, was proceeding from town to the court house, in the terrible storm prevailing at that time, he was struck by lightning and instantly killed. When found, the umbrella, which he carried, was considerably burned. He was lying on his face, one side of him was blackened, the soles of his boots were nearly torn off, his hat and clothes were badly burned, and his body was considerably mangled. It was a terrible shock. . . . — ***Saline County Journal*, September 12, 1872.**

Among all the frightening confrontations with mother nature, lightning seemed to be extraordinarily capricious to the settlers. A lightning strike could cause instantaneous death for some, while others sometimes survived physically unharmed.

During the heavy storm of Sunday evening last the residence of Mr. Joseph Shroeder . . . was struck by lightning, and two sons of Mr. S. were instantly killed. Three of the brothers were sleeping in one bed, and one of them escaped almost miraculously with a severe burn on the back. The ages of the deceased were nine and ten respectively. . . .

— ***Arkansas Valley Democrat*, September 14, 1878.**

An attempt to resuscitate a lightning-strike victim by use of a "galvanic battery," which presumably was the pioneer version of shock paddles, was ineffective for the man described in the following account.

During the severe thunder shower prevailing at the time, "Mack" Vest, a young man well and favorably known to all our Southern readers, started out to the stable to feed the pony, accompanied by his cousin. He had proceeded about half a dozen steps from the house when he was suddenly struck by lightning and instantly killed. The bolt struck him a little above the right ear, and passing downwards tore his right shoulder all to pieces; tore great strips of skin from his right side and breast, and passing down his right leg tore the boot from his right foot and passed into the ground. His cousin, who was walking by his side at the time, escaped comparatively unhurt, only being slightly

shocked. Dr. O. W. Hughes of Jewell City, was called immediately and did all in his power, by the use of a galvanic battery, and otherwise, to revive the unfortunate young man, but all to no purpose. The terrible bolt had too effectively accomplished its fatal work. . . . In this severe affliction the family have the earnest and heartfelt sympathy of our entire community. Truly, "In the midst of life we are in death."

— *Jewell County Monitor*, September 12, 1878.

Rain

Summer storms in Kansas sometimes bring documented reports of six or more inches of rainfall in localized areas, generating enormous runoff from the surrounding terrain and creating dangerous flash flooding along low-lying areas. Many of the prairie waterways are ephemeral and thus are dry, dusty gullies most of the time. However, after a downpour, even though the rain might have fallen miles upstream, these normally placid creeks rapidly can become raging torrents. The danger to livestock, buildings, crops, and human life is increased because many of the thunderstorms occur in the late afternoon or early evening, thereby generating floods during the night.

A contributing factor in drownings during the pioneer times was that few bridges had been built across the streams and rivers of the region. Most of the crossings were "low-water bridges" or fords, where people could walk, ride a horse, or drive a buggy or wagon through the water. Such traverses functioned well during most of the year, but obviously could be treacherous during times of high water.

Many of the pioneer settlers, who had moved from the Eastern part of the United States to the Great Plains, were undoubtedly familiar with the dangers posed by floods. People who had grown up in Ohio, Pennsylvania, Virginia, and Kentucky, for example, would have encountered many large rivers. However, prairie waters that were normally low and easily forded during most of the year may have lulled many pioneers into a sense of false security, even when they began to be filled with runoff. It would be easy to be overconfident about crossing a stream that rarely had water flowing in it, that had not been a danger or obstacle most of the year.

Last Thursday Mr. Pattison living near Bosland, in attempting to swim in the Smoky was drowned. Mr. Pattison had some

horses across the river and he and his men had been talking about getting them over, but the river being so high concluded not to get them. But Mr. Pattison, being a good swimmer, and a Mr. Blair, [*were*] determined to have a swim anyway. The current was strong and the Smoky was at it highest point. Blair soon after going in called for help from three or four men on the shore and was pulled out. Mr. Pattison said he was all right and he would swin [*sic*] down the stream and come out at the ford. He seemed to be all right and fearless. One of the men from shore asked him "how are you getting along[*?*]" He answered all right, and at that instant went down into the raging waters and was seen no more. All efforts to recover his body have, as yet, been fruitless.

Mr. Pattison's mother and wife saw him go into the river and urged him not to, his mother going into the house weeping before the accident; his wife witnessed his sinking to rise no more. . . .

— *Ellsworth Reporter*, August 1, 1872.

Many times entire communities turned out to help search for the bodies of drowned victims.

Last Tuesday afternoon our citizens were startled by the report that William T. Spence had been drowned in the river, near Mr. Rees' Mill, a short distance south of town. A large number of men immediately hurried to the spot, and a rope being stretched across the stream, Mr. C. L. Pierce and Mr. N. B. Rees were soon in the water, making search for the body. After dragging about with their feet for a few minutes, they came across it, lodged in the top of a driftwood tree, about one hundred yards below the dam. A rope was thrown the gentlemen above named, who, with great difficulty made it fast to the lifeless form, when it was pulled to the shore. Mr. Spence was in the employ of Mr. Rees, and in company with Mr. Laf. Rees, had been doing some work on the opposite side of the river. It being dinner time, they quit work and started for the house, on this side of the stream. The river had been rising rapidly all the morning, and a very strong current was running. Mr Rees, being a good swimmer, had no hesitation in crossing, but made the remark to Mr. Spence

that unless he was a good swimmer, also, he had better not attempt to make it. Mr. S. replied that he had often swam it, and thought he could safely do so again. So saying, he pulled off his shoes and threw them over to this side, and started into the water. By this time Mr. Rees had crossed, and on looking back saw his unfortunate comrade struggling hard with the obstinate current. He started back to assist him, but was forced by the mad waters to use every exertion in his power to save himself, and could render the drowning man no relief. He immediately gave the alarm and assistance hurried to them, but ere it came the murky waters of the treacherous stream had washed him down and closed over his inanimate form. The river, where he was drowned was not over eighty feet in width, but was running very swift [*sic*] and was ten or twelve feet deep. It is thought Mr. Spence was either not a good swimmer, or that he became frightened or cramped. . . . **— *Saline Valley Register*, August 30, 1876.**

Although many drownings resulted from misjudgments of swimming ability, some victims were simply caught by rapidly rising flood waters.

Mr. Amos Hugh, a resident of Kill Creek, Osborn [*sic*] County, called upon us this afternoon and gave us the sad particulars of a terrible visitation of water which inundated Kill Creek bottom, destroying property and life, last Saturday evening.

Four persons were drowned: Mrs. Brighton . . . and her two children and a Mrs. Green. The fearful rush of waters which caught the unfortunates, was occasioned by the bursting of a water spout, which, apparently, formed up near the head of Medicine Creek, crossed to the head of Kill Creek, and then burst, flooding the valley and raising the creek and its feeders over their banks. Mr. Hugh says that in fifteen minutes after the bursting of the cloud, both sides of Kill Creek was covered with angry, roaring, seething flood. People had barely time to escape from their houses and gain the buffs [*sic*] before the flood was upon them. Mrs. Brighton heard the flood coming and, with her children, escaped to high ground; but, after gathering her family about her, she found she had left one behind, in the dug-out in

which they were living, and, following her motherly instincts, she started back for it, taking a child in arms with her. She reached the dug-out; found her child, and started back; but she was a moment too late. The flood struck her, and, with one long, loud wail, she was engulfed in the muddy waters. After the water had subsided, the bodies were found lodged against a drift, the mother still clasping her children she loved in a last and deathly embrace.

Mrs. Green was asleep in her house (a dug-out), and was not aware of the approaching danger until she was awakened by the rush of water into the house, and then it was too late. She perished where she was, and there her body was found. . . .

— *Hays City Sentinel*, August 23, 1876.

A frequent cause of drownings in rivers resulted from attempts to cross swollen streams in wagons. Sometimes the team of horses pulling the buggy or wagon also perished in the torrent.

On Saturday last, about 9 a.m. the town was startled with the report that a woman [Miss Wren] had just drowned at the lower ford on the Walnut, about one mile from the city. . . . The circumstances of the calamity are as follows: Miss Wren resided temporarily with Mr. Ferman's family, one and a half miles east of Winfield. On Saturday morning she engaged a team (the little roans) and buggy from Will Robinson, and secured the services of John Boylan, a young man living at Ferman's, to take her to the vicinity of Arkansas City in search of employment as a school teacher. The Walnut had raised within the previous twenty-four hours past fording. As the team entered the stream, the current being swift, it was soon swept downward. The young man jumped out seized the team by the bits and tried to pull them ashore. In this effort the horses got him under water, but seizing a bush he saved himself. The next sight he had of the team and lady they were all far below him in the stream, the buggy and one horse under water and the lady was sitting upon the other horse calling for help. The horse she rode was still connected with its mate and the vehicle and before any one could get to her all went down to death. About 5 p.m. the body, team and buggy, were

all found together about one hundred yards above the Tunnel Mills. . . . — ***Sumner County Press*, May 3, 1877.**

It was also precarious to attempt to cross high water on horseback, but for many, it was the only way to get across the prairie streams and rivers. The following obituary explains the death of the Odd Fellow lodge member described in the Introduction.

The sad news of the death of Charles Wolfe, by drowning in the Saw Log, reached the city last Friday morning, about 8 o'clock. . . .

The manner in which the drowning occurred is thus described: On the morning in question about 6 o'clock, Mr. Wolfe attempted to swim the stream, which runs near his house, ten miles northesat [*sic*] of Dodge City. He rode into the stream on horse back. Owing to previous rains the water was very high and the current very strong and swift. When near the middle of the stream, Mr. Wolfe saw that his horse was drifting down stream and would not be able to carry him across. Therefore in order to give the horse a better chance to make head-way he let himself down into the water with the apparent intention of swimming by the side of the animal, but just at this moment, for some unaccountable reason he lost control of himself and was carried down stream, sinking and rising two or three times, then sinking to rise no more. His young wife stood on the bank of the stream, helpless to render any assistance, but compelled to witness the tragic death of her beloved husband.

After the alarm had been given a great many friends of the deceased and officers, visited the river, and all day Friday a vigilant search for the body was kept up. The stream was very high, but it was dragged over and over for considerable distance below the ford. When night came the fruitless search had to be suspended until another day.

Early in the morning, as soon as it was light, Mrs. Wolfe walked down the stream which had fallen considerably during the last twelve hours, with the hope of finding the remains of her husband. She was not disappointed, for, near the place where the accident occurred she espied the body lodged in the brush of the

stream. She notified parties at the house and the body was recovered and prepared for the grave. —*Ford County Globe*, **July 22, 1879.**

We have the painful duty of recording the death, by drowning of a son of Mr. H. Parcell, of Illinois township, on the afternoon of the 21st a short time after the storm. The boy, a lad of fourteen, together with an older brother was breaking prairie with an ox team, on his father's farm; when the storm began, the boys unhitched to go to the house, when the cattle, rendered frantic by the pelting hail, stampeded. After the storm was over they started out on horse-back, to find the oxen, and while endeavoring to cross a small branch near Clear water, which was then a raging torrent, the younger brother was swept off his horse which was swimming, and after a brief struggle for life was drowned. The other boy got through but seeing his brother struggling in the water he rode into his rescue, but the mad torrent hurried both horse and rider down stream. The boy was washed off the horse but holding on to the bridle rein, the noble animal carried him safely to shore. He immediately alarmed the neighborhood and in a short time thirty to forty men were searching the creek for the body. Night intervened without their finding it. The next morning the search was renewed and the body found within ten paces of where they left off the evening before. Even at this time the water was over waist deep to the men who were wading the creek in search of the body. This will give some idea of the amount of water that fell as this creek is simply a drain on the prairie, and is dry three fourths of the year. The deceased was buried on Wednesday, large concourse joining in the sorrowful procession to the grave. . . .

— *Wichita Weekly Beacon*, **May 31, 1876.**

Animals, however, not only rescued people, but sometimes it was the other way around. Livestock were a precious commodity to the settlers, and horses, cattle, pigs, and such, were also endangered by rising waters. Sometimes to save their animals, ranchers found that the cost was extreme.

We learn that on Saturday night last, during a severe rainstorm, two elderly gentlemen named Price living on Salt Creek, just over the line in Republic county, went out to their corral to rescue their cattle and hogs from drowning in the rise of the waters. They had saved the cattle we understand, and returned to get some hogs that were struggling in the flood, when one of them, James V. Price, becoming unable to escape the rapidly-rising stream, was drowned, the other succeeded in saving himself. . . . — ***Concordia Empire*, June 16, 1876.**

Prairie Fires

One of the most fascinating aspects of the prairie frontier is the grassland fires. Burning is used as a grassland management tool in many parts of the Great Plains, particularly in the Flint Hills of Kansas, where fire on the hillsides in the early spring is a common sight. Burning preserves the unique nature of the Plains by favoring the grasses and killing shrubs and trees, which would otherwise invade and ultimately dominate the area.

Natural prairie fires are most common in the early spring when lightning can set the grasses aflame, and in mid- to late-summer and early autumn when the vegetation is often tinder dry. In addition to lightning, fires are caused by careless smokers, pieces of glass that magnify and focus the intense rays of the summer sun, and cinders that escape from burning trash or piles of brush. Regardless of their origin, prairie fires have always evoked a sense of awe.

In an article entitled "Some Features of Kansas Farming," in *Scribners* [*Monthly*] for November, Mr Henry King gives the following vivid description of that beautiful scourge — a fire on the prairie:

Next to calamities like that the homesteader's wife told of . . . is the coming of the autumn prairie fire, which so frequently menaces their stacks and cribs, their helpless stock, their stables and cabins, and even their lives. Were it not for its known danger and power of havoc, this tempest and scourge of fire would be a spectacle of commanding force and beauty. First, you will catch glimpses of what you take to be gray wisps of haze away off on the horizon; and watching, you will see these vagrant particles

deepen gradually, and gather into a definite volume of smoke, black like a rain cloud, and bronze about the edges. Then the strange, somber bulk starts forward across the prairie, and you hold your breath at sight of the rapid progress of it. (A mile in two minutes is not an exceptional rate of speed for a fire once fairly under headway.) It halts an instant, you note, over a broad swale where there is standing water, but it is for an instant only. The next moment it reaches the upland again and the dry grass; and directly it grasps a belt of the tall, thick blue stem, and the flame leaps suddenly and madly out above the smoke, then subsides again, and the black mass grows blacker than ever, and rolls higher and higher, and you can scent the burning grass, and hear the distant roar of the fire — an awful roar, resembling the sound of artillery in heavy timber. And it is so calm immediately about you that you do not so much as miss the ticking of your watch in your pocket; there is no breath of air stirring, and the sun is shining, and the heavens above you are blue and placid. But the stillness will be broken soon. The oncoming cloud is only a few miles away now, and you easily trace the scarlet and terrific energy at its base; the smoke begins to hurt your eyes, too, and the heat becomes heavily oppressive. And then, all at once, the wind smites and staggers you, that appalling roar deafens you, and the sun is blotted out, and you are in a darkness as of midnight without moon or star. It is an experience of but a dozen seconds or so, this sudden plunge into darkness, though it seems an hour, and when you look out again, you find that the fire has passed you a mile or more to your right, and is still rolling desperately onward; and there in its tracks are charred and smoldering stacks of hay, and an occasional house aflame and tottering to its fall, and a group of men and boys beating back the outer line of the fire with brush and old clothes, and sending forward little fires to meet it and if possible keep it at a safe distance. The creek may stop and smother it when it gets there, though such a hope has mere chance for a warrant, sometimes these mighty conflagrations vault across streams twenty to thirty yards in width, so swift and resistless is their momentum; and as a rule they are eflectually [*sic*] stayed only when they reach a wide extent of

plowed land, and have to yield, sullenly, for lack of anything more to feed their inexorable fury. — *Kirwin Chief*, **November 5, 1879.**

The foregoing eloquently depicts the excitement and terror of a prairie fire, but it does not capture how it feels to be alone in the midst of one. Many times the pioneers had to battle with the fury of a violent fire. Sometimes they won, sometimes they lost; and sometimes it was a standoff.

It was the seventeenth of November at ten o'clock p.m., the wind was blowing at a fearful gale — I was in my garden some three rods from my sod cabin, when I heard a roaring in the southwest; looking up I saw a most appalling sight, broadspread and high, the air was filled with lurid flames, mingled with living cinders, smoke and ashes, urged amain by the mighty breeze. It came rushing down upon me, roaring, crackling, thundering! — on it flew with lightning speed like a devouring demon, I had barely time to get into the lee of my cabin before it struck where I had been. A sheet of living red-hot flame was above my head — all around was fire! Beneath my feet, in front, on both sides was fire! My only protection was a little space scarcely eight feet wide and six feet long, in the shadow of my little home. I had only two buckets of water, for which I had traveled two miles south and back to obtain, and a long handled dipper to fight with. I would reach around the corner of my cabin in the smoke and flame, holding my breath — for no man could inhale such an air, — and dash the water on the roof, and thus by assiduous efforts save my little home and myself. I was hemmed in by two more walls of fire than the fire of death, into which rode the immortal "six hundred" — fire above my head, and fire beneath my feet; and though there were no cannons to roar and thunder yet, there was plenty of both. To a "Second Adventist" this might not have been much of a scene for they are looking, praying, hoping for a spectacle far more terrible than this, even for the burning of the whole world. I fought the flames for six mortal hours trying to save the little I had about my building. I fought with hands and feet, stamping and rubbing until they were bloody and sore. All my crops, and over twenty-five hundred forest and fruit tress were burnt dead and sear[*ed*] — seven hundred fine apple,

peach, cherry and plum trees all black and dead. The loss of my crops was hard, taking away from me the means I had drawn around me for my winter's subsistence, placing me in a poor, and penniless condition, yet the loss of my trees seemed more, and harder to bear. I had tended them with great care, and well had they repaid the pains: such attention as I had bestowed begets a sort of affection, and there is in them a kind of comfort ownership, and sociability for one all alone, that they seemed an oasis on this otherwise treeless plain. At seven o'clock the wind lulled and changed to the northwest — I had got all safe around my cabin, and sat in the door for a few moments when I saw the devouring flame coming down upon my neighbor, Mr. Burdick's house; armed with a corn-knife and gunny-bag and with bloody feet I started for its protection. The wind not being high, gave me time to clear away all the inflammable stuff contiguous and throw it back, so as to make the house secure. For an hour I watched, until all was safe, then, with exhausted, weary limbs, puffing like a horse at the end of a race, I got back to my cabin, the door of which had been open and threw myself upon a bed, black with cinders and ashes, which I had not the power to brush off, for a little of "nature's sweet restorer — balmy sleep," — I got the sleep, but the balmy want there. — I suppose on account of the presence of so much cinders and ashes. For an hour I rested, got up and looked out doors; that night, and all night long, fires glimmered and glared on all sides round, lighting up the broadspread ruin.

Next morning, Nature as if conscious and in mourning for the outrages committed upon her fair face, had changed her waving robe of russet brown for one of somber black. All things had a different aspect, dark, drear and saddening. My very soul seemed to be at times, appalled and dismayed, as the thoughts went to these awfully grand, but destructive scenes, and the blackness of the earth, adds poignancy to the sadness, which down, down, deep in my heart, still lingers. But I know that God still lives, I put my whole trust in Him, and therefore my faith is well founded, for "His loving kindness and tender mercies are even over the children of men." A. S. KIMBALL.

— *Chronoscope*, January 22, 1879.

The sweeping extent of prairie fires was remarkable. The fast-moving inferno disregarded distances or political boundaries and often inflicted its wrath on several counties. It was often impossible to predict the exact path of an oncoming blaze, because of the vagaries of the winds on the open Plains.

A common method of preventing the spread of prairie fires was to plow a guard around an area to protect it. These bare spots, if wide enough and without sufficient fuel to support the fire, would often prevent flames from spreading.

Rumor brings us the sad news of two ladies being burned to death in a prairie fire, on the Solomon, recently. As we have stated, this is but rumor, and we most sincerely hope that it is without foundation. The heavy clouds of smoke that have been hanging about us for the past two weeks, is evidence sufficient of the terrible work of the fire-fiend, somewhere; and we would again urge upon our farmers the necessity of fire-guards. Remember, "prevention is better than cure;" a few hours labor to-day, may be the saving of hundreds of dollars' worth of property tomorrow. . . . — ***Norton County Advance*, October 19, 1878.**

However, not even protective barriers could always keep death at bay. One man tried to prevent an intentionally set fire from escaping, but the fickle winds thwarted him and the embers jumped the firebreak that he had prepared.

A Mr. Bowman, living a mile north of John W. and Joseph W. Antrim, began plowing around a piece of land on Thursday and continued on the same a day and a half, plowing a strip some three rods wide. The grass being high [*on*] the land, he concluded to burn it, and supposed the strip of plowed ground was amply sufficient to keep it within bounds, but just after he had started the fire the wind suddenly changed into the north with such fury as to carry the fire clear across the plowed strip. All will remember that it blew a gale on Friday evening. The Antrim brothers being south started to go to Mr. Bowman's assistance, but before going far discovered the fire coming upon their place and hastened back to save their premises. Before they reached

their place the fire was upon them. Their first efforts were to release the horses, three in number, from the stable, which was on fire. One horse was extricated without any trouble, the second one gave some trouble to John at the door who was trying to get him out, whereupon Joseph kicked the horse in order to get him out, which was finally accomplished and he returned, as is supposed to release the third horse. He was not seen again for five minutes, as John had to seek the open air to catch his breath. On returning he saw Joseph some two rods from the stable lying on the gronnd [*sic*] about ten feet from a haystack the flames from which were lapping his body, but they could see that life was extinct, and nothing could be done to extricate him. It is supposed that when he came out of the stable he inhaled the hot air and never breathed again, just having time to run where he fell. It is supposed that he did not untie the third horse, as it perished where it was tied. The loss in property was one horse, some two hundred and fifty bushels of corn, seventy-five bushels of oats, and all their hogs and chickens.

— *Wichita City Eagle*, March 20, 1879.

Domestic animals were not the only valuable assets lost to fires. Machinery and wagons, crucial to the sustenance of the pioneers, were also destroyed. The following account of a prairie fire depicts the appalling consequences to people trying to save their livestock and a wagon in a barn.

Last Sunday forenoon, about 11 o'clock, a prairie fire from the southwest passed across section two of Lincoln township, Sedgewick [*sic*] county, causing the death of two valuable citizens of that township, Edward Felter and Joel Knight. Our information is that Mr. Felter had been married just four weeks to a sister of Mr. Knight's, and that Mr. and Mrs. K. were there that day for a visit. The man [*sic*] saw the fire coming with furious strides and ran out and cut their mules loose from in or near a straw stable. They then attempted to draw their wagons from about the same, but seeing they hadn't time to do this, started for the house, a short distance off. But the dense smoke and heat from the fire smothered them down and they fell to the ground

insensible. Both men had every particle of clothing burned from their bodies; still more, all their flesh was burned off, and the doctor reports that the fleshy fat under the same was actually cooked brown for a half an inch deep. Mr. Lew. Barr was the first man on the spot after the fire, and took the bodies to a Mr. McGorkel's and medical aid was at once summoned, but Mr. Knight died in seven hours afterwards and Mr. Felter in thirteen hours. To the women: As soon as they saw the fire coming both ran out of the house, Mrs. Knight going some distaoce [*sic*] and becoming tired out, put the shawl over her head and sat down in the grass, but a Mr. Baker coming along with his wagon took her in, and thus saved her life. Mrs. Felter, after leaving the house ran back to it again and as soon as the fire passed by ran out again and the house burned to the ground. We learn that Mr. Felter, before falling the last time, placed his pocket book, containing one thousand dollars, for which he had just before sold a farm, under him, thereby saving the money. Shortly after the fire was over he got up, picked up the money and handing it to his wife, said he had saved her that much.

— *Hutchinson News*, April 3, 1879.

In some pitiful circumstances, the attempt at a rescue did not involve horses, machinery, or wagons, but a dearly loved one. Such were the fearful hazards of living and working on the inflammable grasslands in pioneer days.

Last Friday evening, the fire on the south side of the river, some nine miles from this place, was coming up pretty close to the house and stacks of Mr. Poteka, who at the time was away from home. Mrs. Poteka had secured the safety of the stack and was looking after some stock with the assistance of her little girl, when the fire came suddenly upon them. The little girl ran to get away from the fire, and in her flight fell into an excavation which had been dug for a cellar. The mother, not so fortunate in her escape, cried to the girl, "do not leave me," and these were the last words she was heard to utter. On the return of the father, the alarm was given and the neighborhood turned out in search of the missing woman, and about 12 o'clock at night, she was

found within a few rods of some braking, with every particle of clothing burned from her body and the flesh so badly burned as to almost drop from the bones. She was buried last Sunday.

— *Kirwin Chief*, October 31, 1877.

The dry landscape, the uninterrupted vastness of the grasslands, the unfamiliarity of many of the pioneers with the changeable winds, and sheer carelessness all contributed to a high incidence of prairie fires. These disasters often wiped out years of tireless struggle to develop a sustainable living on the harsh and sometimes unforgiving land.

Each spring and fall the press of the west is frequently called upon to record the destruction by prairie fires of thousands of dollars worth of property, the results of years of toil and accumulation, and not infrequently of cases wherein many lives are sacrificed in efforts to preserve from destruction the earnings and savings of years. The prime cause of these disastrous conflagrations can generally be attributed to carelessness. People fresh from the east are not as familiar with the devastating and uncontrollable element as those who have continually lived in a prairie country, and they should be very careful in their dealings with fire. A spark from a pipe may in a few seconds destroy what it will require years to replace. Too much caution cannot be taken in this matter.

— *Cawker City Free Press*, April 5, 1879.

Native Animals

One of the most distinctive features of life on the prairie in frontier times was an intimate daily contact with nature. Today, we tend to believe that native animals are intruding upon our habitat; but in the 1870s, the small human population was clearly encroaching upon native animals. Many of the encounters between pioneers and wildlife were pleasant events for settlers, but some animals brought danger or death. Immigrants were unfamiliar with many dangerous prairie animals — rabid mammals, venomous spiders, scorpions, snakes, and the ubiquitous huge buffalo, all of which could maim or kill the unprepared frontier people. Unfortunately, modern medical treatments were unavailable, and knowledgeable lay people and doctors, who often administered folk treatments, were usually miles away.

Although many dangerous beasts inhabited the land, most reported incidents involved the rattlesnake.

Five species of poisonous snake are indigenous to Kansas (Collins, 1993). The copperhead and timber rattlesnake live in the eastern third of the state, while the cottonmouth is primarily found in the extreme southeastern corner of Kansas. The western rattlesnake and massasauga are the only two species native to western Kansas, the focus of this book.

Of those pioneers who died of snake bites, 83 percent were children (Fleharty, 1998). The majority of adult victims probably would have survived rattlesnake bites without treatment, as their larger body mass could assimilate the poison. Unfortunately, antivenin had not yet been developed, and thus many children perished from the bite.

A little girl of Jacob Herr, 3 years old, living seven miles northeast of Ellinwood, while playing in the yard near the house, was bitten by a rattlesnake about four o'clock Tuesday afternoon, and before eight o'clock in the evening the child died. Medical aid was procured, but too late to counteract the poison. . . .

— *Great Bend Register*, May 1, 1879.

Young children were often bitten because they played outdoors, near outbuildings, corrals, or haystacks, places which — unfortunately for barefooted children — are excellent habitats for mice and rats, a major part of the rattlesnake's diet.

A little son of A. H. Melrose, who lives a half mile west of Sunny Slope, was bitten by a rattlesnake on Tuesday of last week, and died in two hours. He was bitten on the arm and knee. This is the first death resulting from a snake bite we have ever been called upon to chronicle, since the settlement of the county. The child was about two years old.

— *Sumner County Press*, August 2, 1877.

Medical aid was usually sought following a snake bite and a profusion of home cures were often tried in a usually vain effort to save the victim. The treatments commonly involved giving the victim whiskey (the only prescription sanctioned by the medical community) or elixirs made from various plants thought to have medicinal properties, sucking the wound by mouth to extract the poison, and applying poultices to draw out the venom. Poultices were made from a variety of ingredients, sometimes mixed together. Plants and plant derivatives included corn snakeroot, garlic, onion, indigo, tobacco, camphor, and olive oil. Animal products, including milk, hog lard, hartshorn, and eggs, were also used in poultices as were inorganic materials such as salt, ammonia, soda, potassium iodide, iodine, and zinc chloride. Coal oil (kerosene) and mud were also used in poultices (Fleharty, 1998).

Yet, many individuals who survived after being given a folk remedy probably would have lived without treatment. Their survival, after the administration of a home cure, undoubtedly led to the perpetuation of the remedy (Fleharty, 1998).

Seeing an account of a little girl suffering from a snake bite, I thought I would give an antidote which I have found "dead medicine" to snake bites on horses and dogs, and which I have no doubt would be equally effective on a person. Take onions (if green, tops and all) mash them fine, spread on a cloth large enough to cover all the swollen part, sprinkle on some salt, and apply immediately. Change the poultice every fifteen minutes, for the first hour or two. If badly swollen, scarify [*sic*] slightly with a sharp knife.

I had a horse and a mule that were bitten by rattle snakes, and were so bad before I could apply the remedy, that they could neither eat or walk, and in thirty minutes after I applied onions and salt, they were grazing as though nothing was the matter, and the next day made twenty-five miles to a loaded wagon without inconvenience. **W.L.H. — *Wichita City Eagle*, June 3, 1875.**

The risk from snake bite was equally high among older children, because many of them, particularly the young boys, worked in the fields, herded cattle, or did other chores that increased the likelihood of an encounter with a viper.

Last Saturday at noon, when Mr. A B Reynolds and his son Jessie A Reynolds, who live a short distance north of Kiowa, were returning or about to return from the field where they had been engaged in cutting up corn, a huge rattlesnake sprang at the

boy Jesse [*sic*] A Reynolds, a bright intelligent and amiable boy of about sixteen summers, inflicted two stings directly on the posterior portion of the leg near the knee. He lingered in fearful agony until nearly evening when he expired. . . .

— *Barbour County Mail*, September 26, 1878.

However, the threat from snake bite was certainly not confined to children; many adults were also struck while working.

We have seldom a sadder duty to perform than to announce the death of Charles M. Main of Salt Creek township, which occurred on last Monday night.

We are informed that he visited the Ninnescah on business on Friday last. On Sabbath, on his return, he stopped to feed, at noon. After unhitching his team and giving them water he went to the crib to get corn. He reached his hand in the crib through a crack and while thus, a large rattlesnake struck him, the fangs entering on either side of the third knuckle. He went a distance of about four miles to Dr. Fryrear's where some liniment was applied. He was taken home and on Monday forenoon was considered out of danger. He was quite cheerful, and spoke of his recovery, but in the afternoon about three o'clock he became unconscious and gradually sunk until midnight, when he died. . . . **— *Hutchinson News*, June 26, 1876.**

Prairie dog towns were an ideal habitat for snakes, including rattlers. Poor Mr. Maddox discovered this the hard way when he unwisely reached into a prairie dog hole.

Just as we go to press we learn of the death of M. P. Maddox, who lived in Ruella township. It is one of the few deaths from snake-bites that have ever occurred in this county, and it was probably from want of proper treatment that he died. He was bitten Tuesday afternoon by a prairie rattlesnake, as he was returning from the convention at Harper, and died yesterday at 3 p.m. The circumstances are as follows: While passing a dog town he saw two snakes run into a hole, and rashly reaching in, took one by the tail and jerked its head off. He then reached for

the other and was bitten. He leaves a wife and child, to whom we extend our sympathies. — ***Sumner County Press*, November 6, 1879.**

In addition to poisonous snakes, rabies — "hydrophobia" — terrified entire communities. Alarms often were given about the presence of "mad dogs," but few accounts were found of people dying from bites of rabid hounds, although they likely occurred. The madstone, which is referred to in the following account, was a common therapy used as a poultice to combat the dreadful consequences of rabies. The efficacy of the madstone was questioned by many, but praised and fervently sought by others. It supposedly would adhere to the wound and draw the poison from the victim. The May 16, 1879, edition of *The Hays City Sentinel* described the madstone as "about two inches square by one inch in thickness. It presents the appearance of a piece of honey-comb with closed cells, petrified with an even surface and porous throughout." M. M. Coffin, in *Death in Early America* (1976), indicated that the madstone was formed in the heart of buck deer once every generation and therefore quite rare.

Louis Dalton was bitten by a mad dog, as is supposed, on April 29, and went to Hutchinson on next day and got a mad stone from Winslow & Allbright, and applied it, but as it had never been tested, although it stuck and worked well, he and his friends thought it best for him to go to Kansas City where he was told were two that had been tested. I believe medical men generally deny there being curative properties in mad stones, socalled [*sic*].

— ***Hutchinson News*, May 8, 1879.**

Several people were bitten by rabid skunks, a common prairie animal.

We hear of several persons in this section of the State being bitten by polecats and being badly poisoned thereby. In one case, a man died from the effects of the poison.

— ***Saline County Journal*, September 12, 1872.**

Such incidents prompted dire warnings about the dangers that skunks might pose to people.

Look out for polecats. Kill them at first sight and be sure they are dead before you take hold of them.

— *Ellsworth Reporter*, December 12, 1872.

However, not all citizens agreed that skunks were dangerous, and some were more than willing to pen their rebuttals to the editor. Mrs. Page not only took vehement issue with the *Hays City Sentinel* article regarding the dangers posed by skunks, but also submitted her son as living testimony to the contrary.

The following communication comes to us from a well-known lady in Ness County; and we cheerfully give it space. The skunk and its habits are of vital importance to the citizens of Western Kansas, — in fact, so much so that it should be made a study. There is no telling how soon we may all become skunks. It is no more improbable than being metamorphosed into a "long-legged kangaroo, who curls up in a boar's nest:" and, if we may believe a certain newspaper, this has happened. But let us hear Mrs. Page:

EDITOR SENTINEL: I have noticed, several times, in the SENTINEL, articles in relation to sure death from the bite of a skunk. Now in your last issue, you state you are going to prove the truthfulness of your former statements. Now, I do not agree with you. I had lived two score years before I ever heard of such a thing as a skunk biting at all. After my arrival in Kansas I was informed they would bite, and that a speedy death was sure to follow. Some time last fall, my son — James Page — went to Ellis, with the team, and camped out — as is customary with the people in this part of Kansas. Soon after falling asleep, a skunk seized him by his thumb, which awoke him immediately. He jerked his hand away, and sprang to his feet; but in trying to awake his companions, the skunk made off, but only to meet his death at the hands of Mr. Page and others, who were just coming to their camp. The bite was not very deep, but drew the blood sufficient to start the poison in his system, if the skunk was poisonous. In an hour after the bite, Mustang linement [*sic*] was applied; and the next morning, medical aid was obtained. He

followed the physician's directions; and yesterday he was as stout and healthy a young man as you can find in Kansas. Today, I suppose, he is on his way to the City of Hays; and I hope you may get a good, square look at him. If you do, you will come to the conclusion that if the bite of a skunk is poisonous, there is, at least, no necessity for a speedy death to follow. Now let me tell you the idea we have, here, and let us here [*sic*] from you again. There is more or less poison put out for the purpose of killing the howling coyote; and a hungry skunk may dine with, before, or after the coyote and thus becomes poisonous; when a bite from him would prove fatal, unless powerful remedies were speedily applied. **— *Hays City Sentinel*, March 16, 1877.**

Mrs. Page obviously had her facts correct, because the newspaper had previously reported on the bite suffered by her son and commented on the lack of any ill effects.

On last Monday night James Page, a young man living on the Walnut, but who is well known in this vicinity, was severely bitten on the right hand by a skunk while sleeping under a wagon in the rear of Pearson's livery stable. He left for his home on Friday, feeling no ill effects from the wound.

— *Hays City Sentinel*, October 11, 1876.

The newspaper did finally concede that their supposition regarding the perils represented by skunks might be erroneous. However, the editor continued to kindle the fires of controversy by taking issue with Mrs. Page's idea of poisonous skunks and put forward a challenge to her.

We are glad for Mrs. Page and her son's sake that he recovered, and are willing to sacrifice ourselves out of regard for the feelings of the friends of the family; but the above is a terrible blow at our theory. A number of similas [*sic*] cases have come under our notice, and James is the first one we have known to escape. We hardly think the poison theory a good one. If a skunk has the same system of eating and digesting food as other animals who roam the plains — and we know of nothing to the contrary, by the way — poison would have the same effect upon him

as upon the wolf — he would either die immediately or entirely recover. It is preposterous to believe that a skunk secrets [*sic*] a supply of deadly poison — in the crevices of his teeth perhaps — and goes about the land seeking whom he may destroy. A skunk — a sane, fair minded skunk we mean — never fights with his teeth — he has a much more effective weapon. No, we thing [*sic*] our theory to be the better one. Skunks bite only when they have the hydrophobia; and this, owing to some climatic influence, they have very frequently. Shall we hear from you again, Mrs. Page?

— *Hays City Sentinel*, March 16, 1877.

This argument was apparently never settled, but certainly some people were bitten, and while some apparently recovered, many others suffered agonizing effects and eventually died from the bites of rabid skunks.

The Solomon City *Newspaper* says: Last summer a Swede girl in Salina was, while going to a neighbor's house, bitten by a pole-cat. No immediate result following, the circumstance was nearly forgotten. Tuesday of last week the girl complaining of pain in the chest, a physician was called in, who pronounced it a simple "ailment that would pass off in a few days." On Wednesday she was seized with fearful paroxysms, it required three strong men to hold her. It was then evident that hydrophobia was doing its horrid work. Morphine was administered to alleviate the suffering girl's agony, who died the next day.

— *Ellsworth Reporter*, February 5, 1874.

For this hapless girl and many others, the Pasteur rabies vaccine, which was not developed until 1885, came too late.

Skunks were not the only diseased menace. There were also reports of attacks by rabid wolves. Whether these provocations were by grey wolves, which were in the region, or by coyotes, which were often called "prairie wolves," is not known.

A boy named Stockbridge, residing near Bull City [*Alton*], Osborne county, was lately attacked and severely bitten by a wolf, supposed to have been rabid. The boy was lying down drinking from a spring when attacked, and after inflicting several ugly wounds about the boy's legs the wolf made off.

— *Russell County Record*, June 3, 1875.

Tragically the *Russell County Record* of July 22, 1875, reported that the boy died of hydrophobia on the 4th of July. There was even a report of a child who was bitten by a "mad" cat.

Mr. Z. T. White, of Greenwood County, passed through Eureka, accompanied by a beautiful little daughter who had been bitten by a mad cat. He was on his way to Cowley County in search of a madstone said to be owned there.

— *Hays City Sentinel*, July 13, 1878.

The threat of the buffalo (bison) was also prevalent. While most Americans understand that hunting parties nearly made the buffalo extinct on the Western Plains, few appreciate how the size and power of the animal could overpower a single man.

Some parties the other day found the skeleton of a man about four miles west of town. From the shape of the skull it is supposed to be that of a white man. Near this skeleton lie the bones of a large buffalo, and a few feet away the barrel of a very large muzzle loading rifle was found, and a little to one side yet was found the broken gunstock. From the position of things generally, it is very evident that there has here taken place a life and death struggle between a wounded buffalo and a hunter. The broken gun would indicate that the struggle was a bitter one, and that away from camp and friends the hunter had fought the enraged animal until death, and that they had then died together.

— *Norton County Advance*, April 8, 1879.

People were killed by many natural phenomena during pioneer days on the Great Plains, and not all the possibilities were represented in the 1875-1879 time period examined. No fatalities from blizzards were reported during the late 1870s, though, cruel winters undoubtedly killed settlers on the Great Plains. Fatalities from other rarely occurring events, such as earthquakes, were not reported during this time.

Many of these natural hazards continue to plague people presently living in the Great Plains, but we have been able to reduce the risks associated with many of them. With technology, we have increased communication capabilities, thereby providing early warnings of impending storms and floods, and we have better home and bridge construction to resist the threat of earthquakes and tornadoes. We also have placed an emphasis on fire prevention through such things as rural fire districts with community members serving as volunteer firefighters.

Greater medical knowledge has permitted the development of antitoxins and sera to combat bites and diseases, as well as a quicker response time for medical emergencies. And finally, our encounters with wild animals are infrequent because of the fewer number of wild animals and our urbanized lifestyle.

Despite the inherent dangers of living in the Great Plains, people have survived by either adapting their behavior to cope with many of the dangers that exist or by using modern technology to minimize the risks that nature poses to human life.

Chapter 3

It Was Just an Accident . . .

ACCIDENTS WERE ONE OF the principal causes of death on the prairie frontier. Mishaps occurred in and around town homes or rural farmsteads during activities associated with day-to-day living, working, and traveling.

Accidents usually occurred because of someone's lack of knowledge or understanding. For example, one may not have known that the more inflammable benzine should not be placed in a kerosene lantern. However, more frequently, accidents arose from careless, sometimes arrogant attitudes. Many, if not all of the deaths included in this chapter, could have been prevented if someone had been more careful, had listened to wiser more experienced voices, or had more foresight.

Building the Frontier Home

The Pacific Railroad Act of 1861 and the Homestead Act of 1862 provided immigrants with the opportunity to settle on inexpensive land. To satisfy the requirements of the Homestead Act, a quarter section of land had to be developed — specifically, the construction of some sort of home was required. When the immigrants came to the High Plains, they found few trees except for narrow bands extending along some of the rivers. These small stands of timber soon were diminished or destroyed for construction and fuel. As wood became more scarce, the creative settlers built houses of sod or they excavated beneath the earth's surface to construct dugouts. However, both kinds of lodging still required some structural timbers to support the weight of the soil roof. Ridge poles occasionally were not placed correctly or were weakened by knots or rot, and the roof collapsed, killing some of the occupants.

On Saturday last Jacque Walker and wife started for Concordia to do some trading. At about 7 o'clock A.M. they left home, leaving their three oldest children at home to take care of the stock and do chores. It is certain that they had been gone from home but twenty minutes when the ridge-log, of the dug-out, they lived in, broke, burying the three children in the ruins, killing the eldest instantly. She was aged 8 years. The jury of the inquest, after due deliberation and carefully examining the body and the ruins, are in the opinion that the ridge-log struck her first, knocking her foreward [*sic*] onto the stove, and one of the poles falling down caught her head, breaking her neck at the first joint and mangling he[*r*] terribly. The space occupied by the baby hardly seemed large enough to hold a water bucket, yet the girl was squeezed into that small space. The other two small children crawled out under the debris by way of the cellar, crawling through a hole so small that a small sized dog could hardly crawl out of. . . . The clock had stopped at nineteen minutes past seven, A.M., just about 19 minutes after the father and mother had left. . . . I have seen men killed by the shot and shell, but witnessing the body so mangled was more heart rending in the extreme.

God grant that I may never wittness [*sic*] such an other sight.

— *Concordia Expositor*, June 7, 1877.

If settlers did not homestead along or close to trees, they had to travel some distance to locate timber. After the logs were cut, they had to be loaded on a wagon for transport. But wood had to be properly stacked in the wagon to prevent the top log from rolling off those below and perhaps causing a fatal accident.

Mr. H. Dunham was hauling a load of wood on last Monday; he had the wagon bed on the wagon, and placed two small logs in the bottom and one log in the centre of the bed. He then got on the lead and started home; he drove in a little sidding [*sic*] place and that started the top log, throwing him off with it, and it is supposed that the log struck him in the breast, as he bled profusely from the mouth. The log was about eight feet long and eighteen inches through, and very smooth, the bark being off. I think he never knew what hurt him. Mr. G. Herran came to him first in a few moments after the accident and he knew nothing at all; he died in just five minutes. This is indeed an awful stroke on the family; he leaves a wife and four children to mourn his untimely death. . . . — *Smith County Pioneer*, December 8, 1877.

If the settlers lacked lumber and did not wish to live in a dugout or sod house, some used the abundant limestone that underlies much of the prairie sod to construct homes, sheds, and fences. However, quarrying rock can be a dangerous operation if one is careless.

One Thomas Lowe, residing about seven miles from Bull City, Osborn [*sic*] County, met a horrible death recently. He was quarrying stone from a hillside, when a huge boulder was detatched [*sic*] from above him, cruishing [*sic*] his head into a shapeless mass. — *Hays City Sentinel*, November 29, 1876.

Little surface water existed in western Kansas and unless the homestead was adjacent to a permanent stream, wells had to be dug for fresh water — a potentially dangerous task. One person was usually in the hole digging and the removed soil was lifted to the surface in a bucket by another. A wall of stone usually was constructed around the edge of the well to prevent the surrounding soil from slumping into it. But at times, when men were digging and constructing the well, the bucket could become loose and fall, injuring or even killing the man below.

On Wednesday last, one of those unfortunate affairs which are almost daily occurring around us, took place on the farm of Thos. Farley, one mile northwest of town, resulting in the death of an esteemed citizen — Mr. Larkin Cullins. He had just finished digging a well for Mr. F. and had commenced walling it up with stone, which were [*sic*] being lowered to him in a heavy wooden bucket, Mr. N. B. DeArmond having hold of the windlass. The bucket had been safely landed at the bottom, emptied of its contents and started on its upward course, and was near the top, when suddenly Mr. DeArmond felft [*sic*] something give away. He called loudly to Mr. Cullins to "look out," but before he had time to realize the cause of the outcry, the heavy bucket, weighing seventy-five pounds, and descending with lightning speed, struck him on the head, fracturing the skull. As soon as the alarm could be given to men near by, Mr. D. was lowered, where he found Mr. C. insensible in the water, which was about eighteen inches deep. Ropes were fastened about him and he was drawn up and conveyed to the residence of his brother-in-law, Mr. J. T. Barnhart, where Drs. Bryant and Vernon were immediately summoned, who did all that could be done for the suffering man. Unconscious and in deep pain he lingered until near midnight, when he passed over to the other shore. . . . The funeral services were conducted by Father E. Bradbury, assisted by his son, Henry C. Verily, in the midst of life, health, vigor, and seeming security, we are but one step from the portals of that "mysterious realm" that lies in boundless expanse but a little ways beyond. — ***Saline Valley Register*, April 11, 1877.**

Uncovered dug wells at the homestead also invited accidents.

As the father was going out to dig potatoes the child followed him nearly to the well, and, after cautioning it not to go near the well, he went on to the field. The mother, supposing that the child was with its father, gave it no thought. In half an hour, Mr. Bemis returned, when both realized that the child was missing. He felt almost sure that the child was in the well, and, after feeling for it was a long stick, he jumped into the well, which had seven or eight feet of water in it, and taking hold of the rope let himself to

> **the bottom. He found the body, and with his feet brought it to the surface, where he held on to the rope. The mother and her sister, who were watching him, were too much overcome to draw him up. Mr. Ash happened along just at this time and they called to him, and he pulled the father and his dead child out. For nearly an hour they tried to restore animation, but without avail. The well was uncurbed with loose boards thrown over the mouth.**
>
> **— *Wichita Weekly Beacon*, August 27, 1879.**

Occasionally, as the settlers were excavating for water, they would encounter small veins of coal. This was reported by the local newspapers, and small coal mines subsequently became a fuel source for nearby settlers. Usually these mines were relatively shallow, but one was deep enough to cave in on a mother and her children searching for coal for her stove.

> **Mr. Menzes, who is working a coal mine about eight miles southeast of here went, yesterday, to Bunker Hill on business, and while he was absent his wife, followed by two of her children, went to the mine for coal. There was plenty of it outside, but it being wet from the rain which was falling at the time, Mrs. Menzes went a little to one side of the main drift to pick out some dry coal from the bluff, where an excavation of about three feet had [*been*] made; she had procurred her fuel and was about to return, when the bank caved down, burying her about two feet deep and covering one of the children all except one hand. The other child, who had barely escaped being buried alive, went to work with his hands to uncover the bodies but finding himself inadequate to the task, ran to the house of a neighbor for help. Assistance having arrived, a messenger was at once sent for Mr. Menzes, while others applied themselves to the work of recovering the bodies of the unfortunate mother and her child; to whom death, by suffocation, had come long before the task was completed. . . .**
>
> **— *Russell County Record*, February 8, 1877.**

Most Happen at Home . . .

Fire was a necessity in the daily routine of living in the frontier home. Flames, for cooking and heating, were often in an open hearth, stove, or both, and presented a hazard to the unwary. Many frontier children died when their clothing was ignited.

Because women and girls spent more time in the house than men and boys, they were exposed more to domestic fires. Women added fuel to the stoves and refilled the kerosene lanterns. This handling of fuel coupled with their loose, often full-length, dresses provided the necessary ingredients for disaster.

Last Thursday evening a four year old daughter of John Long, living in Macon Township, was burned so badly that she died that night. She was standing in front of the stove when her clothes caught fire, and before her mother could be called, who was just outside the door, and the flames be extinguished the almost entire front of her person was burned to a crisp. Dr. Coleman was called to attend her. —***Newton Kansan*, December 12, 1878.**

Last Monday, about noon, Mrs. Frank Patterson . . . was so seriously burned as to die about 7 o'clock of the same evening. While preparing dinner, with her back to the stove, her clothes caught fire, and the flames quickly flared up and enveloped her with fire. A bucket of water stood near, which she dashed over herself without doing any good. She then rushed out of doors and rolled on the ground, finally putting out the flames, but not before everything but the band of her dress, her corset and shoes was completely burned off of her. Mr. Patterson was at the School House some distance off, and had just started home when he met his little girl, about three years old, who ran to her papa crying, "Mamma fire! Mamma fire!" but Mr. Patterson not knowing what the child meant, thought something must be wrong, and hastened to the house, finding his wife, all burned, sitting on the door step. He laid her on the bed and sent the hired man, who had come in to dinner, for the Dr., doing in the meantime all he could to alleviate her sufferings. She lingered on in the greatest agony, until about 7 o'clock in the evening, when she died. She was buried next day in the Cemetery west of this city. . . . —***Great Bend Register*, September 26, 1878.**

The careless use of inflammable substances around the house also led to a number of deaths. The kerosene, or coal-oil-lantern, a primary source of light for after-dark activities, was often responsible.

The record of another accident comes to us from Washington County. Susie Black attempted to fill a lighted lamp with benzine and was killed by the explosion which followed.

— *Jewell County Monitor.*

Susie had a little lamp,
'Twas meant for kerosene,
She undertook to fill it full
and has not since benzine.

— *Hays City Sentinel*, March 21, 1879.

Another tragic accident occurred when the vapors from a container of a hot inflammable mixture ignited.

An unusually sad occurrence was the burning of a two-story frame house in Wilson on the 26th inst., owned by Mr. Isaac Wilson, and occupied by the family of Mr. J. W. Haffa.

It was about 9 o'clock a. m. when Mr. Haffa was preparing some varnish composed of turpentine and gum asphaltum, for which purpose he was heating one half gallon of spirits of turpentine on the cook-stove. Fearing that the mixture would get too hot Mrs. Haffa lifted the kettle containing it from the fire for her husband to replace the stove-lid. Instantly, as the kettle was lifted, the hot compound flashed into flames which enveloped Mrs. Haffa in a sheet of fire, compelling her to drop the kettle in the middle of the room in her attempt to carry it out of the house. The scene which then followed is indescribable. The burning fluid was dropped alongside of a three-year-old little daughter whose clothing was ablaze from head to foot in an instant, and who, from fright and agony fell helpless to the floor. At the first flash of flame an older daughter, about 9 years of age, ran into a small pantry under the stairway, and hearing the cries of her little sister ran to her assistance, trying to pick her up and carry her out. But she failed in accomplishing so heroic an

undertaking and burnt her hands severely in her attempt to do so. In the corner of the room, just behind the door into the pantry from which this girl made her escape, stood a crib with a sleeping babe some six weeks old, which might have been rescued by the little girl if her mind had not been directed to the cries of her sister. But it perished, no cry from it having been heard. That the little girl ever passed from the pantry to the assistance of her sister, and then escaped with so little injury is marvelous. Up stairs in a front room an elder sister of some thirteen summers lay sick in bed. Hearing the screams below she ran down stairs only to find her escape cut off, narrowly escaping up the stairway followed by long tongues of flame. Fortunately for her Mr. McCoy, the first to arrive to lend a helping hand, seeing the frightened girl in the room above, who by this time had thrown open the shutters and window, directed her to leap, which she did, being caught safely in his arms.

To return to Mr. Haffa it should be said that quickly as possible after aiding his unfortunate wife to escape into a rain barrel just outside of the house, he returned to the rescue of others whose fate was imperiled. The writer, among the first to arrive on the scene of the disaster, saw this poor distracted man rush away from the door of the flame-filled room, the one side of his face burnt to a crisp, his hands burnt black and the blood oozing from the fingers, piteously exclaiming, "Oh! my God! My poor children are burnt up alive!"

Although Mrs. Haffa received medical and surgical aid immediately, so extensive were her burns that she survived her injuries only about six hours.

Yesterday, the 27th, at 3 p. m., the remains of Mrs. Haffa and of the little girl and babe, whose charred bodies had been recovered from the burning debris, were interred in the cemetery, after which appropriate services were held in the school house listened to by a large audience of sympathizing neighbors.

As a bright lining to the dark cloud whose gloomy shadow rested on this community yesterday, it is pleasant to note this generous impulses of our people in giving substantial aid to the grief-stricken family, for which they are sincerely thankful. Samaritan. Wilson, June 28, 1879. — ***Ellsworth Reporter*, July 3, 1879.**

In an attempt to rekindle a fire, a woman, who apparently did not understand the volatility of kerosene, poured it directly from the can onto the flames.

We come to record another frightful accident which occurred in this city last Thursday, resulting in awful death to a beautiful young wife who but a few weeks since took the man of her choice confidingly and lovingly by the hand and came out upon the border to build up a home and name for themselves. Mrs. Jennie Henry, on that day, in attempting to renew the fire with wich [*sic*] to prepare her husband's dinner, took up a can of kerosene and poured some of the contents upon the smouldering fire. An explosion followed quick and frightful enveloping her dress and entire person in fluid flames, but not before she realized that the can was about to explode, which at the same instant hurled from her. Wild with intense pain and fright the unfortnnte [*sic*] woman ran up the street shrieking most piteously, which attracted Dr. McAdams' attention, who was passing at the time, and a lady's across the street, who ran with bed clothes with which to smother the merciless flames. Dr. Rentz was also soon upon the grounds, but the poor sufferer was beyond human aid. The doctors could only alleviate in some degree her intense agony, in which she lingered for twelve or thirteen hours. No portion of her body except that covered by her corset escaped the terrible burning. So intense was the fire that from the top of her head to the soles of her feet the flesh was charred and cooked — her finger nails coming off with the bandages. The accident shocked the entire community, and although Mrs. Henry was a comparative stranger she nor her husband lacked for kind attention and sympathy. . . . — ***Wichita City Eagle*, July 24, 1879.**

Children seem to be fascinated with fire, and parents have probably always admonished their children to not "play with it." On the frontier, just as today, some children heeded such words of wisdom and others did not.

News was brought to town last Friday of one of the saddest accidents that it ever becomes the duty of the journalist to place

on record. It occurred on the day previous at about 10 o'clock A. M., and was nothing less than the burning to death of Rosa Thomas, an eight-year old daughter of Mr. A. L. Thomas, whose residence is in Nelson township about eight miles southeast of this place. . . .

Mr. Thomas had determined to burn a lot of corn stalks which he had on his place, and had invited Mr. Mead to his assistance. The fire had been started, and the men were busily engaged in feeding the flames. Mr. Thomas' daughter and two of Mr. Mead's children were present, and playing about the fire. Suddenly Rosa Thomas started away uttering piercing screams, and it was discovered that her clothing was ablaze. Her father and Mr. Mead ran with all speed to her assistance, and using the only means available for extinguishing the flames, finally succeeded by throwing her down and casting dirt upon the blaze, in putting out the fire; but not until the poor child was so terribly burned as to render her recovery an evident impossibility.

Dr. Gilmer was at once sent for, and repaired to the bedside of the dying child, but the best he could do was to leave such remedies as would have the effect of deadening the pain. The Doctor found, however, that the child's nervous system had been destroyed, as she experienced but little pain.

The victim of this saddest of accidents lingered until about 11 P. M., when the spirit passed from earthly to celestial scenes. The agonizing pains, which had she been a little less burned might have racked her young body, were mercifully spared, and we understand her death was almost painless. . . .

P. S. — We understand that only two weeks previous to her death, this fated child, in her play, had her clothing take fire, at a neighbor's twice during the same visit.

— *Concordia Empire*, April 28, 1876.

One of the most distressing occurrences that ever happened in our County, transpired last Tuesday. The unfortunate victims are the two children of Mr. F. B. Minner, living nine miles northeast of town. The particulars, as near as can be ascertained, are

as follows: Four children were playing in the stable, and they had somehow got possession of matches; and in lighting them they set fire to the hay. Three of the children escaped from the stable. The oldest of the children, a boy af [*sic*] nine or ten years of age, then went into the stable for the purpose of bringing the little one out, but was caught in the flames and failed in the attempt. Mr. Miller [*sic*] was absent from home, but returned while the stable was in flames. He succeeded in reaching the body and found it burned to a crisp. A portion of the head and one foot fell from the body when it was raised. The little boy who had unsuccessfully attempted the rescue of the little child, was so badly burned that his life is despaired of, his legs and feet being burned to a crisp. It is hard to realize the agony that must be experienced by the parents of the unfortunate children. . . . We trust that the people of that neighborhood will render the bereaved parents all the comfort and assistance that is possible, in their dark hour of trouble. Let us hope that a like occurrence may never again have to be recorded in this County.

— *Smith County Pioneer*, December 6, 1878.

While one typically thinks of fire when hearing of burn victims, hot water that was used for bathing, washing, and cooking sometimes caused extensive injury. Often a child would get too close to the scalding water and death could occur.

On Wednesday of last week, the infant son of Mr. and Mrs. C. H. Glasby, of Nelson Township, a little over two years of age, was playing just outside the door of the paternal residence with a horse's bridle. The mother had just poured some boiling water into a large dish-pan for use in washing dishes, and had placed it temporarily upon the floor at some distance from the door. The child in its play backed into the room and toward the dish-pan, and by some means tripped and fell directly and bodily into the pan of water, and was thereby terribly scalded. We have no particulars of the scene which followed: It is needless to describe it. Every parent will be able to appreciate somewhat the feelings of the parents of this little one at sight of the terrible suffering they were powerless to avert from their innocent little one.

A physician was called speedily, and the child lingered. At one time a successful issue was hoped for, but the scalding element had done its work, and on Monday evening another infant spirit was called away and another home made desolate. . . .

The record of such deaths is a long and sad one, and calls for the exercise of greatest care and caution on the part of parents with reference to their little ones. . . .

— *Concordia Empire*, May 19, 1876.

Even when care was exercised, accidents still occurred. In this case, the broken handle on a tea-pot resulted in the scalding death of a small child.

While Mrs. Boone, the wife of a farmer in Sedgwick county, was pouring out tea last Monday evening, the handle of the tea pot which Mrs. Boone was holding, suddenly gave way and the scalding contents poured down upon the head of her little eighteen month's old child, scalding its face, arms and breast in so frightful a manner that the little sufferer died the next morning.

— *Saline Valley Register*, July 31, 1878.

Another mealtime death was recorded when the parents, who had been exercising caution in removing the bones from a fish, left the table and the untended child secured a portion that had not been deboned.

On last Thursday, a little girl about a year and a half old, belonging to Mr. T. C. Sowers, who lives on Main street, near the bridge, swallowed a fish-bone, which resulted in its death the same night. They had been feeding it some fish and were called away for a moment, when it put in another piece, containing the bone, in its mouth and started to run, swallowing it as it run [*sic*]. Dr. Sidlinger was called, but the bone was too far down to be reached, the folds of the trachea protecting it from reach from above. Dr. McKee and others were called and consulted, and it was decided to cut into the trachea, but with little hope of saving

the child's life. The operation was performed, the child being under the influence of ether, but the bone was not removed and the child died about midnight.

It was a beautiful, sprightly child, and its death cast a gloom over the hearts of all who heard of it. After its death the bone was removed and was found to be a jagged, crooked bone with two or three prongs, altogether about a half inch long. It was found hooked under the left vocal cord, and could not have been safely removed. . . . **— *Hutchinson News*, August 15, 1878.**

Don't Drink That . . .

Some accidental deaths resulted from ingesting substances — like strychnine — that were kept around the home to control pests such as rodents, or a substance like lye, to be used in household chores and for washing clothes.

A prescription was filled out at a drug store in Lyons for Mrs. J. W. Givens. On taking the medicine, she was thrown into vomiting and soon died, when it was discovered that the medicine had been put up in a strychnine bottle.

— *Rice County Gazette*, August 28, 1879.

Sometimes, the nature of the accident was not always clear. A child was accidentally poisoned when given medicine used previously by her mother, but which now was laced with strychnine. Considerable mystery surrounded the case. The coroner concluded that someone had placed the strychnine in the medicine in the hopes that the mother would continue to use it and perish. But no evidence supported this assertion, and no charges were filed.

I was called upon last Tuesday evening late, and informed that there had been some children of Richard Bobier's poisoned. I went and held an inquest. The following facts were developed: Drs. Head, Elliott and Sutton, made a post mortem examination of one of the children that had died, and found that death was caused by strychnine. The mother had been giving them some medicine, which she had kept in the house. The doctors examined the bottle of medicine and found five grains of crystallized

strychnine yet undesolved. They found particles of strychnine in the child's stomach. The other child, by prompt attention, was in a fair way to recover. The facts elicited showed a bad state of feeling between some parties, and while the jury were agreed that there had been a terrible crime committed, and that the guilty party or parties were not far off, yet the evidence failed to point clearly to the guilty ones, they gave it as their verdict that the poison was accidently given by the child's mother, but did not say whether the poison got into the bottle by accident or not. The father of the children, Mr. Richard Bobier, is now in the Black Hills country. The whole evidence and circumstances proves clearly to me that the poison was intended for Mrs. Bobier, and not for the children, as she was in the habit of taking medicine from this bottle frequently, and had taken some from it only a few days before. This thing needs more investigation. Ora Jones.

— *Smith County Pioneer*, July 13, 1878.

Lye poisoning was also a common problem. A concentrated solution of either potassium or sodium hydroxide, lye was commonly used by the settlers in making soap. Lye is highly caustic and can result in death if taken internally.

A little son of John Martin, Esq., of Westminster, died on Wednesday of last week, under the following circumstances; Mrs. Martin had been sick for over a month and the child which was about a year old had been sent to the residence of Mr. Thos. Hoppings . . . [*who*] was taking care of it. On Tuesday Mrs. Hoppings was washing. She had a box of concentrated lye setting on the table near. She had just poured the water off of it, leaving a little in the box. She went and sat down to rest for a little while, and, suffering with a headache she leaned her head on the bed. While there the child had got to the box and drank the lye. Medical aid was called at once but no relief could be given. It died the next day. . . . While the circumstances cast a gloom over the entire community no blame attaches to Mrs. Hoppings.

— *Hutchinson News*, March 2, 1876.

They Were Just Playing . . .

Other tragic accidental frontier deaths occurred as children were happily playing amongst themselves.

> **A four year old son of Mr. Robert Moore, living north of town, was choked to death a few days ago. He with his little brothers and sisters were trying to see who could eat the most shelled corn and a kernel of corn lodged in his throat, strangling him.**
>
> **— *Saline County Journal*, November 15, 1877.**

> **Last Monday three children, aged respectively nine, eight and four years, of Andrew Harms, a Mennonite who lives eight miles east of here in Pleasant township, section 33, were smothered to death. The parents had come to town that day to do their usual trading, leaving the children at home, and while playing the children for some reason got into a large Russian chest which had a double spring lock, and when the lid came down it fastened them in, and where their parents found them [*the*] next day, after a long search, smothered to death. The children in the agonies of death had torn quanities [*sic*] of flesh off of each other. Another child aged two years was left at home also, but fortunately did not get into the chest.** **— *Newton Kansan*, July 4, 1878.**

Frontier children, like those of today, will play with almost anything. Playing with the running gears of a wagon was great fun until it rolled down a hill and over a young girl.

> **Last night a child of Mr. WHEATLEY, aged about nine years, who lives northeast of the city, was accidentally killed by a wagon. It appears that Mr. WHEATLEY and his brother had been using the running gears of the wagon, and after unhitching, the children commenced playing with it, the little girl having hold of the tongue when it started down hill, and the girl in letting loose, fell, the wagon passing over her neck, killing her almost instantly. . . .** **— *Beloit Weekly Record*, November 7, 1878.**

One would not anticipate an accident while watching a baseball game. However, bats could slip from the player's grip and speeding balls could travel considerable distances into the spectators.

L. Haven, a lad aged 14 years, was killed near South Haven, Summer [*sic*] county recently, by a blow from a ball club which had slipped from the hands of a striker engaged in playing ball.

— *Edwards County Leader*, December 20, 1877.

Accidental deaths were also caused by a variety of poisonous native prairie plants, such as loco weed, milkweed, and larkspurs. The beautiful flowers and foliage could be very tempting to inquisitive children.

A son of Mr. Miller, living southeast of town, died last week from the effects of eating some poisonous weed growing on the prairies. — *Ellsworth Reporter*, May 8, 1879.

Dangers of Farming

Livestock, as always, were sometimes dangerous to be around. All of the accidental deaths caused by domestic animals and reported in the early newspapers were of men and boys — not an unexpected discovery as primarily frontier males worked with livestock. Numerous reports of settlers being kicked by animals were found.

On the 4th of July a little son of Mr. Miller, 12 miles south of town, recently from Texas, was kicked in the breast by a Texas pony, from the effects of which he died in a few moments. The little fellow was playing with his sister, and passing near the pony, he playfully hit it with his hand when he was instantly killed. The little boy was 12 years old; his death was a terrible blow to the parents. — *Inland Tribune*, July 12, 1879.

A sad accident occured [*sic*] near Wilson on the evening of the 15th. A little boy, son of Rueben Palmer, was found on his range lying on the ground dead. It is supposed that he was thrown from the horse and killed instantly. He was sent by the father on horse back to turn some cattle in an opposite direction that were approaching some hay stacks that stood about half a mile from the house, late in the evening. The boy not returning as soon as was expected, search was made and the boy was found by his uncle and taken to his house, who then carried the sad news to the bereaved parents. The uncle says when he found the boy (which was about an hour and a half after he was sent out) the faithful horse and dog were both standing within a few feet of his body. In the midst of life we are in death. We never know when we have spoken the last word to our children and our friends. Little did that father think when he told the boy to go and turn the cattle back, that it would be the last words he would speak to him, and the last time he would see him alive. The bereaved family have our heart felt sympathy. A. A. Jellison.

— *Ellsworth Reporter*, March 21, 1879.

Horses and mules were not the only animals to inflict damage.

Through Dr. Owen we learn that a ten year old son of Mr. Wm. Thompson, who lives above the fair ground, met with a violent and sudden death last evening. He had brought in the cow from the pasture and was holding the rope while Mrs. Thompson was milking. Thoughtlessly and boy-like, he tied the end of the lariat around his wrist. The cow becoming frightened at something suddenly started off with mad speed, dragging the poor boy by the arm. The mother screamed and called her husband who was cutting cane not far off, and he rushed to the rescue. By that time the cow had made a wide circuit and returned to the house, with the boy still attached to the rope. The little fellow breathed but two or three times after his parents got to him. His back was broken and his body terribly bruised about the head and shoulders. The funeral will take place to-day. . . .

— *Wichita Weekly Beacon*, September 10, 1879.

A fatal accident occurred at Logan, one day last week, which terminated in the death of a son of Mrs. Larrick. He was picketing out a cow, which getting frightened, threw him to the ground, and the picket pin striking him in the neck, entered the windpipe, killing him almost instantly.

— *Phillips County Herald*, June 14, 1878.

A boy in Ashland was killed by a hog on the 7th inst. He went out to gather cobs where the hogs were, when one struck him under the left arm, near the heart, severing the artery. The boy bled to death in a short time. — *Ellinwood Express*, July 20, 1878.

Although farm implements on the frontier were of much simpler design than modern equipment, they also were hazardous if precautions were not taken.

Andrew Lovindall, living about five miles from town, near Marcot's was found by his brother lying insensible in his field on Monday, with a terrible wound in his thigh. Near him stood his team attached to a revolving hay rake the teeth of which were bloody. Dr. Campbell being called, said that the femeral [*sic*] artery was severed, which necessarily proved fatal. The man died on Monday night. — *Clyde Herald*, September 19, 1878.

Saturday morning last, about 9 o'clock, a sad and fatal accident occurred in Grove tp., by which Mr. Frank Brown lost his life. It appears lhat [*sic*] he was plowing with a gang plow and two yoke of oxen, when he was thrown from and under the same, one shear running into the right leg laying it open to the bone, the other shear passing into the left hip severing the main artery.

He was taken to his home and a messenger dispatched for the medical assistance, but it arrived too late to be of any service, and with the closing of the day the angel of death came and took his soul to that eternal home from whence there is no returning.

— *Hutchinson Herald*, August 3, 1878.

Stay Away from the Water . . .

In addition to death caused by weather-related flash-flood waters, the widely scattered permanent rivers and lakes of the prairie tempted and sometimes trapped Kansas pioneers into watery graves.

A very sad accident occurred here last Thursday evening, by which the only son of Rev. J. M. Vetter's, a bright promising little boy ten years old, lost his life. He, in company with three other small boys, had gone fishing in Sand Creek, but had left their fish-poles and went to the pond near Dr. Floyd's, where they began wading in the water. Two of them went in beyond their depth, and sank to the bottom, rising to the surface and sinking three times, as near as can be ascertained. The screams of the two others brought a young man who was at work for Dr. Floyd, to the scene just in time to see Johnnie Ragan sinking the last time. He plunged in and brought him out in an apparently lifeless condition; and instantly rolled him on the ground, thus saving his life. When told that there was another boy in the water, he again went in, but it was some time before he could be found. A large crowd was soon on the spot, and every remedy tried to resuscitate him, without avail. He had been in the water so long that life was extinct. The family have the heartfelt sympathy of the entire community in this their sudden bereavement.

— *Newton Kansan*, August 16, 1877.

We learn that Bertie Vetter, son of Rev. John Vetter, of Sedgwick, formerly of Sterling, was drowned on the 9th inst. in Sand creek, which runs near Mr. Vetter's house. Bertie had been in the habit of playing in the water, but, being somewhat uneasy about the safety of his son, Mr. Vetter had forbidden him going into the

creek. A playmate, however, dared him to go in. He went. The two boys got to scuffling and ducking each other. Before they knew it they were beyond their depth.

— *Rice County Gazette*, August 16, 1877.

Edgar Nunamaker, son of H. Nunamaker, Esq, sixteen years old, was drowned in the Smoky on Saturday evening. This sad calamity has cast a gloom over the whole community, and the afflicted family have the earnest sympathy of every one, — but how little consolation is contained in this sentence to the hearts that have been crushed by the loss of a bright and promising child. Several boys, as is the custom, had gone to the swimming hole, in the river at the mouth of Hencke Creek, and while in the water, it is supposed that young Nunamaker was seized with cramp, and carried to the bottom. Noble efforts were made to save him by his companions Masters Dave Fox, Frank Foster, Willie Hank, Frank Fox, and Geo. Minnick, but they were all lighter in weight than him, and the water was fifteen feet deep, so their efforts which came near resulting in their own deaths were futile. The body was recovered after it had been in the river nearly an hour, and strenuous appliances made to resusitate [*sic*] life made, but to no purpose. The funeral which took place on Sunday afternoon was largely attended. Young Edgar was a particulary good boy and full of unfolding hopes, and his quiet, unobtrusive character will long be remembered by those who knew him. Life is made up of just such sad episodes, and all of us have our own silent griefs. In almost every household there is an enshrined memory, a sacred casket, where a lock of shining hair, a ring, or faded picture, tells us of some one that is gone. The younger children as they grow up learn to look upon the picture of the dead, as on the face of an angel, and wonder if they will ever be as good as they were. They look with tender care upon the various relics — the broken playthings, the bat and ball, the unfinished piece of work — and seeing their mother's tears, and hearing her talk, they wonder meekly if they shall ever deserve to be loved as much as he who is now in heaven. When by death

some one is removed, then only can we measure the real depth of affection that was cherished for them. One beautiful trait of humanity is the tenderness with which we cherish the memory of the departed. His playmates long for their dead companion with real and tender grief — though it may not be demonstrative — they "wish he was back again." They are surprised to find how much they loved him. To look upon the domestic and social life of this afflicted family it seems hard that this separation should take place. Death has taken from this household a splendid child, and all now remember his loving ways, his excellent qualities, and his manliness. How strange it is that as soon as we are severed from those we really love, they seem more than ever desirable and necessary to us, but such is the inevitable of this life. There are scars that time cannot heal — the heart does not become callosed [*sic*] to such grief as this, and there is only the promise for us left — "he shall live again."

— *Ellsworth Reporter*, July 19, 1877.

It is supposed that the drunk woman described below fell into the river at Salina, but one wonders whether she might have committed suicide.

Poor Maggie Murphy must have lived in a cozy little home once, and she had a good husband and a little son who filled her cup of happiness to the brim. But she had just tasted of those sweet peaceful joys of home, when the cup was dashed from her lips. She raised her hands again to drink, but how changed the contents of the cup. Death called her loving husband first. She then struggled hard to raise her boy to be a man and take the father's place in the world. But when he was just upon the eve of manhood, he too was chosen from among the living, at the remorseless beck of death. Then came woe to the widowed and motherless woman. She tried to drown her sorrow in liquor, and soon the habit of drinking was fastened upon her, and she become [*sic*] known as a drunken woman who came to Salina on periodical sprees. Last Friday she came again on a spree. Saturday morning she filled herself up and wandered about town, across the bridge and over to the brewery. But just before arriving at the latter place she fell by the road side, too drunk to walk.

Some men working at the brewery discovered her as they were going to dinner, and conducted her to the stalls on the Fair ground, where they covered her with a dress she was carrying in a bundle, closed the doors to protect her from the cold, and went to dinner. On their return they went to the stalls, but found she had gone. On Sunday two young men were rowing a boat up the river, when one of them discovered the body of a woman floating in the water. They at once reported the fact to Coroner Groger, who summoned a jury and proceeded to the place where the body was found. Upon drawing it from the water it was identified by witnesses as that of the woman whom they had placed in the stalls. She was known to others in town and had given her name as Maggie Murphy and Sarah Burgess. Upon her person were found three photographs — her husband, son, and her sister's two children, — together with a little money and some trinkets. Nothing could be ascertained of her relatives or where she lived. It is supposed that as soon as the men left her the [*sic*] had crawled out of the stalls and staggered off down the river bank back of the stalls, and being so helpless was drowned without an apparent struggle. The body was buried at the county poor farm on Monday. It was indeed a sad case. Her only fault was, she was a drunken woman. — ***Saline County Journal*, November 6, 1879.**

Handle with Care . . .

Firearms were involved in many accidental deaths among the settlers. Hunting was important on the frontier. It secured meat for the table and for market, and provided recreation for many. Although there were no hunter safety courses or publicized warnings about guns on the frontier, concerned citizens, parents, and others warned the settlers about the dangers of being careless with firearms. However, sometimes inexperienced hunters became excited with the flush of wild game and forgot even the rudiments of gun safety.

"One sorrow doth tread upon another's heels,
So fast they follow
"When sorrows come they come not single spies,
But in battalions."

Last Saturday evening Benny Eldridge, in company, with

Sammy Heller and Henry Woodcock, all schoolmates and playfellows, started out for a plover hunt south of town. It was past the middle of the afternoon, and the three had but one gun — a breech-loader — between them. It was nearing sundown, and the party were [*sic*] about three and a half miles south of town, near the Greenlee farm, and while young Heller was putting in a cartridge, with the muzzle of the gun turned from the other two, a flock of birds got up. In his excitement Benny ran round in front of the gun, and Sammy, in attempting in his haste to close down the barrels had failed to half-cock the weapon and it was discharged by the concussion. The whole charge tore through the fleshy part of young Eldridge's thigh, about half way down to the knee, completely severing the femoral artery. His companions were frightened so badly, as not to know what to do, while the life-blood of young Eldridge gushed out at each pulsation of his heart. By the assistance of the other two he walked to a school house near at hand when he told them to tie something around his leg to stop the blood, which they did; but even then his life had almost run out. By this time the shadows of evening were falling. The assistance of a farmer living near by and his wagon were secured, and Mr. Clark Kincaid, who was returning home, learning of the accident rode back to the city with the heartrending news to his parents and brother. Mr. J. W. Eldridge, the father, in company with others, started to meet the wounded boy. He was lying in the wagon, his head supported by young Heller, his face covered up and his eyes closed, making no attempt to talk until his father spoke to him. As soon as he arrived home several physicians were summoned, but they determined that it was too late. Hardly an ounce of blood remained in his veins. He continued to talk until half past nine o'clock, complaining of an oppression about his heart and pain in his stomach, when he quietly passed away. His sister, Miss Matie, is at the Cheyenne Agency, in the Indian Territory. After he had received the wound he spoke to the boys and said he would die, and expressed an anxiety for the welfare of his dear sister. The following day was the anniversary of his birth, and his sister had sent him a bundle of Indian arrows and other trinkets, and a congratulatory letter that he had reached fifteen, which

things arrived at the post office the same hour that he received the fatal shot. . . .

His funeral and burial took place on Monday, Rev. John Kirby delivering an address of much feeling. The public schools were dismissed, and his body was followed by a long cortege of carriages, and by fellow-schoolmates by twos on foot. He was loved by all who knew him for his many manly and gentle qualities. We can say nothing of the deep grief of the father, mother, brother, and sister. The calamity was so unexpected and so sudden as to be almost unsupportable. It is a heavy hour, in which untold sorrow eclipses all things else, nor words nor tears can mitigate its poignancy. As to the companions of the ill-fated little Benny, their anguish has been touching. There can be no possible blame attached anywhere. Sammy Heller has been almost wild, the unfortunate affair having preyed upon his minds until fears are entertained for his life. He cannot rid himself of the horror, and for a day or two past has been in a critical mental and physical condition. ***— Wichita City Eagle*, April 10, 1879.**

Wm. Howard, a lad aged sixteen years, died last Monday, from the effects of a wound received from the bursting of a gun he was trying, on the previous Friday. He was working for Mr. Becker in Union township, before his death. On Friday, a neighbor boy came over with his gun to Mr. Becker's, and proposed to trade with Howard for his gun. The boys went across the road to Mr. Burris' farm, and were testing the guns. Howard had young Fritz's gun when he fired, the breeching burst, a sliver striking and enbedding [*sic*] itself in his forehead. He did not fall, but picked the iron out and walked over to Mr. Becker's, not seeming to be seriously hurt. On Sunday he was up and walking around. Monday morning he took worse and sank rapidly, dying about noon. He, with his father, was lately from Missouri.

***— Wichita Weekly Beacon*, February 13, 1878.**

Frank Albert, son of Chas. Albert, was accidentally shot, last Sunday, with a pistol in the hands of his companion, Jas. D. Varble, while they were amusing themselves shooting at a mark, on the west side of the river, half a mile below town. They had been practicing for sometime and Frank had fired the last shot at the target, and what they both thought was the last load in the pistol, and Varble remarked that if there was another shot in the pistol he thought he could beat it. Frank handed him the pistol and Varble says that he took it and as he turned it towards the mark, the pistol went off. He did not dream that it was loaded and does not remember whether it was cocked or not when he took it. The ball passed through the biceps muscle of the left arm and then into the chest below the sixth rib.

Be [*sic*] was brought home in a wagon and medical assistance procured. There was some difference of opinion as to where the ball is located. The wound was probed but without finding the leaden missle. Frank is about twenty years of age, bright, active, and popular with his associates. At the time of this writing he lies in a precarious condition, suffering great pain, and undoubtedly bleeding internally. It is a very serious occurrence and gives us another warning in regard to the careless use of firearms. Dr. Owens is attending the case.

LATER — Frank died Monday at 12 o clock. A coroner's inquest found a verdict of accidental killing. The funeral took place yesterday at eleven o'clock. . . . This ends the most woeful tragedy in our history. — ***Wichita Weekly Beacon*, February 26, 1879.**

On Wednesday afternoon, 5th inst., Fritz Walckley aged about twelve years, son of John Walckley, residing in Republic township, was instantly killed by being shot through the head. It appears his father and mother were absent, and young Fritz, with boyish curiosity, was handling the gun left by his father, when by some means it was discharged and the whole charge passed into his head. From the appearance of the wound, he may have attempted to blow into the muzzle, or look into it, or have carelessly handled it in some other way when it exploded. He was

alone in the house, his younger brothers and sisters being at play outside. He was a bright, intelligent boy, beloved by all who knew him, and his sudden death has saddened the whole community.

— *Concordia Expositor*, September 27, 1877.

On Tuesday of last week a little daughter of Mr. and Mrs. M. H. Kibbay, who reside near Austin in this county, was shot and instantly killed by a seven year old brother. The father was away from home, and the mother and older sister were at work in the garden, leaving the little boy in the house with his two year old sister.

The report of a pistol brought the mother and daughter to the house where they found the child dying and the little brother vainly trying to staunch the flow of blood from a ghastly wound in the head. He had taken the revolver from the top of the safe where it had been left by the father, and presented it at the head of the child, pulled the trigger with the fatal effect above described. This is another terrible warning to parents who are in the habit of leaving firearms within reach of their children.

— *Sumner County Press*, June 8, 1876.

Many settlers were in the habit of keeping their guns loaded even when they were not being used. However, one of the more curious behaviors that led to accidental firearm discharge was the practice of handling loaded guns by the muzzle. Thirteen newspaper reports during the years of 1875-1879 indicated that someone was killed in this manner. Usually they were retrieving the firearm from someone or someplace, or they were trying to put down the gun.

About five o clock in the afternoon the deceased [*Ole R. Moe*] and Evan Rosencrist and his son, a boy about eleven years old passed through town on their way to Concordia, when about half am ile [*a mile*] below town, they saw a prairie chicken, and [*the*] deceased jumped from the wagon with the intention of shooting

it. He went to the rear end of the wagon and took hold of the muzzle of the gun and drew it towards him when it was discharged, the contents striking his arm near the sholder [*sic*], destroying the muscles, nerves and tendens [*sic*], severing the axilary [*sic*] arteries and fracturing the bone badly. Portions of the bone and muscles were carried away by the charge, which passed out back of the shoulder. All he said was "I am gone," which he repeated three times. He did not fall immediately, but took several steps. Mr. Rosencrist sprung from the wagon and went to his assistance, and tried to get him into the wagon, but was unable to do so. He finally eased him to the ground, and then sent his son to town to get assistance. A large crowd gathered in a few moments, but he was unconcious [*sic*] and ceased to breath[*e*] in about fifteen or twenty minutes, when his body was brought to town and deposited in the old saloon building.

— *Scandia Republic*, March 28, 1877.

Loading a gun could also be a danger. To prepare a muzzle-loader gun, the powder, wad, and shot were pushed down the barrel, which meant that unless care was taken, the barrel could be pointed at the person loading it.

Last Friday afternoon, about five o'clock, p.m., Newton C. Cartright, aged fifteen years, a son of Mr. V. C. Cartright, while out hunting accidentally shot himself. The fatal accident took place near the Cowskin Creek some two miles from his father[']s house. He was standing [*on*] a log reloading one barrel of his shot gun, the other being loaded, and in ramming the charge home, the gun slipped off the log, and the hammer striking it, the whole load was discharged into the lower part of his abdomen. Ranging upwards it lacerated the blood vessels and viscera of the abdominal cavity producing an internal hemorrhage that terminated in death, at ten o'clock p.m. Friday night. He was seen by a neighbor near whose place he was hunting, and was carried home. To make this heart rending calamity more bitter his father and mother were absent in the southern portion of the county and did not get home until after the poor boy was dead. Dr. Furley was summoned to his side, but he was beyond human aid. He

was buried on the farm, on Sunday, Mr. Ashbaugh preaching the funeral sermon. . . . — ***Wichita Weekly Beacon*, October 25, 1876.**

A thrill of horror passed through this community, last Monday evening, upon hearing the fact and manner of the death of Grant Matthews. He was a young boy of fourteen or fifteen years of age, and at the time of his sudden and tragic death was with a hunting party, consisting of his brother, Geo. Matthews, Judge S. M. Tucker and Mr. Stancer, who were hunting on Stachell creek, in Butler county, about forty miles from this city. At the time of the accident George was out on the prairie, hunting, and Tucker and Stancer were preparing to change the camp, and had loaded their traps in a wagon. Among other things lying in the wagon was a loaded shot gun, with the muzzle towards the endgate. Grant had taken an axe out to cut a sapling [*sic*], after which he approached the hind end of the wagon and pitched the axe in. It struck the hammer of the gun and the heavy load of buck shot was discharged, the entire contents striking the unfortunate boy in the right side of the face, carrying away the whole lower half of the face. Death was instantaneous. His body was placed in the wagon, and Judge Tucker, after finding George and informing him of the terrible event, started on horseback to bring the news to his family. He got into the city about 6 o'clock and the wagon followed, arriving at about 10 p.m. The corpse was taken to Matthew's drug store and prepared for burial, and yesterday morning taken to the residence of his mother. His mutilated face was covered to conceal it from the bereaved friends. This is one of the most terrible and heartrending tragedies it has ever been our duty to record, and the entire community join in tendering their deep sympathy to the stricken friends of poor little Grant. . . .

— ***Wichita Weekly Beacon*, December 12, 1877.**

Transportation Accidents

Travel, sometimes over great distances, was necessary on the frontier. Most settlers were farmers and lived far from neighbors or from town.

While crossing the broad expanse of prairie on horse, mule, buggy, or wagon, it was common to not make destination by nightfall, and many was the unfortunate settler who had made the prairie his bed.

Yesterday morning, in coming to town, Messrs. Cheneworth and McFarland, of Ness County, sighted an object on the prairie, about ten miles south-west of Hays, and upon investigation, found several blankets, a saddle, a coat, vest, and pair of overalls; and from the position of things, it was evident some weary stranger had made his bed there. The blankets were spread out upon the grass; and the clothing and saddle had been used as a pillow. In the pocket of the coat was found a pocket-book, containing several letters, some addressed to the owner, and one written by him to his brother in Medicine Lodge, Barbour [*Barber*] County, stating that on Monday morning the writer (J. L. Murdock) would leave Ellis for Dodge, on horseback, in quest of work. He had evidently made his bed at this spot on Monday night. From the appearance of the grass at the foot of his bed, it was evident that the horse had been tied by a short halter-strap to one of his feet; and from the same indications, Cheneworth and McFarland are confident the man was dragged away by his horse, — frightened, perhaps by a wolf. It is almost certain the man was killed, as he would not willingly abandon his clothing and property, and nothing had been seen of him at the ranches or camps in the vicinity. A search was made for his body, but failed to discover any thing. Accidents of this kind are very frequent on the prairies; and if, someday, the skeleton of a man is found in one of the gulches bordering on the Smoky, it may safely be set down as belonging to J. D. Murdock. . . .

— *Hays City Sentinel*, June 29, 1878.

"Equipment failure," then as today, was another hazard to the pioneer. Wagons, drawn by a team of horses or mules, were the major means of transportation and often cause for concern.

Another dreadful calamity has brought grief and almost despair into a happy household. Allen Lawrence, aged fifteen years, son of Mr. Henry Lawrence, of West Wichita, met his

untimely and sudden death, last Tuesday, a little before noon. He was driving the wagon used in hauling wheat from the field to the stack, and the loading was nearly completed when the ladder on the front of the wagon gave way, precipitating the unfortunate boy on to the double trees. The frightened mules started on the run, and Arther [*sic*] clung with desperation to the single trees until his strength failed him, when he fell to the ground. Both wheels passed lengthwise over his body, inflicting such injuries, external and internal, that death ensued in less than an hour. Thus is added another to our list of sudden and cruel deaths that have shocked the hearts and called forth the deepest sympathies of our community, within the past year.

— *Wichita Weekly Beacon*, June 25, 1879.

And poor road conditions precipitated accidents on the frontier, just as they do today. Local newspapers reported several instances of wagon accidents caused by rough terrain or objects in the roadway.

On the night of the Fourth, as Mr. and Mrs. Flint were returning home from the celebration, when within a short distance of their residence, the night being unusually dark, their team wandered off from the road, and in crossing a ravine the front part of the wagon was suddenly pitched into a gulch, throwing the occupants to the ground. Mrs. Flint was holding her infant daughter in her arms, and the little one fell under the front wheel and it is presumed that the wheels passed over its head, the skull being considerably crushed. A messenger was immediately dispatched for Dr. Cannon, but before the Dr. had arrived, the spirit of the litte one had passed to the [*sic*] THE OTHER WORLD. This is indeed a sad affair, though the fatal calamity is only one of a thousand that transpires everyday, throwing across the threshhlds [*sic*] of happy families a shade of sorrow that time cannot erase. **— *Smith County Pioneer*, July 13, 1878.**

A distressing accident occurred in Beaver township on the night of the 25th ult., resulting in the death of Nellie, an [*i*]nfant,

13 months old, child of Ed. Weitzel. The parents with infant and several other persons were in a wagon returning from a Christmas party, and were approaching the Arkansas for the purpose of crossing. Before arriving at the stream the wagon passed over some object and upset throwing its contents upon the ground and frightening the team to a runaway. The child's clothing caught in the wagon some way, and it was dragged violently along and far out into the stream, where the team stopped from exhaustion, before its distracted parents could recover the little one. It was so injured that it died on the 27th.

— *Sumner County Press*, January 11, 1877.

Wagons and buggies in town, where activity and "traffic" were increased, also necessitated care by pedestrians when crossing the roadway.

Occurred on Friday afternoon, Dec. 19, near the lumber yard of Edwards Bros. & Fair, in Sterling. The details of the circumstances vary with each eye witness to the event; but after a careful comparison of what has been said by those who were immediately on the ground, the following facts seem clearly evident. The day was extremely cold, and the wind blowing almost a gale, a team owned by Edward Bros. & Fair, were [*sic*] just entering the lumber yard from Broadway, when Rev. F. S. Buckner's two boys, Henry and Rollo, came running along the sidewalk. Rollo was in the lead, and facing the keen winds, he turned his face partly backwards looking towards his older brother who was following near his side. In this way, and without observing whither he was going he ran against the horse that caused his death. He doubtless observed this way of running that he might better protect himself from the cold. Escape was impossible. He was already between the horses and the wagon. Had not the horses been stopped in a moment another turn of the wheels would [*have*] crushed the noble child.

The driver who is a sober and competent teamster, realized the situation and stopped the team. But the horse, which was never known before to kick, struck the child, some say once while other say twice. Be that as it may there were two heavy bruises one on his leg, the other on his chest. Drs. Harriman, and

Trueheart attended the child, but after much suffering he quietly expired, Saturday at midnight, Dec. 20. His father had left on Friday morning to attend dedicatory services at Medicine Lodge. He was sent for on Friday night and returned home on Sabbath to find his boy already twelve hours in the embrace of death.

The boy was a promising lad of six years. The accident seemed unavoidable. Blame rests upon no one, and the bereaved parents and brother have the heartfelt sympathy of the entire community. . . .

— *Rice County Gazette*, December 25, 1879.

Yet, even out of town, on country roadways, some tragedies occurred.

We are pained to record an unhappy accident, which resulted in the death of a young farmer named Christopher C. Shaw, who is known to many of our readers. On the 20th ult. [*ultimately*], Mr. Shaw, accompanied by C. S. Eberhart and Rosal Hugobon, were driving in a wagon to their home in Walnut township. At about sundown when near the farm of Henry Rosemond, Shaw and Eberhardt [*sic*] jumped out of the wagon in to the road and commenced a frolic in the snow. While they were just engaged the team carrying the U. S. Mail, coming north, passed their wagon, and came quite suddenly upon them. Both the mail carrier and Eberhart called out to Shaw to get out of the road. He was slow in acting, and the pole of the wagon struck him in the stomach. He was speedily taken in charge and driven to his home. Everything was done that could be done to save his life, but his recovery was out of the question. He died on the 27th inst. This is one of those unavoidable accidents which sometimes occur when no one was really to blame. . . .

— *Saline County Journal*, January 2, 1879.

Driving under the influence of alcohol also led to accidents and death on the frontier. However, in the following case, the condition of the team of horses certainly did not improve the drunk's chances of reaching his destination.

A Swede by the name of Peter Johnson was killed at the bridge near Mr. S. Carlin's — nine miles south of town — last Saturday night. As near as we can gather them the facts are that Johnson started from Salina that evening with a small load of lumber. He was intoxicated. One of his horses was totally blind and the other blind in one eye. The night was dark and when the team came to the bridge the wagon was hauled only partially on the approach of the bridge and was thus capsized. The next morning the wagon and its load was found upside down and under it the dead body of Johnson. One horse was also pinned down by the wagon, but managed to regain it[*s*] feet when assisted, and was not very much injured. The other horse was grazing near by. . . .

— *Saline County Journal*, December 23, 1875.

In some places, ferries were used to provide transportation across the prairie rivers. But they were not always safe for man or beast.

From R. W. Stevenson, who left Tuesday morning for Wichita, with a party of boat builders, we received on the afternoon of the same day the following note by the hand of a private messenger:

We arrived here (London crossing,) about 11 o'clock a.m. As we came in sight of the ferry, we discovered twelve or fifteen men running down the north bank apparently greatly excited. On arriving at the ferry, we were informed that John Broderick was drowned. They had put two horses on the boat. When in the middle of the river, the horses became restive, and upset the boat. Three or four men were in it and all went out with Broderick and the horses. It is supposed that one of the horses struck Broderick. He swam for some time, holding to a paddle. He went under some tree tops, came up for a moment and then went down out of sight. . . .

— *Sumner County Press*, June 7, 1877.

The "Iron Horse"

By the 1860s, railroads were beginning to push westward into the Great Plains. The first track in Kansas was established in the extreme eastern region of the state in 1860, but extensive construction was delayed until the close of the Civil War in 1865. The first major line in Kansas, the

Union Pacific, began in Wyandotte in September of 1863 but did not reach Topeka until 1866. This railroad, which became known as the Kansas Pacific in 1869, extended westward up the Kansas and Smoky Hill valleys and reached the western border of the state in 1867.

The other major railroad, the Atchison, Topeka, and Santa Fe, began in Topeka in 1868, and by December 1872 stretched to the western border of Kansas. The railroads were vital links to the Eastern U.S. markets, with thousands of head of cattle shipped annually (Richmond, 1992).

But, on the frontier, deaths were associated with the new "iron horse," and included wrecks, work accidents, and falls.

Frank Glover, an old colored man, heretofore employed as a porter at the Douglas Avenue House, was run over and killed by the 9:45 p.m. train, last Sunday night. He was shockingly mangled, his body literally torn to pieces. An inquest conducted by Coroner Munger and County Attorney Stanley, was held on the body at the scene of the death, about 11 o'clock at night. Two ladies returning from church a few minutes before the train came in, saw a man sitting, in a stooping position, on the track. Mr. C. C. Wheeler, in following the train into the depot, almost fell over the body of a man lying on the track. He immediately reported the fact to Dan. Parks, and the two returned to the place where it was lying, when it was seen to be a colored man, afterwards identifed as old man Glover.

The engineer, fireman, and conductor were examined and testified to using the usual precautions of blowing the whistle and ringing the bell. It seems that the old man had been on a spree for a day or two previous, and on this particular evening, was seen to be under the influence of liquor, by several parties, and in that condition wandered along the track and, either sitting down or falling, remained there in a state of semi-consciousness until he met his death. He was shockingly mangled, both legs torn from the body, and the latter crushed and almost severed in twain just below the breast. His face and chest were not mutilated. We give below the body of the finding of the jury:

An inquest held in the city of Wichita, Sedgwick county, Kansas, the fourth day of June, 1876 . . . [*found*] the said person came

to his death by being run over by the cars while sitting on the track, supposed to have been asleep. . . .

Since the finding of the jury is silent as to whether the death of the man was caused by the culpable negligence of the railroad employes [*sic*] or not, we are constrained to say, that, from a personal examination of the locality of the tragedy, from the end of the curve to the place where the body was found, and examining the width of light on the track from the head-light, and taking these in connection with the sworn statement of the engineer, that he could, if he had seen the body, stopped the train inside the length of the engine, that, though there was no criminal negligence, the death of this man was the result of a lack of the extraordinary care and precaution which the law contemplates and demands from all railroads, running through thickly populated towns and cities. We think this fact should have been included in the finding of the inquest. — ***Wichita Weekly Beacon*, June 7, 1876.**

And youngsters would frequently hang onto the railroad cars for fun, as the cars were being shifted about in the rail yard.

A boy named Cartwright was clinging to the rear of a freight car as the train was making up in Hutchinson on last Saturday morning. When the cars came together his hold was shaken loose and he fell on the track and was run over. His leg was mashed off close to his body, and he died in about half an hour. So far as we could learn, no blame could be attached to the train men. Parents should be careful to keep their children away from such danger.

— ***Rice County Gazette*, October 23, 1879.**

Several accidents resulted from individuals attempting to board a moving train. It wasn't always easy to gauge the speed of the train, and many overestimated their own agility.

A very sad accident occurred at Dodge City yesterday morning, a half hour after midnight, by which a well known traveling salesman of this city, Mr. H. C. Page, lost his life beneath the wheels of a passenger train. Page had been out upon the road since the first of the present month, and was returning to this city

for the purpose of being here during fair week. The train was just pulling out of Dodge City when he ran toward it an [*sic*] attempted to get aboard. He grasped the hand-rail of the platform upon the forward end of the last coach but one, but by some means he failed to get his foot upon the step, his body swung downward beneath the platform, he lost his hold of the railing and fell beneath the wheels. The car under which he fell and the Pullman coach followiug [*sic*] passed over the body of the unfortunate man. The train was at once stopped and asistance [*sic*] sent to the victim of the accident. His head had been crushed beyond recognition and his body was terribly mutilated. When found Page was quite dead. It was too late then to prepare the remains for removal to this city and they will arrive here today. . . . — *Ford County Globe*, September 23, 1879.

Instances of brakemen being killed also were reported by the area newspapers. Working around large moving railroad cars and locomotives was always dangerous, but even more so during inclement weather.

Last Thursday afternoon, at about half past three o'clock, Louis F. Parker, aged 25 years, brother of Mrs. R. B. Lynch, of this city, had his legs run over at Peabody by two empty flat cars, from the effects of which he died after five hours of intense suffering. Mr. Parker was a breakman [*sic*] on the freight trains between this city and Emporia, and at the time of the accident was assisting in making up a train at Peabody, and was making what is called a "running switch" with two empty flat or coal cars. It was raining at the time and he went to the forward end of the cars as they were rapidly running and with one foot on the car and the other on the "draw head," which holds the car link, was in the act of putting in a link, when his foot slipped and he fell upon the track. It so happened that the bumpers and the break [*sic*] of the car were on the hinder wheels as the forward end passed over him simply bruised his head and back. He then attempted to get off the track before the hinder wheels and the bumpers came upon him, but only partially succeeded; the wheels catching him just above the knees. The wheels of second car also passed over his legs, and in some unknown manner both

his legs were broken in three different places. . . . Both legs were amputated in hopes of saving his life, but it was a hopeless case, and he died at 8:20 P.M. The body was conveyed to this city, where the funeral took place last Friday afternoon. . . .

— *Newton Kansan*, October 25, 1877.

Three train wrecks were reported on the prairies of Kansas from 1875 to 1879 that resulted in death. One of the worst accidents occurred just east of Great Bend, with three individuals being killed.

On Friday morning, May 18th, 1877, an Excursion train left Topeka for the Arkansas Valley. About 300 people were on the train. The day was exceedingly rainy, and the whole face of the earth was flooded. But this train met with no mishap until it reached a point of 1½ miles east of Ellinwood and 11½ miles east of Great Bend. The engine was there ditched and the baggage car telescoped by the smoking car. Three persons were killed and about twenty wounded.

An Inquisition held and taken for the people of Kansas in the town of Ellinwood in said County began on the 19th day of May, 1877, before me, B. S. Lewis, Coroner . . . upon the view of the body of Elmore Miller and there lying dead. . . . Miller was about 28 years of age and the jurors . . . do say that he came to his death by reason of said accident to said train, which occured [*sic*] May 18th, 1877, near Ellinwood in said county and that he was instantly killed in said wreck, that the said accident was caused by a washout in the track of the A. T. & S. F. R. R. [*Atchison, Topeka, and Santa Fe Railroad*] and which was produced by a heavy rain fall. And we further find, that A. J. Nelson was killed and Sherman H. Bailey died on the evening of the 19th day of May, 1877, from wounds received in said wreck, and we further find that there have been no other deaths occured [*sic*] by reason of said accident up to this date, May 29th, 1877. And we further find that the general arrangement of the Road has been good; and we further find by the evidence given, that the track at 7 o'clock on the evening of said accident, where said train was ditched was in an unsafe condition for trains to pass over. And we further find that if the section Foreman, John W. Conroy,

and the Station Agent, M. Dick, had performed the duties as imposed on them by their employers, the A. T. & S. F. R. R. as shown by the evidence given, could have prevented said accident. We do further find that at 7 o'clock of said day the section master, J. W. Conroy, with his employees passed over the track where the accident occured [*sic*] and found the same in an unsafe condition and that necessary steps were not taken by them before the arrival of the train to stop it, or notify it of the danger and that said Conroy was guilty of great negligence and error in judgement and his conduct clearly censurable in the premises, and further, that he had ample time to pass over the washout and go beyond far enough to stop the train and have prevented the accident. And we further find, that the station agent, M. Dick, delayed more time than necessary in taking his meals and had he been at his post at the time he was looked for, he could have prevented the accident by telegraphing to station east of this and that we censure him in the premises. And we further find that the conduct of the officers and train men on said train at the time of the subsequent to the accident was commendable in all respects. And we further find, that the prompt attention of the officers and managers of the R. R. Company given to the dead and wounded after the accident, has been all that could be required or expected of them and is deserving of the highest praise.

In testimony, whereof we have here unto set out hands this 29th day of May, A. D. 1877. — ***Great Bend Register*, May 24, 1877.**

In the Work Place

In the growing pioneer village, the lumber yard was a lucrative business, but could be an unsafe place for youngsters to play.

A sad accident occured [*sic*] on last Saturday evening. Two of Mr. Huff's children were playing about a lumber pile in Clarke Bros'. yard, when little Harry, a bright boy about six years old, was caught under a falling pile and killed. It is supposed that he was trying to climb upon the lumber pile and pulled it over on himself. When found a few minutes afterwards life was extinct and although restoration was attempted it was impossible to effect it. — ***Rice County Gazette*, May 25, 1879.**

And grain elevators sprang up, as soon as the early settlers began to harvest their crops.

Last Friday evening Arthur Signor, six-year-old son of a widow lady residing in Russell, got into a bin of wheat in Knight and Bradshaw's elevator, and was drawn into the chute through which the wheat was running. His position was not discovered until the chute became clogged; and an investigation revealed his dead body. He had been smothered to death.

— *Hays City Sentinel*, August 31, 1878.

Even such an innocuous place as the General Store could present a hazard. The store clerk in the tale that follows had probably stood on a stool countless times without incident, to hang advertisements on the outside of the store.

On last Friday morning, Mr. A. N. Brewer, who had been engaged for some time, assisting J.H. Read, Esq., in his store, came down to open the store and get ready for business as usual. He was boarding with Mr. Read and it had been customary for Brewer to come down town before breakfast of mornings, open out and make a fire in the store while Mr. Read would remain at home till after breakfast when he would come and relieve Brewer, and he would go and get his breakfast. On this morning, Mr. Brewer came down about as usual and opened the store, made a fire and started to hang out the usual goods as signs. He placed a small four legged stool in the recess, at the entrance, the floor of which about a foot higher than the sidewalk, and mounted it, goods in hand. While reaching up to place the signs in position, one leg of the stool which, it seems, was near the edge of the door sill, slipped and the stool split and gave way letting him fall full length with that part of his breast or side directly over the heart, striking on one part of the stool. He arose quickly and went in the store, looking around as if to see if any one saw him, as he got inside he fell. Some one who saw him fall first, watched him and saw as he entered the store, his knees give way, and he went over to see if he was hurt. He found him lying on the floor, near the door, complaining of coldness and great pain.

Quite a crowd soon collected and he was taken to the Reno House where medical aid was summoned, but it was of no avail. He said he could feel the blood flowing in the inside of his body and that "he knew his heart was bursted." He suffered great pain until nearly noon, when he died. His cousin, living in McPherson county, came after his body and on Saturday took it to that county, where it was buried. . . .

— *Hutchinson News*, February 17, 1876.

Dangers lurked in other places of employment as well. Initially, Kansas rivers had provided the power necessary to run early grain mills. Eventually, however, steam was used to power the equipment. If not operated properly, the boiler heating the water to produce the steam could explode.

About 9 o'clock yesterday morning, a loud sound of explosion was heard, coming from the vicinty of the depot. A crowd of people hastened in that direction and it was found that the boiler in the new corn grinding mill, formerly owned by Messrs. Smith & Nellands, had exploded.

Mr. Charles Smith, one of the owners, Mr. Rankin, temporary engineer, Mr. J. B. Semple, miller, and Mr. David Kettle were in the mill at the time of the explosion.

Mr. Rankin, who stood near the furnace, was thrown through the engine house, over a coal house about 12 feet high, and struck the ground about ninety feet from the mill. He was instantly killed, and his body was badly mangled, one arm torn off. He was a native of Indiana, from Milford, Elkhart county, and was in this county without money, having worked in the mill only one day. He was unmarried, as was Mr. Smith.

Mr. Smith was thrown about thirty feet from the mill, and his body horribly mangled, his jaw bone being broken in two places, one eye torn out, his skull badly bruised, and it is probable that other bones were broken. He died after breathing about two hours, being unconscious to the last. Mr. Smith had two brothers here.

Messrs Semple and Kettle miraculously escaped without serious injury. The former was knocked down and dragged some

distance by a belt in which he became entangled. His injuries are a badly bruised leg, a cut on the head and a painful eye, filled with dust.

Mr. Kettle was badly stunned and he received a hard blow on the arm. Drs. Huffman and Buck attended these gentlemen. . . .

The causes of the explosion were, high pressure of steam, and low water. As is too often the case, this shocking occurrence is the price paid for the handling of steam power machinery by inexperienced men. There was not a practical engineer connected with the mill. — ***Newton Kansan*, February 15, 1877.**

Accidental deaths were responsible for many of the graves that frequent prairie cemeteries. Like today, no matter the setting — around the home, working in the fields or with livestock, traveling across the prairie on steed, wagon, or train, conducting business at the local store, or swimming, riding, or hunting — human error and consequent accidents always presented a risk to prairie settlers.

Gravestone north of U.S. Highway 40, west of the creek, southwest of Victoria, in Ellis County, Kansas. The monument was erected by the Union Pacific Railroad in remembrance of five track workers killed in 1867 by Indians, a few miles west of Victoria.

Kansas State Historical Society, Topeka

The weather was a significant part of the "unforgiving environment" in frontier Kansas. This tornado was photographed in Anderson County, near Central City, April 23, 1884. *Kansas State Historical Society, Topeka*

Tornado damage in Russell County, n.d. Note one wagon tossed into the home and another apparently untouched to the left.
Kansas State Historical Society, Topeka

The Moser Brother Sheep Ranch after a tornado, near Claflin, Kansas, *ca.* 1900. *Kansas State Historical Society, Topeka*

A woman in horse-drawn carriage passes over a "Low Bridge Crossing" at Osborne, Kansas. Creeks such as this were a hazard to settlers in frontier Kansas after a rain, due to the dangerous flash-flooding. *Kansas State Historical Society, Topeka*

Buggy coming through a water hole at Ellis County, Kansas. A routine crossing could be dangerous if a horse faltered and the buggy upset in water deeper than anticipated. *Kansas State Historical Society, Topeka*

The Santa Fe Trail crossing on Pawnee Creek, Pawnee County, in south-central Kansas, *ca.* 1880s. Established creek crossings such as this were always more reliable for a safe passage.

Kansas State Historical Society, Topeka

The Santa Fe Trail coming in to Dodge City, Kansas, showing two loads of buffalo hides being brought to town, in 1872. Hunting the native bison was productive, but carried an element of risk and danger from the huge stampeding animals.

Kansas State Historical Society, Topeka

Building the frontier home was not free of hazard. Three unidentified men appear in this view of an unidentified stone-front dugout in Osborne County, Kansas. Cutting the timber and quarry rock was not without their occupational dangers. *Kansas State Historical Society, Topeka*

The L. A. Mead family at their dugout one mile north of Bloom, Ford County, Kansas.
Kansas State Historical Society, Topeka

The interior of the Mead family dugout. *Kansas State Historical Society, Topeka*

Two young boys stand outside their sod house near Claflin, Barton County, Kansas, n.d. It was not unusual for the weight of the sod on the roof to collapse the roof timbers, killing the family within.
Kansas State Historical Society, Topeka

Breaking the prairie at Victoria, Kansas, in the 1870s, like farming today, was a high-risk occupation.
Kansas State Historical Society, Topeka

"Strawberry," the cow, on an old homestead near Victoria, Kansas, *ca.* 1880. Working with livestock could be the cause of accidental death on the frontier.

Kansas State Historical Society, Topeka

Recalcitrant hogs could be a danger to the farmer. This Barton County settler is tending his pigs, *ca.* 1900.

Kansas State Historical Society, Topeka

Unidentified boys swimming in a Russell County, Kansas, creek. Underestimating the depth of the water was a common cause of drowning, then and today.

Kansas State Historical Society, Topeka

A team of horses pulls a covered wagon across the Arkansas River at Great Bend, Kansas, in 1872 — always a risky venture. *Kansas State Historical Society, Topeka*

A Kansas River ferry, location not identified. An occasional overturned ferry or a careless passenger falling into the water was sometimes cause of death on the frontier.

Kansas State Historical Society, Topeka

Camping out, in Russell County, Kansas, could pose its share of hazards — from rattlesnakes, unexpected groundhog holes into which horses stumbled, or flash-flooding adjacent to creeks.
Kansas State Historical Society, Topeka

Chapter 4

The Wild, Wild West

MURDER CAME TO THE frontier in many forms and often under unusual circumstances. Firearms were most often responsible for these deaths; a large number of frontier-period murders likely occurred because guns were readily available. Almost every man or family had at least one pistol or rifle, both for survival and food gathering. Many firearms were leftover from Civil War service. These firearms were almost routinely taken along when the head of the household went outside or into town.

Many men during 1875-1879 carried a gun out of habit, without giving much thought to whether or not it might continue to be necessary. Ten or fifteen years earlier, firearms had been considered essential for protection against warring Indians; but by the late 1870s, most of these confrontations had passed. However, the lawlessness in the region, the dangerous animals, and the opportunity to bag game were important aspects of frontier daily life, and required firearms.

During the settlement period of the Plains, transient people moving into and through the region occasionally fell victim to foul play, whether by firearms or other weapons. The identity of these victims, the murderer, or the motive might be unknown. Reports of such events were usually accompanied by a physical description of the deceased, in the hopes that a reader might be able to identify the dead.

> **Last Thursday the remains of a man apparently about twenty-five years old, was found floating in Salt Creek, at a point about one mile west of Salt City, in this county. George T. Walton, acting Coroner, having been notified, summoned a jury and held an inquest. The body had apparently been in the water two weeks or more, and was consequently much disfigured by the natural process of decomposition. Two gun shot wounds were found in the head, near the apex of the skull, the balls ranging downward. The man, whoever he was, had evidently been murdered, and afterward thrown into the water. A wagon track was discovered, leading from the road to the water, and afterward returning to the road. The remains are those of a man five feet ten inches in hight [*sic*], with dark brown hair, light mustache and weighed about one hundred and fifty pounds. The body when discovered was only partially clothed in a striped cheviot shirt, cotton socks and a pair of number nine Congress gaiters. The rest of the clothing had doubtless been removed by the murderers and carried away to conceal the identity of the victim. If this was the object it was successfully accomplished, as nothing was found to indicate in the slightest who the unfortunate man was, whence he came or who were his murderers. . . .**
>
> **— *Sumner County Press*, November 2, 1876.**

Sometimes the victim was known, but not the assailant.

> **It is rumored that a fearful tragedy was enacted at a school house about three miles and a half south of Red Stone P.O. on Monday night. After school was dismissed in the evening, the young lady teacher remained, as it is supposed, to sweep. A storm came up soon after, and although the lady did not come home her parents felt no uneasiness concerning her, supposing**

she had stayed at the house of one of the neighbors, on acconnt [*sic*] of the storm. But ln [*sic*] the morning, when the school children came to school, they found their teacher lying on the school room floor with her throat cut, and perfectly dead. It is not yet known whether the deed was done by her own hand or by that of an assassin. We can not vouch for the authenticity of the above statement, as our informant was unable to gain full particulars.

— *Clyde Herald*, June 27, 1878.

Self-defense

The omnipresent firearms were unfortunately seen by many as a quick solution to settle differences that arose between individuals. Sometimes, quarrels set off a tragic series of events.

In many printed reports, self-defense was given as the reason for a death. However, there were cases where it was unclear whether this was a legitimate claim.

Last Sunday night word was received in town that a murder had been committed over in Solomon township, in this county. On Monday the Coroner was notified, and he, with the County Attorney, proceeded to the place where the dead man was lying. The dead man was Charles W. Manus, and after the inquest the jury returned a verdict that the deceased came to his death by reason of a revolver wound [*sic*] fired by one Andrew J. Wyatt, and that the said Wyatt fired the same with a felonious intent. The Coroner then issued his warrant for the arrest of Wyatt, and after he was brought before J. W. Langford, Justice of the Peace, he waived the preliminary examination and was committed for trial at the district court. Wyatt does not deny the killing, but claims it was in self-defense. There had been trouble between the parties for some time past, originating from Wyatt allowing his stock to trespass upon Manus' crops. No witnesses were present or in hearing of the report of the revolver at the time, and it is a case in which circumstances alone must govern.

— *Norton County Advance*, November 13, 1879.

Charlie Manus was shot and instantly killed on last Sunday the 9th inst., by another man named Wyatt. The scene of the tragedy was about 15 miles west of Logan, near Edmund city, in Norton county. Manus had taken up a horse belonging to Wyatt, which had been in the habit of trespassing upon his (Wyatt's) premises. After the shooting Wyatt got on to his horse and rode to Modell, and in the absence of the justice gave himself up to constable Watson. We understand that Wyatt claims the shooting to have been in self defense. As Manus was shot in the back of the neck, his counsel will probably have trouble in making this count stand. **—*Logan Enterprise*, November 14, 1879.**

Violence was sufficiently common on the frontier that some newspaper editors commented on the frequency of killings, though such admonitions seemingly did little to halt the bloodshed.

C. P. Johnson, near Phillipsburg, was shot dead, last Saturday night. The shooting was done in self-defense, it is claimed. We refrain from making comments, at present, but it seems this shooting business is getting too frequent. Various rumors are afloat as to the prabable [*sic*] cause. It is reported that the difficulty grew out of a dispute over a claim, each of the parties claiming a better right to the same.

—*Kirwin Chief*, September 18, 1878.

In a few cases, public acquiescence was evident in the killing.

On Saturday last a little "onpleasantness [*sic*] occurred at the above station [*Trego*], some thirty-three miles west of this point, resulting in the death of a frontier negro. The particulars as far as we could learn are that this colored man had earned the reputation of being quarrelsome, and "on the shoot." On Saturday, he, without cause or provocation, commenced abusing a young lad, and a bystander, who lives on the Solomon told him to let the boy alone; when the colored man with a rock in his hand, approached him threatening to kill him. The white man pulled his revolver and told him to keep back or he would shoot him. The negro kept advancing, and the white man fired, the ball

taking effect near the left nipple, producing death almost instantly. The party who did the shooting left for parts unknown. The jury returned a verdict of justifiable homicide. No effort has been made to arrest the white man, and those who were acquainted with the deceased are of the opinion that a vote of thanks is due to him. — *Ellis County Star*, August 10, 1876.

Alcohol and Firearms

As always, the consumption of alcohol could make some people more belligerent. This was evidently what precipitated Mr. Turner's pugnacious attitude toward Mr. Hitchcock and Mr. Neal in the 1875 *Sumner County Press* report.

Another one of those horrors generally enacted only upon the frontier, was played to the death last Tuesday in London township, about twelve miles northwest of this city. The election for that township was held at Porter's school house, and had progressed quietly until noon, when J. H. Turner, who was present and, as usual, heavily armed, challenged Mr. Hitchcock's vote. At this Mr. H., who is an old resident of the township, was justly indignant, and accused Turner with having chalenged [*sic*] only with a view to provoke an altercation, but that he was not afraid of his pistols. After indulging in mutually abusive language, the parties separated, and Hitchcock started for home. Turner then mounted his horse and, in company with J. C. Aitkin, rode off in the same direction. After leaving the school house a few hundred yards, they overtook R. M. Neal, a neighbor of Turner's, who had voted, and who was now walking in the direction of his home. Turner was excited and indulging in threats against the life of Hitchcock, when he recognized Neal, against whom he has had a long and deep-seated grudge, and at once began to apply to him the most abusive epithets. Neal, angered, at length retorted warmly, and told Turner that he had better dismount and make his boastful words good. The latter at once dismounted with revolver in hand and commenced firing. Neal drew a revolver and returned the fire, until each had fired five shots. Turner than attempted to draw another pistol, when Neal, clubbing his weapon, knocked him down, and wresting the revolver

from him, fired, it is supposed, another shot. Messrs, Hitchcock, Givens, and Porter had arrived upon the scene by this time and at once proceeded to separate the combatants, when it was discovered that both were wounded. Mr. Neal had received a grazing shot on the forehead, and Mr. Turner was shot through the arm, the ball penetrating and lodging in the lungs; and also in the mouth, the ball passing quite through the lower part of the face and coming out in the neck. Either wound was probably fatal. Dr. Beeler was at once dispatched for and arrived in time to pronounce the wounds of a fatal character, before the soul of J. H. Turner took its flight to the God that gave it. Neal was not, as we understand, dangerously wounded. He had only fought in sheer self-defense, and the act, though most deplorable, is conceded to be a justifiable one, and that the killing of J. H. Turner saved another valuable life. We were assured by Mr. Aitkin, from whom we have obtained most of these particulars, that Turner had left the school house threatening to kill Mr. Hitchcock as soon as he overtook him, and that Neal was all, in his opinion, that saved the former, as Hitchcock was not armed. It is a most lamentable affair, and plunges a wife and large family into a helpless grief that ought to have been averted. But the senseless habit of carrying weapons, and indulging in bad whiskey, are continually multiplying such results. . . .

— *Sumner County Press*, November 4, 1875.

Gambling and Firearms

Gambling was commonplace in many of the frontier towns. Adding gambling to drinking and firearms certainly increased the likelihood of violence.

News was brought here Monday morning by R. A. Bishop, just in from Windfield [*sic*], of a terrible and fatal shooting affair that occured [*sic*] there as follows: L.G. Webb, attorney at law, of Winfield, and a member of the last legislature, from Cowley county, became enraged, through drink and loss at gambling with one Page, a saloon keeper, and arming himself with a two-barreled Derringer, he took the life of Page, a quandom [*sic*] friend, mercilessly, in cold blood, while he was talking with a

customer in unsuspecting defencelessness [*sic*]. The gambling that led to so fatal a result occurred several days before, when Page succeeded in winning, a sum of money from Webb, the latter asserting that it was done by unfair means, or that Page cheated him. This dispute however, it is said, was settled the evening before, yet Webb reiterated the statement that he had been cheated, Saturday afternoon, and went out remarking that he would make it all right, that "Page would pay for this, yet."

Webb returned in the coarse [*sic*] of a half hour coming through the rear door he approached Page, who was leaning upon the end of the bar counter talking with a stranger, while Jesse Herrington, a colored man, formerly of this city, was behind the bar as an attendant[.] Webb waited until Page finished his talk then drew a derringer and without a warning voice, discharged its contents into Page who immediately wheeled and ran out of the door towards a drug store, but fell dead upon the sidewalk a few yards from it, his heart having been pierced by a bullet. The affair caused intense excitement throughout Windfield [*sic*], threats of lynching Webb were openly indulged, thereupon the mayor closed all the saloons for the day. . . . The sad lesson taught in this, grown to be familiar episode, is only one more among a thousand never to be heeded nor regarded until too late. The moral goes with such a show, every time, but is so little heeded that . . . has grown to be folly to indulge any longer in words, written as a warning against the pernicious practices of gambling and drinking. These are the two posts that have supported every gallows-tree in the land from time immemorial, and despite the warnings will so continue for all time to come. — *Wichita Weekly Beacon*, June 5, 1878.

There is seldom witnessed in any civilized town or country such a scene as transpired at the Long Branch saloon, in this city, last Saturday evening, resulting in the killing of Levi Richardson, a well known freighter, of this city, by a gambler named Frank Loving.

For several months Loving has been living with a woman

toward whom Richardson seems to have cherished tender feelings, and on one or two occasions previous to this . . . they have quarrelled and even come to blows. Richardson was a man who had lived for several years on the frontier, and though well liked in many respects, he had cultivated habits of bold and daring, which are always likely to get a man into trouble. Such a disposition as he possessed might be termed bravery by many, and indeed we believe he was the reverse of a coward. He was a hard working, industrious man, but young and strong and reckless.

Loving is a man of whom we know but very little. He is a gambler by profession; not much of a roudy [*sic*], but more of the cool and desperate order, when he has a killing on hand. He is about 25 years old. Both, or either of these men, we believe, might have avoided this shooting if either had possessed a desire to do so. But both being willing to risk their lives, each with confidence in himself, they fought because they wanted to fight.

Together with all the better class of our community we greatly regret this terrible affair. We do not believe it is a proper way to settle difficulties, and we are positive it is not according to any law, human or divine. But if men must continue to persist in settling their disputes with fire arms we would be in favor of the duelling system, which would not necessarily endanger the lives of those who might be passing up or down the street attending to their own business.

We do not know that there is cause to censure the police, unless it be to urge them the necessity of strictly enforcing the ordinance preventing the carrying of concealed weapons. Neither of these men had a right to carry such weapons. Gamblers, as a class, are desperate men. They consider it necessary in their business that they keep up their fighting reputation, and never take a bluff. On no account should they be allowed to carry deadly weapons.

Richardson was buried on Sunday afternoon in the cemetery north of town, and his death, be it said to our discredit, adds another grave to the already long list filled by those who have met death in a violent manner. . . .

. . . Below we give the evidence and verdict of the jury:

Adam Jackson, bar-tender at the Long Branch, testified as follows:

"I was in the Long Branch saloon about 8 or 9 o'clock Saturday evening. I know Levi Richardson. He was in the saloon just before the fuss, standing by the stove. He started to go out and went as far as the door when Loving came in at the door. Richardson turned and followed back into the house. Loving sat down on the hazard table. Richardson came and set near him on the same table. Then Loving immediately got up . . . says to Richardson: 'If you have anything to say about me why don't you come and say it to my face like a gentleman, and not to my back, you dam [*sic*] son of a bitch.' Richardson then stood up and said: 'You wouldn't fight anything, you dam——' could not hear the rest. Loving said 'you try me and see.' Richardson pulled his pistol first, and Loving also drew a pistol. Three or four shots were fired when Richardson fell by the billiard table. Richardson did not fire after he fell. He fell on his hands and nees [*sic*]. No shots were fired after Richardson fell. No persons were shooting except the two mentioned. Loving's pistol snapped twice and I think Richardson shot twice before Loving's pistol was discharged. A. A. JACKSON. . . .

Wm. Fickensher, sworn, says: "I was at the Long Branch when the shooting occurred. Saw Loving coming in at the front door. Richardson was just going out at the same door. When Loving came in Richardson followed him back. It was then a few minutes before anything was said, when Loving said something to Richardson about saying things to his face. I was still behind the piano. Richardson was sitting on the table near the stove and Loving standing before him near the end of the bar. Richardson said 'I don't believe you will fight'. Loving said 'just try me and see.' They both then drew pistols. Richardson had his pistol out and had fired a shot just as Loving got his out. Loving's pistol snapped the first time. Loving then ran around the stove, Richardson after him. Richardson fired two shots, one of them passing over Loving's head. Loving then fired and hit Richardson in the left brest [*sic*]. Loving fired twice more, one of the

shots hitting Richardson. Richardson fell back but kept on shooting at Loving. W. F. FICKENSCHER. . . .

Wm. Duffey testified: "I was at the Long Branch saloon. I know Levi Richardson, who is now dead. I know "cock-eyed Frank" (Loving). . . . I heard no words pass between them. They had fired several shots when Frank fell by the table by the stove. I supposed that he was shot. I then had a scuffle with Richardson, to get his pistle [*sic*], and threw him back on some chairs. Succeeded in getting his pistol. There might have been a shot fired by one or the other while they were scuffling. Cannot say whether Richardson had been shot previous to that time, but think he had, as he was weak and I handled him easily. Richardson then got up and went toward the billiard table and fell. . . .WILLIAM DUFFEY. . . .

P. L. Beatty testified: About a month ago Richardson stated that he had had words with Frank and that he had struck at Frank; said that he would "shoot the guts out of the cock-eyed son of a bitch any way." P. L. BEATTY. . . .

W. H. Harris testified: I was sitting at the table to the north of the stove. Richardson was sitting on the table south of the stove. Heard Richardson say in a sneering tone "you won't fight." Loving replied "you try me and see." Richardson raised up, pulled out his pistol and commenced shooting, and then both commenced dodging around the stove. . . . W. H. HARRIS. . . .

— *Ford County Globe*, April 8, 1879.

Duels

Many murders on the frontier obviously resulted from reckless acts of passion, but there were instances in which the killing was the outcome of a formal duel between two individuals. Although duels are usually associated with the 18th and early 19th centuries, one account was found in which the disagreement between two individuals was settled via a duel in 1876.

Hugo [*Colorado*], a station on the K.P. [*Kansas Pacific*] road, some two hundred miles west of this city, on last Thursday was the scene of a deadly combat between Orbena Davis, of River Bend, and Albert Jessup, of Deer Trail. All the particulars we are

able to gather are, that the two men were sitting in the depot engaged in what seemed to be a business or friendly conversation, talking low, when they got up and started down the railroad track arm in arm, Jessup with a Colt's Improved revolver in his hand, while Davis carried a Winchester rifle. Had it not been for them carrying their weapons, their movements would not have attracted the attention of the several persons who were present. When they had proceeded about two hundred yards down the track west of the depot, they shook hands and Jessup continued his walk fifty paces when he turned and fired three shots at Davis in rapid succession, by which time Davis had fired two shots, the second of which passed through Jessup's body so near his heart that he fell forward upon his face and expired before Davis could get to him. By this time the lookers-on, who had made their way as near the battle ground as safety would suggest, were gathered around the body. Davis refused to tell anything concerning the trouble between them which led to the shooting, further than that while talking in the depot Jessup had challenged him to a duel, and he either had to fight him or show the white feather; and he preferred the former. After assisting in carrying the body of his deceased antagonist to the depot, Davis got on his horse and left, but was afterwards overtaken, arrested and taken to Donver [*sic*] where he awaits a hearing. . . . Davis is a young man, not more than twenty, and seemed as cool and collected when exchanging shots with Jessup as though his position was attended with no danger. — ***Ellis County Star*, June 15, 1876.**

"Random Acts" of Violence

Many Americans believe that drive-by shootings of the 1980s and 1990s are a result of a general moral decline in modern society, but apparently, such violence has been a part of our culture for a long time. The gangland slayings that occurred during the roaring '20s are familiar as Hollywood put to film the exploits of Al Capone, John Dillinger, and many other gangsters. Today, we continue to hear of drive-by shootings as urban street gangs attempt to control their "turf." Yet, frontier drive-by shootings occurred where the horse served as the vehicle from which the shots were fired. We found two incidents that could be classified as drive-by shootings.

At about half past four o'clock this (Friday) morning, two pistol shots were fired into the building occupied by Dora Hand, alias Fannie Keenan. The person who did the firing stood on horse back at the front door of the little frame south of the railroad track. The house has two rooms, the back room being occupied by Fannie Keenan. A plaster partition wall divides the two rooms. The first shot went through the front door and struck the facing of the partition. The remarkable penetration of a pistol ball was in the second shot. It passed through the door, several thicknesses of bed clothing on the bed in the front room occupied by a female lodger; through the plastered partition wall, and the bed clothing on the second bed, and striking Fannie Keenan on the right side under the arm, killing her instantly. The pistol was of 44 calibre, nearly a half inch ball. . . .

The pistol shot was intended for the male occupant of the bed in the front room, but who has been absent for several days. The bed however was occupied by the female lodger at the time of the shooting, and narrowly escaped the ball that went through the bed covering. The cause for the shooting is supposed to be for an old grudge. The officers are in pursuit of the supposed murderer, to whom circumstances point very directly.

— *Dodge City Times*, October 5, 1878.

On last Saturday our quiet community was shocked by an occurrence so terrible and so unexpected, that it could not but hold its breath in pitying horror as it noticed this fresh entry in the records of crime. The following, as near as we can learn is a true statement of the

AWFUL TRAGEDY:

On the evening of Friday, the 23rd of May, Mrs. Steadman and her mother, Mrs. Champion, were returning from hunting their cows. When they neared the river on the north side, they saw a young man by the name of John Garten, on the opposite side, riding toward the river, yelling and

SWINGING HIS REVOLVER.

As he rode into the stream he fired once into the water, then rode across, still holding the weapon in his hand. On his coming up to Mrs. Champion and her daughter, one stepped to one side of the road, and the other to the opposite side, to let him pass. Garten rode by but had gone only a few paces when he turned in his saddle and

PRESENTING HIS REVOLVER

snapped it at Mrs. Champion. The pistol missing fire, he turned on Mrs. Steadman, again drew the trigger and shot her through the breast. Mrs. Champion heard her exclaim:

"MOTHER I AM SHOT!"

as she fell to the ground, and before she could reach her daughter's side the bullet had done its work and her pulses were stilled forever. Garten, not seeming to realize what a terrible deed he had committed, rode on home, ate his supper, and then went back to Parson's Ranche [*sic*]. Here he spent the rest of the evening and the night. Nothing unusual was noticed in his actions and his companions at the ranche [*sic*] had no intimation of the shooting until about daybreak, when Sheriff Simmons arrested Garten on the charge of murder. The Sheriff brought his prisoner to Medicine Lodge and placed him in the structure which passes for a jail. About 11 o'clock he was taken before Squire Wise, but waved examination, and about one o'clock the Sheriff and his deputy, started with the prisoner for safer quarters, there to wait his final trial. We would also say that Garten says he did not know his revolver was loaded, and claims to have no recollection of the occurrence. **—*Medicine Lodge Cresset*, 29 May 1879.**

In several incidents individuals were killed for trivial reasons, the result of random violent circumstances or events.

About 9 o'clock Monday night last, City Marshal Meagher shot and instantly killed Sylvester Powell, a 'bus driver employed by the Southwestern Stage company in this city. About noon of that day somebody threw a snowball at Powell while he

was riding down Main street near Douglas avenue, striking him on the head and knocking his hat off. He supposed it was Dennison, who at that time was standing in a wagon in front of Mr. Robert's store auctioneering it off. He jumped off his horse, picked up the neck yoke of the wagon and hurled it at Dennison, striking him on the right fore arm, fracturing it. Dennison made complaint, and a warrant was issued and placed in Mike's hands. About 6 o'clock that evening Powell was arrested and taken before the police judge, fined twenty three dollars and having no money, was sent to the calaboose. About 8 o'clock Brownie went to the Marshal and offered to bail Powell out which was accepted and the prisoner was released. About 9 o'clock or half past the Marshal was standing alone in the rear of Hope's saloon and while standing there he saw Powell coming around the corner of the building where he was and about ten feet off. He said to him, [']Hallo, Syl, what's the matter![?]' Without speaking Powell fired. Mike jumped for him and endeavored to wrest the pistol away. The Marshal seized the pistol with his left hand when it was fired, burning his hand. Powell then jerked away and ran. As he was passing down the alley between Houck's and Allen and Tucker's store, the Marshal fired at him and he returned the fire. Meagher then started back, ran around by the New York store, and as he turned the corner, he saw Powell approaching with his right hand in his pocket. Supposing that he meant to make an attack Mike shot, the ball taking effect through or near heart, causing almost instant death. As he fell he exclaimed, "My God, what have I done?"

Powell was about twenty-seven years old, and had been in Wichita about a year. . . . When sober he was quiet and unobtrusive, but a regular demon when excited by drink.

Of Marshal Meagher, the man who fired the fatal shot, the Eagle [*Wichita Weekly Beacon*] says: In all the trying and exceedingly dangerous positions into which Mr. Meagher has been thrown as an officer in times past, he never before resorted to arms to protect his own life. During the earlier days of our town when it was infested with bands of known desperadoes and murderers, and upon occasions when deadly weapons were cocked and leveled within a foot of his face, he always succeeded by his

imperturbable coolness to not only come off without a scratch, but to hold and confine his assailants without resort to deadly means, and although we have neither seen nor talked to him since the fatally sad rencounter [*sic*] of Monday night, from our knowledge, of the man's character we know he regrets as much as any one, the sad issue. — *Sumner County Press*, January 11, 1877.

"Irreconcilable Differences," Assault, and Murder

Abuse of one person by another frequently resulted in death, usually to the victim, but not always.

Wm. Creeks being duly sworn, testified as follows: I am the defendant in this case; knew Thos. Williamson in his life time; he threatened my life on several occasions; the first time was about the 15th of September, between El Paso and my place. He came up facing me, right in front of me, and told me to stop; I stopped; he says, "I suppose you hav'nt [*sic*] got any money to loan me at all." I said "no." Well, says he, "G— d—n you how do you come to loan money in the neighborhood, and can't loan me anything?" I told you several times that I had no money to loan; he said, "G-d d—n you;," I told him I did not want to quarrel with him; he says, "I will see your latter end." I started off and looked back: he had his revolver swung to his saddle; I drove on, and the next time I met him was on Dog creek; he there stopped me again; he says, "you are coming back again, are you?" I said, "what do you quarrel with me all the time?" and he said he intended to quarrel with me so long as I stayed in the country; he called me all the names he could think of, I drove off and left him; he came down to my stables in May; I was at the well watering my horses; he was standing at the house; directly he came down to where I was: I did not pay any attention to him; I went into the stoble [*sic*]; after I came out, he was standing outside; he says, "Creeks, G-d d—n your old soul, what in h—l have you been talking about me? G-d d—n you, come out here until I whip you;" I went on unharnessing my horses; I never gave him a cross word, never; I have not quarreled with any man in thirty years; he kept on calling me all kinds of abusive names; the woman came out; my niece came where I was, she says, "what's

the matter, uncle![*?*]" I said, "nothing, only Williamson was talking to me." Mrs.——— was standing in the peach orchard; I went down to the house and then went back to the granary after some feed for my horses; he was coming out; he says, ["]G-d d—n you, stop, until I talk to you;" I paid no attention to him; he went to his house; mother Quinell went to him ane [*sic*] told him not to make any trouble; afterwards he came down to where I was; he was carrying something when he came up; my niece was washing some clothes; he called to her, and said, "where is that d—nd old uncle of yours[*?*];" she said he was in the house; he did not see me; I judged he was about half intoxicated; he then went to his house; I met him several other times when he passed me in company with others; he never would say anything to me when he was with anybody; I have gone off my farm in order not to meet him; I went out of his way because I did not want his abuse; I didn't know whether he would take my life; after that time, I met him on the prairie; on the 27th of October, I had just finished sowing my wheat; I finished about 9 or 10 o'clock; I had my gun with me; I took it with me most all the time; was in the habit of doing so; I shot at the chickens, to scare them off the wheat until I got it in: I saw Williamson, that day on a hill, when he was coming home; he went up to his house; got a bucket and went to the well; then he came up to my house and set down; I then went to shuck some sacks of corn; when I came back with the corn I went into the granary; I turned around to my wagon and looked down the road and saw him coming up; I went to the house for a drink of water, talked with Nealey's folks and think I then started back to the granary; my team was in the stable which is by the granary; I went to my horses; I wanted to open my granary and get my sacks of corn inside, and get out some straps belonging to my harness; I brought them out and put them in the wagon; I hitched the traces of off horse, then I came round and was putting the reins on the horses; the horses were headed east, on the south side of the granary, next to the road; my wagon was standing a little west of the granary; well I was hitching the lines when Williamson spoke to me; I did not see him coming; I saw him standing at his house when I first came out with my horses; the first thing he asked me, "Creek what

have you done with my cattle chain[*?*]"; I said, "I haven't got your chain"; he said, "you're a d——d old liar, you have"; I didn't say anything; he went on to curse me; don't recollect all he did say; did not have a plane or trowel belonging to him; I passed around on the near side of my near horse, and took up his tug; my water bucket was sitting under the wagon; I walked around to get it, and just as I stooped to get it a rock just grazed my head; says I, Jim stop that business, throwing rocks; he said, "G-d d—n you," and threw another rock, which hit me on the shoulder, and at that time he started towards me, still talking and says, "G-d d—n you, I will kill you," and reached into his pocket; I got my gun. drew up and fired on him, and he fired on me; the shots were both at the same time; he was so mad, he was black, and trembled like a leaf; I fired on him for the protection of my life; I was in the most lonely place I ever knew; he knew I was down there at my work and he determined to have revenge; I never quarreled with him; I did not pay any attention as to the fire arms he had; he was shot; he walked across the road angling; he put his hand down on the grass and sat down; I saw then that he was bleeding; I drove around then hitched my horses; I then saw Mrs. Carter going up, and Mrs. Nealy [*sic*] asked me what was the matter; I said nothing in particular; I got a bucket of water and went up to Williamson and washed his face; he wanted to lay down; I told Mrs. Carter she could take the bucket back; I then went to Arkansas City; was gone two weeks; I went awap [*sic*] to freight to Cheyenne; I did not want to be in jail.

— *Wichita Weekly Beacon*, January 3, 1877.

Sexual Assaults

Rapes of adults and children certainly occurred on the frontier, although most editors seldom used the word in their articles, preferring to use phrases such as "revolting crime" or "committed an outrage."

On Thursday morning, the 10th inst, Mr. Garvey who lives on Battle creek, in Long Island Township, discovered the body of a man lying on the prairie near his house. He at once recognized it as the body of a man known by the name of General Lane Cooper, and immediately reported his discovery to the proper

authorities. A Coronor's [*sic*] jury was impanelled and ascertained the following facts:

"The deceased came to Long Island Township from the Black Hills about two months ago, and took a claim on Elk creek. For a short time past he had been paying his attentions to Miss Alice Grover, a girl about fifteen years of age. Cooper proposed marriage to the girl and was accepted, and the marriage set for the 23rd inst. On Sunday the 6th day of this month Cooper visited Miss Grover, and as Mr. and Mrs. Grover were preparing to start the next day to Franklin County, Nebraska, where they designed to purchased some corn and a wedding suit for their daughter. Cooper said he would stay about the place and see to furnishing wood and caring for the stock in their absence. The proposition was accepted, and the parents started on Monday. On Wednesday Cooper and the girl quarreled he accused her of criminal intercourse with Garvey who lives on an adjoining claim. The girl denied the accusation, saying the [*sic*] Mr. Garvey had only been living there about two weeks and that he had never kept her company. Cooper persisted in his accusation and told her she must go over to Garvey's dug-out and he would prove it. She told him to go out and see how high the moon was, and if it was not too late she would go. While he was out she put an old butcher knife in her pocket. While going he threatened her frequently as he had been doing during the day. When they arrived at Garvey's Cooper tried to elicit some confession from her, but she still denied his accusations and Garvey told him that the [*sic*] was hardly acquainted with the girl, and had never kept her company. Cooper was enraged at his failure to implicate Garvey, and as they returned continued to threaten the girl. When about 80 rods from Garvey's house, Cooper assaulted the girl and outraged her person. The girl said she intended to tell her father, Cooper said he would kill her if she did, but the girl reiterated her intention. Cooper then struck her in the face, knocking her down. When she got up he asked if she would tell, and she said she would, at which he grasped her throat with his right hand, choking her till she could not speak, and said "D__n you, I'll stamp the life out of you!" at the same time striking her again in the face. The girl had been unable to get hold of her

knife during their struggle so far, but at this juncture she succeeded in taking it out of her pocket and striking him with it. The knife struck the collar bone above the left breast and passing below the first rib entered the region of the heart, possibly cutting the heart itself. Cooper fell forward upon his face exclaiming, "Great God! you have stabbed me!" The girl released from his grasp, ran away some distance, but returned, and not receiving an answer when she spoke his name, she turned him over and felt his pulse, then put her hand over his heart to ascertain whether it beat. Being satisfied that he was dead, she went home. She instructed the children to say to any body who inquired, that she had gone to a neighbor's house, after which she took the smallest child, about two and a-half years of age, and started to meet her parents. She met them at Turkey creek, in Nebraska [*Furnas County*], early the next morning, having walked more than thirty miles. Cooper was doubtless a very bad man, as he had made indecent proposals to other young ladies in the neighborhood. The evidence shows that he was compelled to leave Indiana for seducing a girl, and that he repeated his crime in Nebraska and was shot through by the girl's father. The scars made by the bullet were plainly visible at the time of the inquest. . . . The Coroner's jury which was composed of some of the best citizens of Long Island township, fully exonerated the girl, and the citizens generally think she was perfectly justifiable in committing the deed. — *Kirwin Progress*, January 19, 1878.

In the following article, the man who allegedly molested a little girl was James Sanders, who subsequently was beaten by the child's father but allowed to live. However, in the second article, although likely referring to the same incident, Johnson is named as the guilty party and was later hanged.

A findish [*sic*], brutal and terribly revolting and sickening crime was committed last week about three miles east of Salem by a young man, herder for J.F. Hurst, named James Sanders, upon the person of a little girl only five years of age. This fiend went to the house from his herd for a drink and in returning met the little girl, a daughter of a new comer, and committed the

revolting crime. The child reached home nearly dead and told her story. Her father went and found Sanders, knocked him down and beat him considerably and left him. Subsequently the neighbors went to arrest him but he had gone. At last account he had not been captured. The physical condition of Sanders renders this horrid crime still more horrible.

— *Jewell County Monitor-Diamond*, August 21, 1879.

A herder by the name of Johnson [*Sanders?*] was lynched in Jewell County, on the 27th, for committing an outrage on a 5-year-old girl. The child's father had previously beaten him almost to death. **— *Inland Tribune*, September 6, 1879.**

Spousal Abuse

As we know, spouse abuse can be mental or physical, but in the pitiful case chronicled in the *Ellinwood Express*, the abuse took the form of extreme neglect and abandonment.

A tale of starvation and death comes to our ears, which, for brutality and fiendishness, surpasses anything ever dreamed of, the recital of which makes the heart sick.

A man named Baumer, or Broomer living about fifteen miles north of this city . . . is reported to have let his wife actually starve to death. The couple have been living in a dug-out, and some five or six weeks ago the woman took sick. and finally became so weak as to be entirely helpless. All this time her brutal husband would do nothing for her, and she had to depend upon her neighbors for nourishment and help; but even this was denied her at last, for the husband forbade any one coming to the house, saying that he could take care of her himself, and he didn't want any G_d d__n Yankees around his house.

As time passed, and the woman was not seen about the premises, some of the more venturesome neighbors asked Broomer about his wife, when he told them she was still sick. When asked if he had employed a physician he replied: "No, it costs too much money for doctors; besides, I think she'll die anyhow."

This state of affairs was made known to the Commissioner, and last Thursday Mr. O. O'Blennis and a neighbor entered the hovel to see what could be done for the woman. On opening the door their nostrils were assailed with a horrible stench and it was some time before they could summon sufficient courage to approach the miserable couch upon which lay the victim of this devil incarnate. Upon being questioned as to her illness she stated that she had been bedfast for nearly six weeks, and was not able to help herself, that her husband had repeatedly refused to give her nourishment, or even a drink of water, nor would he allow any of the neighbors in to see her. She further stated that the night previous her husband struck her in the mouth because she had begged him for a drink of water. Hearing this both men turned to go in search of some of the neighboring women to attend to the poor creature's wants seeing which the woman called them back and begged them not to leave her, for if she was left alone with her husband after what she had disclosed, he would kill her. The men then decided that the woman must be removed at once, to which the husband objected, and wanted to know what authority they had for doing so; but he was told to interfere at his peril, and he slunk off into one corner of the hovel and sat down, muttering curses against all intermeddling Americans.

On attempting to lift the unfortunate woman from the bed, — horror of horrors! — these strong men well nigh fainted. For over five long weeks had the poor creature lain there in her own excresences [*sic*], until the flesh upon the back, buttocks and hips was in an advanced stage of putrifaction [*sic*]! Great God! do we live in a civilized country, and yet harbor wretches worse that [*sic*] barbarians?

The poor creature was finally taken to the house of a neighbor, where she was carefully bathed, clothed in clean linen and put to bed. But these kind offices came too late: the tortured spirit was fast nearing dissolution, and notwithstanding everything was done that could be to alleviate her suffering and save her life, she passed away on Saturday morning to that abode where troubles never come.

We understand that Broomer is under arrest; and if there is a

law covering such cases we hope it may be enforced to the letter, and that our fair county may never again be cursed by the presence of such a brute, — aye, he is worse than a brute, for brutes will protect and care for their kind.

— *Ellinwood Express*, October 2, 1879.

Child Abuse and Infanticide

Few events evoke more anger than those where violence is directed at a child. Child abuse and infanticide remain a bane of modern society and were certainly present on the frontier.

Although the death of the youngster depicted below was caused by a rattlesnake bite, the inquest into the child's death ruled that if the beatings had not first occurred, the child might have survived the bite.

Last Sunday, Mr. Craig, who lives on the south side of the river, whipped his little son, a child about seven years old, for permitting a hog to stray from the premises. It seems that he lost all judgment, and very cruelly whipped the child with an ox whip and then sent him out in search of the hog. The little fellow wandered about the prairie and was bitten on the toe by a rattle snake, when, from exhaustion he fell on the ground, where he was picked up by Mrs. Lewis, and taken to her residence. Medical aid was not had until noon, Monday, when everything was done for his relief. He was insensible most of the time, except when roused by extra efforts. On Thursday evening he died. The coroner at once summoned a jury . . . and proceeded to hold an inquest.

The father came in during the night and gave himself up to the sheriff and is now in jail. The general impression among those who have seen the child is that he died from the effects of the whipping. But, though death may have resulted from the snake bite, the father's conscience will never forgive him for his unguarded, not to say cruel, treatment of the child. Mr. Craig is a very industrious man; and having taken a claim on the South Side this spring, had been hard at work. We have not heard of any harsh treatment by him toward his children before this. In an unguarded moment he seems to have lost his self-control, and doubtless suffers intense anguish for the rash act. . . .

The coroner's jury have returned a verdict, finding that the child came to his death from blows inflicted with an ox-whip in the hands of his father. . . . — ***Inland Tribune*, July 7, 1877.**

Infanticide, willfully killing a child, has always been repulsive. Three accounts of infanticide were found in the newspapers examined. The *Saline County Journal* of July 4, 1878, carried a brief report about finding a decapitated body of a child in the Smoky Hill River near Lindsborg. Other tragic incidents are similiar to those reported in modern newspapers.

What few words I shall say will be about the tragedy that took place on F. creek, a short time ago — you no doubt have had some notice of it. It is the poisoning of a child by its mother, and her confession of the crime, and some other things connected with the matter that call for a rigid investigation of the matter by the proper authorities; we, the people here, have been informed that the father of the child, went to Salina and consulted the officers of the county about the matter and wanted to know what to do about it, and was informed that he had better let the matter drop. Now Mr. Editor there has not in my opinion been a blacker murder, or one more cruel and heart-rending than was committed by Mrs. Pearson. It is claimed she is insane; suppose she was, (which many doubt) should not her sanity be investigated, and if she is insane to the extent that she can take the life of her own child, is she a fit person to have charge of children or even be permitted to run at large[*?*]. She may be insane again, and the other child that God has given her may pass away in like manner, and it may not stop here; her husband is not safe; or I will ask is the community safe when such things can be done without investigation. Infanticide or child murder is one of the most shocking of all murders, and no christian people should tolerate it. The county is investigating and prosecuting criminals, the crimes of which will dwindle into insignificance when compared with the one committed on F. creek; all christian people call for a rigid investigation, and if she is insane, send her to the asylum, and if she is not let her pay the penalty which the law inflicts.

— ***Saline County Journal*, February 25, 1875.**

Tuesday morning about seven o'clock the coroner, Dr. Sieber, was notified by Charles Quine, who keeps a restaurant on Douglas avenue, that something resembling a new born child, was in the vault of an out-house belonging to him, situated in the rear of his building. Dr. Sieber immediately proceeded to the place and finding sufficient evidence to indicate that a dead body was concealed there, empaneled a jury . . . who proceeded to further investigate. Some women's clothes covered with blood were taken out of the vault and the body of a male child of recent birth was discovered. An examination of the body showed marks as of strangulation, which made it necessary to ascertain who was the mother. The clothes were recognized as belonging to one Maria Vanis. She was found confined to bed in the back room of Quine's restaurant. Maria Vanis is a Bohemian women, about the age of 26, very dark skin with a comely countenance. She acknowledged to have given birth to a child Monday night about 12 o'clock, while she was in the privy and throwing the clothes in after, as they were dirty. The father of the child she stated to have been one Jacob Schultz, a blacksmith and railroader, living in Kansas City, but for a time in Wilson, where she had lived till within two months as a servant in the Wilson House. She had complained of a severe headache the afternoon previous, and had been allowed to go to bed. About nine o'clock she was suffering so that Dr. Minnick was sent and as she stated positively that nothing else was wrong the Doctor gave medicine for that complaint. Several witnesses were summond [*sic*] but nothing definite was concluded and a post mortem examination over the body of the child was determined on and Dr. Fraker examined the body as directed, finding the following evidence: The body was a male child 16 1-2 inches long, found on the left side of the neck, just below the jaw, a mark as of a finger, and and [*sic*] on the other side two marks of the same character, face livid, tongue blue, one section of the brain was found to be congested, in base of brain, same, neck and chest spots corresponding, lung slightly expanded by entrance of air, base of lung completely collapsed, heart normal, ventricles and oracles [*sic*] filled with dark blood

and stomach empty. And in his opinion death was caused by strangulation. The child was alive and fully matured when born.

The jury gave in a verdict that the child came to its death unlawfully at the hands of some one, supposed to be its mother, Maria Vanis. She will have a preliminary examination today.

— *Ellsworth Reporter*, June 12, 1879.

The Troubled West

The ready availability of a rifle brought sorrow to a new bride and death to one of the young men involved in a supposedly innocent "shivaree." The serenaders certainly exceeded the boundaries for such activities, as the men actually entered the bedroom of the newly betrothed. Evidently the father of the dead youngster felt that his son's behavior was inappropriate because he put up most of the bail money for the bride's release.

On the 2nd inst., Probate Judge H. H. Reed, issued a marriage license to Robert P. Maginness and Miss Amanda J. Groom, of Pawnee Township in this County. On Thursday, the 3rd inst., they were married. On Friday, the 4th inst., a party of young men in the neighborhood had made it up to give the newly married couple an old-fashioned charivari, with the usual tin pan and horn accompaniaments [*sic*]. But from some cause or other the majority of the party failed to put in an appearance, and the "fun" was postponed until the next Thursday evening, the 8th inst. On that evening seven young men, among whom were Owen Henry and his two elder brothers, assembled at the house of Mr. Maginness, at which place the bride and groom were stopping, and at once commenced the "fun" of charivaring them.

They made two or three circuits around the house, firing off pistols, and ringing bells and rattling tin pans, &c. No one responding to their "racket" they at length demanded admittance into the house. Old Mr. Maginness got up and struck a light and let them into his room. They then made the inquiry:

"WHERE IS BOB?"

The old gentleman informed them that he was in the other room, in bed. A partial sod partition separated the two rooms. The three Henry boys led the way and passed into the room

where the bride and groom were in bed. The two elder Henry boys took a position near the foot of the bed, and Owen, the younger, stood at the foot of another bed on the opposite side of the room. The two elder boys done all the talking on their side. They told Maginness to get up, and show himself. He told them he would not. They told him the second and third time to get up or they would pull him out of bed, but he told them he would not. His wife then told them to get out of the room, or she would shoot, at the same time reaching for an old rifle, loaded with a paper wad that stood against the wall on her side of the bed. They failed to heed her, and still insisted on "Bob" getting up, or they would pull him out of bed.

THE EXCITED BRIDE

then leveled the gun and commenced pulling back the hammer, as she says, when the gun was prematurely discharged, missing the two elder boys, and striking the younger brother in the abdomen, about two inches above the navel, tearing a hole through his stomach the size of a silver dollar. One of the elder boys only escaped receiving the charge himself, by pushing the gun to one side with his hand, when he saw the excited woman was about to shoot. The poor boy, after being shot, walked into the other room with the remark:

"I AM SHOT."

Mrs. Maginness, the woman who done the shooting, then remarked that it couldn't have hurt him very bad, as the gun was only loaded with a paper wad. The sequal [*sic*], however shows that she was terribly mistaken. The boy's parents and a doctor were immediately sent for and were soon on the scene of

THE TERRIBLE TRAGEDY,

and everything was done for the poor sufferer that parental love and surgical knowledge could suggest, but all to no purpose. After enduring the most excruciating agony until three o'clock Wednesday afternoon, death kindly relieved the poor boy of his sufferings, and his young spirit took its flight for another world. Owen was only 13 years of age. . . .

— *Smith County Kansas Pioneer,* April 18, 1879.

Murders also resulted when quarrels or jealousies occurred between two men for the affection of the same woman — the "eternal triangle."

Our town was intensely excited last Saturday over the examination of a man named Scott, for the killing of one Howard, in the unoganized [*sic*] county of Hodgeman, which is attached to Pawnee County for judicial purposes. The two men were young and unmarried, and it seems were both "struck" after a girl at the ranch where they had been stopping, which engendered feelings of jealousy in both of them. On the morning of Tuesday of last week, the two men started with a wagon and team for Dodge City, and according [*to*] the statement of the survivor, they camped about twelve miles out, and that as he was returning from picketing the team, with an ax, the other man attacked him with a knife, and that, in self-defense he struck him with the ax, hitting him on the head and killing him. His story seemed so preposterous that he was sent to jail to await his trial, and a coroner's jury proceeded to the scene of the tragedy, and exhumed the body. It was then found that the head was literally cut and mashed to pieces, and the cuts and bruises indicated that they were done when he was lying on the ground, and most probably the attack was made when he slept.

— *Hays City Sentinel*, August 9, 1876.

Infidelity was also a problem on the frontier, and some of the resulting romantic tragedies read like modern television soap operas.

Information "came over the wires," Saturday afternoon of a shooting affray which took place at Waterville, the particulars of which we find in the Champion to be as follows:

Dr. Humpheryville is a well known and well-to-do physician, living a short distance from Waterville, the thriving little Central Branch town, and enjoys a large and lucrative practice in that vicinity. He is considered one of the straight forward and upright citizens of Marshall county, honorable in his dealings and respected and admired by all who know him. He is very well off in this world's goods, owning a fine farm and a most excellent

practice, and the prospects before him for a future life of ease and comfort were every good. Among his other possessions, however, and as it has developed, the most unfortunate of his gains, is a wife — a buxom young woman, fair to look upon and comely in appearance, but, as developments show, of a disposition not intended to make the Doctor's home that immaculate abode of virtue that he desired. In his employ Dr. Humphreyville had a young man who served him in the capacity of teamster and man of all work, who did the chores and made himself generally useful during the Doctor's professional trips. It seems that during the Doctor's absence Mrs. H. looked on the trim built young man with the same description of eyes thro' which Mrs. Potiphar observed Joseph, but unlike Joseph the teamster would not allow the Doctor's wife to tear his clothes, and a criminal intimacy soon sprang up between them. In time the Doctor's suspicions were aroused that every thing was not just right between the wife of his bosom and the man of all work and he accused her of the infidelity and discharged the servant. With tears and protestations she declared her innocence, and upbraided him for his cruel suspicions. The doctor kept watch around the premises, and in a day or two his perseverance was rewarded by his intercepting a messenger going to his house with a letter for his unfaithful spouse from the discharged teamster, which in his mind fully established the guilt of the pair. He made no outward demonstration, but continued to keep a watchful eye out. Yesterday he came to Waterville on some business, and and [*sic*] returning home before dinner, met the teamster coming away from his house. There was no hesitation in his act, nor any parleying. He simply pulled out his derringer and emptied it into the man's body, the ball passing clear through his lungs. At four o'clock the man was still living, but his physicians pronounced his case absolutely hopeless. — ***Concordia Expositor*, April 11, 1878.**

Last Saturday the citizens of Brant township were thrown into a state of great excitement by the discovery of one of the most cold-blooded, fiendish murders on record. The Coroner was

notified and on Sunday proceeded to the place, a jury was empaneled and Drs. Slagle and Saunders made a post-mortem examination of the body. We repaired to the place to learn all the particulars of the terrible affair which are as follows: Mrs. Danalson lived on a homestead with her two children, a girl of 8, and a child of 18 months. She is separated from her husband, but he had been attending to her during a recent severe illness. and staid [*sic*] at the house. Last Friday she told him she was well enough to do her own chores and he need not stay there any longer, and he went home to his own farm about three miles away. The next morning a neighbor, Wm. Schwartz came to Mrs. Danielson's [*sic*] about 9 o'clock to take back her horse which he had found loose, and the little girl came to the door and told him her mother was dead. He went into the house and found Mrs. Danielson [*sic*] lying on the floor weltering in blood. He gave the alarm and soon neighbors were on hand. The news spread like wild-fire and soon the whole country was aroused to the fact that one of the most horrible murder, ever known, had been perpetrated in their midst.

It appears that the murderer crawlek [*sic*] up to the window of the house at bed time, before the light had been put out, and just as Mrs. Danielson [*sic*] was in the act of putting on her night gown, and putting the muzzle of his gun within a few inches of the glass fired direct at her breast. The gun was loaded with shot and one ball or slug. The slug struck her about two inches to the left of the right nipple and crashed through her heart and must have caused instant death. One of the shot also entered her breast at the center of the breast-bone and passed through her heart. Several other shot entered her breast in different places. She evidently stood for the briefest moment and fell without a groan. The children were in bed asleep but both were awakened by the noise of the gunshot, and the little girl says she was scared and jumped up in bed and called "ma," "ma," and she did not answer. The baby cried and she told it not to cry, and she would get up and light the lamp, which was standing on the table, by the window and must have been put out by the discharge of the gun. The little girl, Carolina Augusta Minos, showed such wonderful bravery and tells her story so clear that we will tell it as near as

possible in her own words. "I got up and tried to light the lamp but the wind blew into a hole in the window so hard that I had to move it to the secretary. When I got the lamp lit I saw that ma was lying on the floor dead. I got some play things for Emma and took her up and held her. I asked her if she would go to sleep, and she said no, and pretty soon I asked her again and she said yes, and I put her to bed and put out the light and went to bed and went to sleep and slept till morning. Then I got up and built a fire, and mixed some biscuit and tried to get some breakfast for Emma, for she was hungry. Then I saw Mr. Schwartz out doors and I went out and told him that ma was shot dead. He ran in to the house and looked at ma, and then went out. He told me he would go and get somebody. To the question "Were you not afraid and did you not cry when you lit the lamp and found your mother dead?" she answered "No, for ma used to tell me when she was sick that if ever I found her dead to not be afraid, nor cry, and not to leave the house, but to take care of Emma and God would take care of me." Then the poor little girl broke down and sobbed, but checked herself by a powerful effort.

The little girls' story was very affecting, and her exhibition of courage and devotion most wonderful.

THE MURDERER.

Whoever he is, rode to the vicinity upon a horse, and turned into a corn field north of the house, dismounted, tied his horse to a corn stalk near the roots, walked stealthily to the house, took his position about four feet from the window, took his aim with the muzzle of the gun within a few inches of the glass and fired at the bared breast of his victim, then ran back to his horse, mounted and rode off on a run. A more cowardly, fiendish crime was never perpetrated in any country on the globe, and the murderer must have been one of the community. The woman's husband, Danalson, was arrested on suspicion, on a warrant sworn out before a justice at Omio [*Jewell County*] and held to await the action of the Coroner's jury. . . .

The motive for the murder no doubt lies in domestic affairs. Some five years ago the woman's former husband, Mr. Minos, was drowned in Buffalo creek [*Southeast Jewell County*]. Since

then she has lived on her husband's claim, until she married Danalson. Previous to her last marriage she became engaged to a man named Schwartz, and accorded him the privileges of a husband. For some reason the engagement was broken and the woman became the mother of a child out of wedlock. Danalson was informed of the condition of the woman while prosecuting suit for her hand but that made no difference with his affections. He married her soon after her child was born. She married him to mitigrate [*sic*] her disgrace and to get out of trouble. But her affection remained with the father of her young child and finally she refused to live longer with Danalson. He hung around however, and tried to live with her. Sometimes she would allow him to assist her, but seemed always to have a divorce in view, probably to the end that she might marry the father of her child. She had had a recent severe attack of sickness and Danalson stayed with her during that time, but on Friday, the day before the night she was killed, she had told him she did not want him any more and he might go home. It is supposed that, having madly loved the woman and having exhausted all his efforts to live with her he was seized with a fit of jeaous [*sic*] rage and determined to put an end to her existance [*sic*] to prevent her living with any one else.

— *Jewell County Monitor-Diamond*, December 5, 1878.

Prostitution also was commonplace, particularly in such cowtowns as Dodge City and Hays City. In some cases, prostitutes would marry. However, the unions were not always successful.

As a reporter, it has become our painful duty to chronicle one of the most scandleous [*sic*], disgusting and cold blood murders that we have any recollection of — The facts as brought out by the Coroners Jury are substantially as follows:

George Palmer, well known in this locality, has been for the last seven years living with one Lizzie Adams, a woman of the town. Within the last year they were married clandestinely, and afterward moved on a farm. — But, alas, how frail the fair; Lizzie brooded over the solitude of the farm and pined for her numerous love-*yers* and a return to the old political faith, as laid

down in the principles of the Victoria C. Woodhull party [*Woodhull, first woman candidate for U.S. President, founded the Equal Rights Party that among other things advocated free love*]. She left the farm, resumed her occupation as Madam of the "nauch," from which time up to last Friday night one Taylor DuBoise seems to have had full sway over the affections and cash of the frail Lizzie. True love never did run smooth, and did not in this instance. Shortly after her return to town her house and its contents were burned, and Palmer was arrested for starting the fire, but the evidence was not sufficient to hold him.

Not to be outdone, Lizzie fixed up another house, and just one month after the fire moved into her new quarters. The same day she sent the following poetry to Palmer:

TAKE ME BACK HOME AGAIN.

Take me back home again, take me back home.
Hopeless and helpless, in sorrow I roam;
Gone are the roses that gladdened my life,
I must toil on in the wearisome strife.
Once I was happy and friends were my lot,
Now I'm a wand'rer, despised and forgot!
Lonely and weary, in sorrow I roam,
Take me back home again, take me back home,
Take me back home again, take me back home.
George, dear George, so gentle and mild,
Look once again on thy pitiful child!
Since we were parted I never have known
Love and affection so pure as thine own!
Days of my childhood, I dream of you now,
While in my sorrow and anguish I bow!
No one to love me neath you starry dome,
Take me back home again, take me back home,
Take me back home again, take me back home.

Oh, could I live but the days that are flown,
Dearest and sweetest that ever were known,
Fondly I weep in my desolate pain,

Longing to be with my George again!
Weary, so weary, my heart yearns for rest,
Poor wounded bird that is robbed of its nest!
Child of affliction! dear George I come,
Take me back home again, take me back home.
Take me back home again, take me back home.

He went, we presume to take her back home again; stayed for supper; drank whisky and got mellow, in fact was drunk.

A short time after dark Taylor Duboise [*sic*] entered the kitchen. George and Lizze [*sic*] were sitting on a bed talking over the things that were, both drunk and happy and unsuspecting danger.

Three shots were heard, parties were seen leaving the house, report spread that Palmer was killed, a crowd soon assembled and found a horrible, sickning [*sic*] sight. Lying on the floor, weltering in his own blood, was the body, all that was left of George Palmer.

From indications, it is thought that he was knocked down and then shot three times through the head, all the balls entering the forehead.

Palmer leaves considerable property, and we have heard it stated, a family in Canada, which, if it be true, will be the cause of considerable litigation.

DuBoise, after committing the murder, went to Sanderson & Whites stable, took a pony belonging to Lizzie[']s son and struck over the prarie [*sic*]. Cap. Whitney and others followed, but failed to overtake him. He made an attempt to steal a horse from Charley Bell, six miles from town but was foiled. He has not been heard of since.

The house in which the murder took place has been evacuated. The girls have moved to Kansas City and Madam Lizzie had taken to the farm. So mote it be. — *Ellsworth Reporter*, March 28, 1872.

During the early years of many of the frontier settlements, men greatly outnumbered women. In 1870, men accounted for 55 percent of the

Kansas population (*4th Annual Report of the State Board of Agriculture*, 1875). By 1875, the proportion of men in Kansas had decreased slightly, to 53 percent. However, some counties, such as Ellis (56 percent), Ellsworth (58 percent), and Pawnee (55 percent) still had a preponderance of men in the area. This differential, along with the isolated nature of the towns, sometimes resulted in men fighting for the favors of a "soiled dove" — often with dire consequences.

A report having been seen that Wm. Thompson, of Texas, was killed, a gentlemen of this city wrote to a lawyer in Waco, Texas, and received the full particulars of the killing of this noted murderer.

During December Ben Gallia and Bill Thomson [*sic*] got into a difficulty, when Gallia shot Thompton [*sic*], killing him instantly. The facts are about as follows: Gallia had been keeping company with a loose woman, and went away somewhere. In the meantime Thompson came; and on Gallia's return he found him in company with his girl. From thence bitter jealousy ensued, as she favored each of them. Gallia gave her a penknife. A few days afterward he saw it in Thompson's possession and claimed it. Thompson told him to prove his property, and cursed him, and said he was the cause of the woman having cut him in the face. Thompson had his face tied up, having received a fearful gash from the woman,and threw up his hands to take off the bandage, when Gallia shot him through the heart. Gallia is now in the penitentiary on conviction for robbery and will be tried in May for murder. Ben Thompson is now in Austin. . . . Bill and Gallia were . . . bad men and gamblers.

Thus died the murderer of Sheriff Whitney, who failed to get his just deserts in this county. He committed many murders; and he finally loses his life in a disgraceful quarrel with a man of his own stamp. — ***Ford County Globe*, March , 1879.**

When romancing a lady, a beau sometimes not only had to win the affection of his intended but also had to be found suitable by the members of her family. In the following incident, frontier violence prevailed when the brothers did not find the admirer of the proper quality required for their sister.

The news of a horrible and brutal murder recently brought to light in Ness county reached this city on Tuesday. All the particulars that we have been able to gather are as follows: A young man whose name we did not hear, was sometime ago missing from his home, and the circumstance created some suspicion of foul play. Diligent search and inquiry was instituted, but for some time without success. This did not discourage the searchers, but serv[*ed*] to increase the interest and their diligence. At last they were rewarded and the body of the unfortunate young man was found in the bottom of a well. A bullet hole in the body and the mashed condition of the skull, plainly showed that he had been foully [*sic*] murdered. Now to explain the cause for the foul deed. Inquiry revealed the fact that as usual there was a woman in the case; that he had been keeping the company of a young girl, the brothers of whom opposed the suit, suspician [*sic*] was therefore directed towards the girl's brothers, and the accumulation of evidence has been suffient [*sic*] to justify their arrest, and a warrant was accordingly issued by Justice A. B. Linn, of this city. What the future developments of the case may bring forth we are unable to say, but we do no [*sic*] that a most brutal and horrible murder has been committeed [*sic*], and innocent blood cries out to the majesty of the law for vengence [*sic*].

— *Larned Optic*, September 19, 1879.

Sometimes, then as now, romantic overtures were made toward an unwilling subject. One man persisted in trying to gain the affections of a reluctant lady. She told her husband of the unwanted attention and he told the interloper to leave his wife alone. However, this angered the unwanted suitor and he murdered the husband.

Willis Jackson, the cold blooded murderer of Phillip McDonald, after nearly two years of hiding, has at last been caught, and if the scale of justice only lightly touches the balance, will suffer the severest penalties of the law. The murder committed by Jackson is pecularly [*sic*] pitiless and horrorfying [*sic*]. It will be remembered by many of our readers that last spring a year ago, while Jackson was in charge of a herd of Texas cattle, on Prairie creek, in Sumner county, near Wellington, he and his herders

boarded at the house of Mr. McDonald. The wife done [*sic*] the cooking for the camp, while his corral was used and his premises generally given up to the dealers in long horns, and McDonald himself employed in tending the cattle. One day during the busy cattle season of that period, Jackson dispatched McDonald here in charge of a bunch of cattle, and during his absence, began an ineffectual attempt on the chastity of Mrs. McDonald who was left at home defenceless [*sic*]. On the return of McDonald he was informed by his wife of what had happened but he agreed, as did she, that it was best to say nothing, as the occurence [*sic*] might never be re-enacted and as no satisfactory settlement short of death could ever be reached between the parties. But on the very next day Jackson seeing that nothing disagreeable grew out of his advances considered himself probably master of the situation and began systematic and open abuses of the rule governing gentlemen while established as guests under the roof of another. The upshot of the matter was that McDonald finally took him to task about it and requested that his impertinences toward his wife cease, that he wanted no difficulty but only what was right, thereupon the bravado of the murderer asserted itself, he grew wrath, and as McDonald went out towards the corral to attend to some unfinished duty, Jackson followed him muttering vengeance and finally drew his six shooter and shot the unarmed McDonald dead in his tracks, then mounting his horse hastly [*sic*], gave loose rein, from which time until recently, he has been unheard of. Thus far, we have given only a brief history of the occurance [*sic*]. But this it is that had to do with the appearance on our street last Friday of Jackson, heavily ironed, and in charge of the deputy sheriff of Sumner county, who landed here with his prisoner last Thursday night and lodged him in jail until Friday morning, whence he was taken to Sumner county for trial.

The deputy sheriff of Sumner county caught and arrested his prisoner while taking breakfast down on the Red River, in Godaloupe [*sic*] county, Texas. There was a standing reward of $500 offered for him. While here he was very nervous, said to be pale with fear, and constantly looking around in anticipation of the fulfillment of some terrible forewarning. His fate, if the

deputy sheriff correctly discloses the feeling of the neighborhood in the vicinity of the crime, is certainly to be dreaded, the bare thought of it enough without the real act to "suspend animation." We hope, however, for the sake of law and good order, that no violence will be done the prisoner, but that he will get a fair and impartial trial, receiving his punishment according to his deserts and only at the hands of the law.

— *Wichita Weekly Beacon*, October 13, 1875.

Law Enforcement

The job of the U.S. Marshal or Sheriff in early Kansas towns could be hazardous, particularly in the cattletowns that sprang up along frontier railroads. Places such as Abilene, Ellsworth, Hays City, and Dodge City were known for their saloons, bordellos, and gambling houses. And, as expected, many confrontations ensued between frontier "toughs" and the local law.

Walter Malone, a reckless character, living at Waldron, Scott county, gave his wife an unmerciful whipping a few days [*sic*]. He then went to his brother's house, got a revolver, and started for home again. Sheriff Leming, learning of the state of affairs, followed Malone, and while getting over Malone's yard-fence, the latter fired three balls into his body, inflicting mortal wounds. He then fled, but was pursued by the citizens, shot down and fatally wounded. — *Ellinwood Express*, August 28, 1878.

The following incidents involving lawmen read like movie scripts or Western novels.

About noon, on Tuesday of last week, it was rumored on the streets of this city that two or three men had been killed in Caldwell on the previous evening.

The arrival of the afternoon mail, brought such confirmation of the rumor, that we at once decided that our duty as Coroner required our presence at the scene of the tragedy. In company with Capt. L.K. Myers Sheriff, and W.L. Chambers, Deputy County Attorney, we arrived at Caldwell at 8 o'clock, Wednesday morning. Before our arrival, Justice J.M. Thomas, acting under a mistaken sense of duty, had proceeded to hold an

inquest, upon the conclusion of which the bodies of the slain men, had been buried. Notwithstanding these proceedings, our duty in the premises, was plain; and proceedings to hold a legal inquistion [*sic*] were at once taken.

A jury was summoned, the bodies were disinterred, and identified as the remains of George Woods and Jack Adams, who had been shot and killed in or near the Occidental Saloon, in Caldwell, on Monday night the 7th inst. After a view of the remains, the inquest was adjourned to the school house, where the afternoon was consumed in the examination of witnesses. According to the testimony the deceased, George Woods and Jack Adams had come up from the Territory Monday, arriving at Caldwell about six o'clock p.m. As is usually the custom of cow boys, as soon as they got to town, they repaired to the most conveinient [*sic*] saloon to liquor up. After they had got up sufficient steam they went out on the street, where the band was playing, and began firing at blazing turpentine balls which some boys were tossing in the air. Being reckless of consequences their firing was at such careless random as to excite the fears of some of the citizens who complained to the authorities, and Constable W.C.B. Kelly, concluded to attempt to arrest them, if they continued to disturb the peace. Summoning to his assistance, his deputy, John Wilson, and a posse of eight or ten armed men, he moved on the enemy's works. In the mean time the cow boys had returned to the saloon where they were proceeding to further quench their thirst. The constable waited at the front door of the saloon, expecting that the festive fellows would make a break for the street again. Tiring of waiting for this, Wilson and Flat, of the posse, entered the saloon. Wilson passed through the partition door into the back room while Flat stopped at the bar and called for a drink. The deceased were at the same time engaged in the same laudable enterprise. After drinking, Flat, took his two six shooters from the bar, where he had laid them while drinking, and as the deceased, who each held a six shooter ready for action, made a menacing movement toward Flat, the latter backed toward the door, only two or three paces distant. Reaching the door first Flat, stepped to the side walk and to the south side of the door. Woods and Adams — the deceased reached the door

and the latter sprang to the side walk when the firing began. Adams received a fatal wound and went out the fight. Woods received two desperate wounds and staggered toward the inner door, where he met Wilson who fired on him. Woods fell to the floor, and was afterward found out side the rear door of the saloon in a dying condition. Wilson, upon leaving the saloon was fired on by Kiser, one of the constable's posse, and slightly wounded in the left arm and left side or hip.

After the conclusion of the testimony the case was given to the jury who returned the following VERDICT.

An inquistion [*sic*] holden at Caldwell in said county and State, on the 9th day of July 1879, before me John H. Folks, Coroner of of [*sic*] said county, upon the bodies of George Woods and Jack Adams, there lying dead, by the jurors . . . say that said deceased George Woods and Jack Adams, came to their death on the night of July 7th 1879; while in or near the Occidental saloon in the town of Caldwell, as the result of pistol shot wounds; that such wounds were inflicted by pistol shots fired by a constable's posse. We further find that said killing was done by the constable's posse in the discharge of duty and in self-defense. . . .

— *Sumner County Press*, July 17, 1879.

We have heretofore mentioned the discovery of the plot to rob the K. P. Express by Mike Roarke's gang of theives [*sic*] and desperados. When the officers made the attack on them, the gang consisted of Mike Roarke, Dan. Dements, Wm Tillman and Frank Brooks. For the past month they have been camping at different points along the K. P. [*Kansas Pacific*] road; and at various stations it was comprehended that trouble would ensue. There was a fifth member of the gang whose name need not be mentioned. While ostenible [*sic*] a member of the gang, he was in the employ of the railroad official, interested in the arrest of Roarke and his band. It was he who gave them away, at Brookville last Thursday night, which resulted in the capture of the leader. When Roarke was captured, Dement [*sic*] took to the timber, and being without a horse made but little headway. It

was presumed that he was wounded, as during the fight he changed his gun from one shoulder to the other. Tillman and Brooks fled towards the Santa Fe track, and a posse of men was at once dispatched from Brookville to capture, Dement [*sic*], in charge of M. P. Wyman, Road master of the K. P. Road. The party also included Evanda as brave man as ever looked down a gun barrel. They struck Dement's [*sic*] trail south of Ellsworth and followed it some distance, and Monday afternoon came in sight of the fugitive. He made his way up Thompson crcek [*sic*][*Southeast Ellsworth County*] and took refuge in the dugout of a ranchman named Buckber. Light was distance ahead of the party, who were scattered out over the prairie, hunting the doomed man as o [*sic*] dog would hunt quail. Light left his horse, and running to the front of the hut, came upon the train robber, with a revolver in each hand. As quick as a flash Light drew a revolver from his belt and exclaimed. "Dement [*sic*], surrender. I've been hunting you six weeks, and by G. — I won't leave with out." In reply Dement [*sic*] pulled the trigger of the revolver in his right hand, but it missed fire and Light sent a ball crashing into his right side. Again and again did the wounded man shoot, but the balls only whistled idly in the air, only one grazing Light's body who the second time fired, his ball hitting Dement [*sic*] squarely in the eye producing instant death. By this time the balance of the party had reached the ground, and the body was placed on a horse and driven to Brookville, where an inquest was held yesterday, and a verdict rendered in accordance with the facts. . . . — ***Concordia Expositor*, November 7, 1878.**

One of the more interesting incidents involved the notorious Chummy Jones and his gang of horse thieves. They were encountered by the law and apparently were being arrested when a gunfight broke out.

A report has reached here that a horse-thief killing was made near Fort Elliott last Saturday. The thieves are thought to be the same who stole Messrs. Lee & Reynold's horses some time ago. All reports agree that two thieves were killed and several more capturnd [*sic*]. One of the killed is thought to be the notorious Chummy Jones, whose name is a thing to shudder at, and is often

used by mothers to frighten their wayward children into obedience. We were told that an officer had command of the squad of men who encountered the thieves, that after two of the thieves had been captured, and the others were making a desperate resistance, the said officer was wounded twice. Fearing that the thieves would overpower his men, he deliberately drew his revolvers and said "I'll make sure of you, anyhow," and with this sent burning lead through the hearts of his festive prisoners. . . .

— *Dodge City Times*, October 13, 1877.

Sheriff Bardsley from Hays City and a detachment of soldiers from nearby Fort Hays took after a group of train robbers near Buffalo Station, Park, Kansas. The account by W. A. Sternberg, agent and operator of Buffalo Station, is typical of crime reports in early days.

About 8:30, Wednesday morning, two men came into the station, and inquired of me if provisions could be procured in the station. I told them yes, and showed them J.M.Thompson's store. The leader of the party threw his bridle rein to his comaade [*sic*], and entered. There was no one at home but Mr. Thompson's hired girl, who did not know the prices of goods; and when I entered the store, he (the leader) was telling her they could come to some agreement, as he was obliged to have the goods. The extravagant prices he paid, of his own accord, attracted my attention; and when, in drawing something from his pocket, he pulled out an envelop [*sic*] bearing the inscription, 'Joel Collins,' I was certain of his being a man the officers wanted. I asked him if he was Joel Collins; and he answered, yes. I had received private dispatches informing me Joel Collins was one of the express robbers. [It is said that Colllins' mask fell from his face while in one of the passenger cars; and one of the passengers recognized him — Ed.] He asked me why so many soldiers were stationed here, I told him, to intercept deserters. He and his comrade had a pack pony; and they loaded on the goods, and, after inquiring where the cattle trail was, leisurely started towards the south. Their ponies were badly fagged out. I at once went to Bardsley, and told him Joel Collins was one of those men; and he saddled his horse, and started after them. In the meantime, they had met

Jim Thompson coming in, and stopped to talk to him. Bardsley approached them, and, after satisfying himself I was right, returned, and called his men to saddle. The posse followed after the two men, and overtook them about five or six hundred yards south of the station. They made no attempt to run. Bardsley's men surrounded them; and Bardsley . . . told them they answered the description of two men he was looking for, and must return to the station. Collins replied, 'all right,' but also asserted that Bardsley was mistaken in his men. They turned, and quietly started to return, but had gone but a little ways when Collins exclaimed, 'by God! we will die game!' and both he and his companion attempted to draw their pistols; but the attempt was the signal for a volley from the soldier posse; and they both fell from their horses, dead. I think about ten shots were fired. The soldiers were close around them when the firing took place. In a short time the boddies [*sic*] were brought to the station.

— *Hays City Sentinel*, September 28, 1877.

Although frontier historians are familiar with the Masterson family, the public tends to recognize only the legendary Bat, Sheriff of Ford County, Kansas. Few realize that his older brother Edward was, for a time, U.S. Marshal in Dodge City. His death represents the epitome of a real Wild West shootout.

On the evening of the 9th inst., at 10 o'clock P. M., six pistol shots "rang out," on the night, on the south side of the R. R. track in Dodge City. Hurrying to the spot to ascertain the cause and result of the shooting, we found them to be as follows: A party of six "cow-boys" who had arrived in town in the evening, had been enjoying themselves with dancing and drinking, some of them evidently getting too much liquor for their own and the City's good. Marshal Masterson and Policeman Haywood, being the custodians of the public peace of the City, were present, prepared to prevent any disturbance or trouble among the boys. One of the boys named Jack Wagner, becoming more intoxicated than the others, got to be very noisy. About this time the City Marshal

observed that he was carrying a six-shooter, contrary to a City Ordinance, and proceeded to disarm him, which he accomplished without much trouble, and turned the pistol over to Wagner's Boss, A. M. Walker.

The dance went on and all appeared to be peace and harmony. The Marshal stepped out the front door to the side-walk where he again met Wagner, and saw that Wagner was again in possession of his pistol. He at once attempted to take it from him, a scuffle ensued, a general rush was made from inside the Hall to the sidewalk; Policeman Haywood stepped forward to assist the Marshal, But just as he did so, two other "cow men" drew their pistols upon him and held him in position. One of them snapped a pistol in his face, which fortunately missed fire.

About this time a pistol was discharged, and Marshal Masterson was shot through the abdomen.

Five shots followed in quick succession. A general rush was made from the scene, and all was over.

Wagner being shot ran into Peacock's saloon and fell upon the floor, where he remained until carried away by his friends. He was fatally shot through the abdomen. He died on the evening of the 10th, and was burried [*sic*] on a hill near town at 4 P.M., on the eleventh.

Walker, the Boss herder, ran through Peacock's Saloon, and fell some distance in the rear of the saloon, from whence he was carried by his friends to a room over Wright, Beverly & Co's store, where he now lies in a very precarious condition, shot once through the left lung and twice through the right arm.

Marshal Masterson walked across the street and entering Hoover's saloon, in the agonies of death he said to George Hinkle, "George I'm shot;" and sank on the floor. His clothes were still on fire from the discharge of the pistol, which had been placed against the right side of his abdomen and "turned loose." Making a hole large enough for the introduction of the whole pistol. The ball passed completely through him, leaving him no possible chance for life. He was carried to his brother's [Bat] room, where in half an hour he died.

Everyone in the City knew Ed. Masterson and liked him. They

liked him as a boy, they liked him as a man, and they liked him as an officer.

Promptly at 10 o'clock on the morning of the 10th every business house in the City closed its doors which remained so until 6 o'clock, P.M. Crape draped almost every door in the City. Never before was such honor shown in Dodge, either to the living or dead. . . .

Four "cow boys" were arrested as accessories to the murder of our Marshal, but all were after the fullest and most complete investigation discharged by Judge R. G. Cook, as it was established that they were to blame only for being in bad company.

Wagner when dying said that he shot Marshal Masterson, and there is now but little doubt in the minds of any but that it was he who killed our Marshal. . . . — *Ford County Globe*, April 16, 1878.

One person was so moved by the death of the Marshal that he or she wrote and published a poem as a tribute to the slain lawman.

On the Death of Marshal Masterson.

BY H. N. LESTER.

Lift him up comrades, and bear him away;
Lift him up comrades, the last honors pay,
As you lay him away in the place of the dead,
Him from whose form the life spirit hath fled.
Honor the man who was faithful and true,
Counting no cost when he'd duty to do;
He is a hero! wherever he's found.
Though no trumpet of fame his praise shall sound.
Comrades! You'll miss him, the generous soul;
Comrades! You'll miss him, at call of the roll;
One place will be vacant that you cannot fill;
A love'd voice is silent, a brave heart is still.
But you'll remember, remember he died
In defence of the law, his slayer defied
And when April comes with sunshine and rain,
You shall deck with its flowers the grave of the slain.

Then lift him up comrades, bear him away,
Lift him up comrades, the last honors pay,
To him who was faithful, loyal and true.
Who peril'd his life when he'd duty to do.
Syracuse, Kans., April 17,'78.

— *Ford County Globe*, April 23, 1878.

Marshal Masterson's contemporaries aptly grasped the unique nature of frontier life and the people who tamed it. The following commentary was offered after the violent and needless death of the Dodge City Marshal.

The loss of Edward J. Masterson, the late murdered City Marshal, has cast a gloom through which is felt the realizing sense of buckling on the armor unto death. The general sympathy and respect for the deceased is deep and heartfelt. As an officer he was vigilant, courageous and conscientious of the important trust in his hands. As we knew him he was kind, civil and steadfast — combined with those qualities that make the brave man, the true friend and good citizen.

While we commend the good qualities that possessed our deceased friend, and deplore the tragic end that so summarily disposed him — and through our sorrows and reverence for the departed, let us go forth girdled with common fraternity for our bodily protection: armed with resoluteness and courage; and guided solely in the axiom: Self-preservation is the first law of human nature.

A frontier life stimulates all the qualities of manhood — the true, the good and the bad. The reckless denizen of the plains is at the mercy of an outraged people. As we see the draped doors, the solemn faces, and the cold, quiet air of remorse, we see depicted that steady determination to give no quarter to the ruthless invader of our lives, peace and prosperity. While we give utterance to our feelings in kindly sentiment, we shall find no mawkish sentimentality in guarding the future conduct of those whose utter disregard of their own lives jeopardize those whose lives are worth living for.

We can forget the animosities engendered through the ordinary courses of life, that we may doubly arm ourselves, by

strengthening the picket lines, and filling to the maximum the ranks of the reserves.

There will be <u>no</u> slow work in protecting the lives of this people against coldblooded assassination.

—*Dodge City Times*, April 13, 1878.

A few months after Masterson was slain, two shots killed another Dodge City lawman, Deputy U.S. Marshal McCarty.

Saturday at 3:30 A.M. two pistol shots fired in quick succession were heard issuing from the "Long Branch" saloon, the first of which it was soon found had summoned the genial, warm-hearted Harry T. McCarty, ex-county surveyor and Deputy U.S. Marshal for Ford county, from this world to another. The circumstances seem as follows: "Mack" has just came up the street and stepped into the "Long Branch;" while leaning on the counter talking to Mr. Jackson, a half drunken desperado named Thomas Roach snatched "Mack's" pistol (A 45 caliber Colt) from the scabbard, and as "Mack" turned to see who had so nimbly disarmed him, the assassin, giving the weapon a flourish or two, fired the fatal shot. The ball penetrated the right groin severing the femoral artery, thence passing through the thigh lodged in the floor. The deceased staggered toward the door where he fell — another shot was almost instantaneously fired at Roach by a bystander, the ball grazing his right side. Roach falling called out "I am shot," and dropped to the floor, thus saving himself from the immediate penalty of his crime from the leveled revolvers about him. In the meantime medical assistance had been promptly summoned to the aid of his unfortunate victim, but it was soon found that he had passed that point when human aid however skilled could be of assistance. He was removed to the rooms of Charles Ronan to breath his last in a few minutes, recovering consciousness but for a brief period of time.

Even a stranger, unfamiliar with the circumstances, would have known as he passed up the streets an hour later that some sad tragedy had been enacted, by the air of gloom that pervaded every countenance, and the groops [*sic*] gathered upon the corners, some with minds too much occupied with the calamity to

indulge in conversation, others in whispers that portended mischief, discussing the propriety of obviating the delays attendant upon legal process, and giving immediate illustration to the saying of our Savior, "Whoever shed man's blood by man shall his blood he [*sic*] shed." But to the credit of Dodge City be it spoken, that the better counsel prevailed and even in the moment of excitement she determined to put herself on record as willing to submit to the law.

An inquest was held in the forenoon and a verdict rendered in accordance with the facts. . . . The prisoner was charged with murder in the first degree [*and*] . . . was recommitted to await trial at the next term of court. . . . —*Ford County Globe*, July 16, 1878.

McCarty's death prompted one to speculate about who was in charge in Dodge City.

Such in brief seems to be the account of the affair, but behind all this is the condition of society, which makes such affairs not only possible, but their frequent occurrence highly probable so long as we have a county board, and Dodge City a city counsel that will continue to license the so called saloons, but more properly speaking, hot-beds of hell, and cesspools of iniquity, for the purpose of raising revenue, without regard to the welfare of society. So long as we have a county attorney that declines to ask that a grand jury be empaneled, giving as a reason that such grand jury would be compelled to find indictments against these nurseries of crime and he would be compelled to prosecute them. So long as the predominating element of Dodge City is made up of theives [*sic*], swindlers and blacklegs, their aiders and abettors such occurrences will be by no means rare.

While the miserable half witted Roach is the guiltty [*sic*] party in this particular matter and should be punished, he is not responsible for the school of crime that has been established, endowed and nurtured in Dodge, through which him and others have become red-handed murderers. The blood of the murdered McCarty is upon the hands of those who consider themselves of the better class of the town and who have encouraged by their voice and purse the congregation of all that is vile, low and

degraded of all clases [*sic*], ages, sexes and conditions. They have sown the wind they are now reaping the whirlwind, they natured and warmed the viper into life, he is now stinging them to death. They whom the gods intend to destroy they first make mad. The[*y*] are ready to heap curses upon the head any one that would encourage settlement of this county by that class of people who would be order-loving law-abiding citizens, instead of lawless desperadoes. Strange as it may seem, we have those among us from whom we should expect better things, who in their inordinate greed for place, power and official position, are ready to join hands with the lawless mob, and with a brazen shamelessness that would disgrace the most degraded harlot, are ready to trade their political virtue (if they ever had any) for a mess of sodden pottage. We have in Ford county one of the noblest heritages on God's green earth, let us see to it that none but those who are on the side of good order, sobriety, and good government are intrusted with office of any position of responsibility whatever. Then, and not until then will such foul crimes cease to disgrace the fair and virgin soil of Ford county.

— *Spearville Enterprise*, July 20, 1878.

In some cases, there was no law in the form of a Sheriff or Marshal, and the people were not disposed to transport the "guilty" party to a venue where formal justice could be dispensed, but rather dispensed their own.

From Mr. Davis who keeps the Red Stables on the river bank, near the bridge, we get a few of the particulars of a terrible crime perpetrated in the Indian territory [*Oklahoma*], near Cheyenne Agency, last week. . . . Nearly two weeks ago a man who had been residing in Reno county, near Hutchinson, separated from his wife and took his oldest boy, aged about fiften [*sic*] years, loaded a wagon with goods and groceries, attached thereto three horses and started for Texas to hunt up a location and go into business anew and among strangers. While on the road and somewhere near the territory line, a colored man on horse back caught up with him and after nearly a day's riding in his company, and towards evening, fell back until the father and son halted for camp when he again came upon them and drawing a revolver

deliberately shot the father dead, then proceeded to murder the boy. He afterwards bragged what a good shot he made in killing the man, stating that he dropped stone dead on the first fire, but said it took three bullets to still the boy in death. After the murder, which he said was done while they were gathering stuff for a fire and too far away from their wagon to get arms. The negro left the bodies lay where they fell and taking the team and loaded wagon drove until he came to an Indian camp, where, feeling akin after his bloody work, he grew wonderous [*sic*] kind, and related to the savages boastingly, his fiendish crime, which proving even too revolting for them was carried soon after by one of them to the agency, when a posse was sent out and the fiend corralled. The captors, after some deliberation over the animal, finally concluded to make him tell all about it, which he did, revealing a soulessness [*sic*] and heartlessness in his premeditations while keeping his victims in sight, and after having partaken of their lunch, on invitation, that is truly in this age of humanity, blood curdling. After which and upon a short consultation, in which they were aided and abetted by the Indians, they concluded to dispose of the gentleman in as brief a manner as possible as no one liked him, nor knew what to do with him if they had thought ever so much of him, and as one old frontiersman remarked when the word law was mentioned. "The law be d__d it don't expect us to build a jail out here." Thus in the most humane way, and much after the style of the gentlemen into whose hands the negro fell, they proceeded to hang him, which was done hurriedly and in silence, but most effectually. One of the Davis boys witnessed the hanging and said that with the barbarity of the crime still fresh upon every mind, no pity was expressed for the fate of the murderer, but on the contrary a general feeling of relief and a unanimous avowal that he deserved his fate pervaded this motley crowd of rangers, half breeds and Indians, coolly surveying their struggling victim while tossing in the throes of death and whirling about in the light and shadow of the flickering flambeau. — ***Wichita Weekly Beacon*, October 13, 1875.**

In another situation, no jail was available to hold the prisoner, and the Sheriff was not inclined to put his life on the line against an angry mob. He allowed vigilantes to try the accused in "Judge Lynch's" court.

Joe North, a notorious "bummer" who made Salina his home a few years ago, and who used to drink whisky at the expense of our citizens was recently hung by mob. He has committed many crimes within the past few years, and for killing a man named Jones about a year ago he was at last brought to suffer in Judge Lynch's court. About dark on Wednesday night last week, the sheriff of Wallace county arrested him at Wallace and handcuffed him, and with assistants was guarding him in a store. About half past ten, several shots were fired in the vicinity of the store, and, although the sheriff's party endeavored to hold the prisoner, the mob finally got possession of him, took him a short distance from the store, and hung him to a telegraph pole.

— *Saline County Journal*, January 7, 1875.

If caught "red-handed," a horse thief was frequently hanged without trial.

On the night of the 20th ult., near 2 o'clock, the team, wagon and harness belonging to Doc. Hancock, a brother of Mr. M. Hancock, of Scandia Tp., was stolen, and ran off. Quite a number started in pursuit, among them Wm. Stanley, who overtook the team, in possession of the thief, some 85 miles northeast of here [*somewhere near Fairbury, Nebraska*]. He immediately took possession of the team and thief by virtue of a navy six [*revolver*]. The thief examined Stanley's authority and found it was correct, therefore concluded to submit. Stanley brought him into Belleville last Friday night, and turned him over to the Under-Sheriff Latham, who brought him before a justice of the peace. Here he waived examination, but owned that he stole the horses. In default of bail he was committed to jail, to await trial at the next term of court.

He gave his name as Fritz Meier and also as Rankin; was evidently a German, was well dressed in a suit of gray, said his home was in Illinois, where he claimed to have a wife and three children, and was apparently about forty years of age.

During the night a mob attacked the jail, breaking down the outer door; but Latham managed to quiet them until he could run the thief off into the country, where he kept him until morning, when he lodged him in jail again. On Saturday evening the mob again broke into the jail, took the prisoner out and down to the creek west of the city, hung him up on a sort of derrick, used by the bucthers [*sic*] in dressing beeves, where he was found Sunday morning. There is no doubt but that he was guilty of stealing the horses. There is no doubt but that he was a sneak thief — at any rate, he bore the marks of one. Still we do not believe the parties who were instrumental in the hanging did right. We have laws and men should abide by them. Two wrongs do not make a right. Myer [*sic*] stole the horses; the mob hung Myer. Myer outraged the law, but the mob did worse: they took the life of a human being.

We are a believer in lynch law, but only in the most extreme cases, and then only after a full, cool and careful investigation. There was no hot blood about this; it was a cool, premeditated job. They apparently went at it as deliberately as they would a day's work.

Now, we don't care how much Myer deserved this punishment, we are very, very sorry that there are people in Republic county who so far forgot themselves as to commit a lawless act of this sort. It will go with them down through their lives, and be ever present with them. It is no light thing to take a human life, cruelly, as this appears to have been done. It not only injures the parties who do the act, but it is a terrible example of lawlessness to set before the young who are to come after us. We have laws — let us obey them, and see that they are obeyed. It cannot be done by breaking them. . . .

We hope never to have to record another act of this kind in Republic county. — ***Republic County Journal*, May 1, 1878.**

Justice and Motivations in the Wild West

The motives for some murders were often not readily discerned and sometimes the reason was to be found in a person's distant past.

Last Wednesday morning our people were horrified at the

report that a foul murder had been committed in town, and large crowds of people in town rushed to the scene. . . . The murder was committed just east of town . . . about twenty steps west of the culvert. We arrived just after the corpse had been dragged out from under the culvert. . . . The man was shot in the lower back part of the head, the bullet ranging upward, severing the spinal cord, and lodging near the bone under the right eye. . . . A coroner's inquest was held . . . and our further report is on the evidence as brought by the investigation. Tuesday night about 10 o'clock a negro and a white man entered Morgan & Sisson's resturant [*sic*] on Main street, and ordered supper. They then asked if there was a saloon where they could get a drink, and on being informed, they went out. They returned in a short time [*and*] ate their supper. . . . The next seen [*sic*] of them was in front of the saloon, the negro trying to induce the white man to go inside and take a drink, and the white man was trying to keep the negro out of the saloon, and have them go down and feed their team. The next seen of them was at Mickey's feed stable, where they went to buy some feed, which they obtained, and asked, Henry, the colored man there, if they could sleep there overnight, and the negro told them yes, the men told him that they were going down in the town and would be back again, and the strange negro told Henry if he did not let them into the stable he would kill him. . . . Henry then closed the stable and went to bed, and nothing was heard of the matter until morning. . . . Now the circumstancial [*sic*] evidence pointed clearly to the negro as the perpetrator of the crime, but the question next arose as to the object of the murder. . . . About five years ago a woman in the employ of B.F. Allen, of Des Moines, Iowa, was murdered and a young man was hung by a mob for the crime, and before they hung him the young man told them he was innocent of the deed, and that a young mullatto [*sic*] negro working at the same place had done the deed, but he was hung by the mob. After the hanging, it was proven beyond a doubt the negro had committed the crime — a young fellow about 14 or 15 years of age. Search was made for him, and he was traced to Colorado, and all trace was lost there. The time of the above murder in Iowa, William Friedrickson, as the murdered man's name proves to be, lived in

Iowa, near Des Moines, and was aware of the circumstances. When the parties entered the resturant [*sic*] at this place Tuesday night, there were parties in the front room of the resturant who had full knowledge of the murder, and the facts in the case — paid particular attention to the negro on account of his rough and brutal manner while there. The negro and white man stepped into the back room and ate their supper, and while eating conversed in a low tone, and after a bit the negro was heard to exclaim in a rather angry voice "I want you to distinctly understand that I ain't driving for B.F. Allen now!" This possibly gives the clew [*sic*] to the murder. The negro knew, or thought Friedrickson knew of the murder, and was afraid that he would give him up to justice, and was prompted to kill him to hide his identity. A party started immediately in pursuit, and found the way he had taken by the wagon tracks, and by one o'clock the same day he was caught in the barn in the rear of Frank McGrath's hotel at Beloit and brought back to Cawker. . . . Over three hundred people awaited his arrival in town, and threats were openly made to hang him, but Col. Whitney brought him in by evading the crowd and taking the prisoner into the back part of his hotel and secreting him. The crowd rushed into the hotel and demanded the negro, but by determined resistance and arguments the crowd was dispersed. . . .

This sad affair has caused the utmost excitement in our city, and it is an occurrence that we hope will never be seen again in our midst. That the negro richly deserved hanging, none will deny who are acquainted with the circumstances, and though it is to be regretted such a frenzy of excitement should seize our people. The indignation was just, though in this, as in all other cases, the law should be allowed to take its course, and much praise should be bestowed on those who guarded the prisoner, for the nerve and bravery exhibited under trying and embarrassing circumstances. The ill feeling engendered is unjust, and should be forgotten, as the officers stood nobly to their duty, at the peril of being overcome by the indignation of the people. We have always claimed Cawker as a city of good morals and common sense, and although the past affair was one that would naturally lead one to do most anything, nothing of a mob character

was really exhibited while the negro was inside the city limits. A black damnable crime has been committed in our midst — the fiend who perpetrated the deed has been captured, confessed his crime, and is now in jail, and it remains with us as law-abiding citizens to see that the law is carried out, and that just punishment is administered. — ***Cawker City Free Press*, April 19, 1879.**

In this terrible incident, lynch mobs made several attempts to forcibly take Charlie Marshall from the law but were thwarted each time. Finally, Mr. Marshall was sentenced to be hanged for his misdeeds.

Though descriptions of African Americans as "Negros" or "coloreds" were not considered pejorative at this time, when they comprised only four to five percent of the population, the undertone of prejudice is clearly evident. The prejudice reflects the racial tensions felt on the frontier and compelled some to speak out against generalized denigrations of black people.

The murder of Mr. Frederickson [*sic*], by a negro, calls forth sundry remarks from our citizens, and the conversation unavoidably ends in the utter condemnation of the colored population in general. Although there is no possible excuse for the murder just committed whereby a good citizen lost his life at the hands of a fiend in human form, yet it is no worse than is often committed by white men. How can we imagine even, a darker crime than the one committed by Olive and Fisher, committing the double crime of murdering and then burning their victims. We do not pretend to be the champion of the colored people, only so far as their good behavior is concerned. But, murder is murder, no matter by whom committed, and we think statistics will prove that the colored people commit less murders, in proportion to the population, than the whites do, and generally are law-abiding citizens. — ***Kirwin Chief*, April 23, 1879.**

Charley [*sic*] Marshall, the colored man who murdered Mr. Frederickson [*sic*], of Phillips county, was arraigned in the District Court, Judge Holt presiding, charged with murder in the

first degree, to which he plead guilty, and was sentenced to be hanged. He was secretly conducted to the courtroom in Beloit, from Concordia, owing to threats made by a mob, should his whereabouts become known. But few were in the court room at the time of his trial. When asked by the court whether he had any thing to say why sentence should not be passed, he awswered [*sic*] that he had nothing to say, but gave a detailed account of the murder, about the same as was published in the CHIEF at the time the crime was committed. The Judge gave him a timely lecture, and concluded by pronouncing the sentence of death upon him. He was remanded back to his cell, to await the awful day when he shall forfeit his life for the terrible crime he committed.

— *Kirwin Chief*, June 25, 1879.

In the five years of frontier newspapers examined for stories related to homicides, over 100 articles were found that dealt with murder in some form — first degree, self-defense, infanticide, manslaughter, and so forth. Many more probably occurred that were never reported by newspapers, tragedies in which someone was killed and no one ever knew what happened or why.

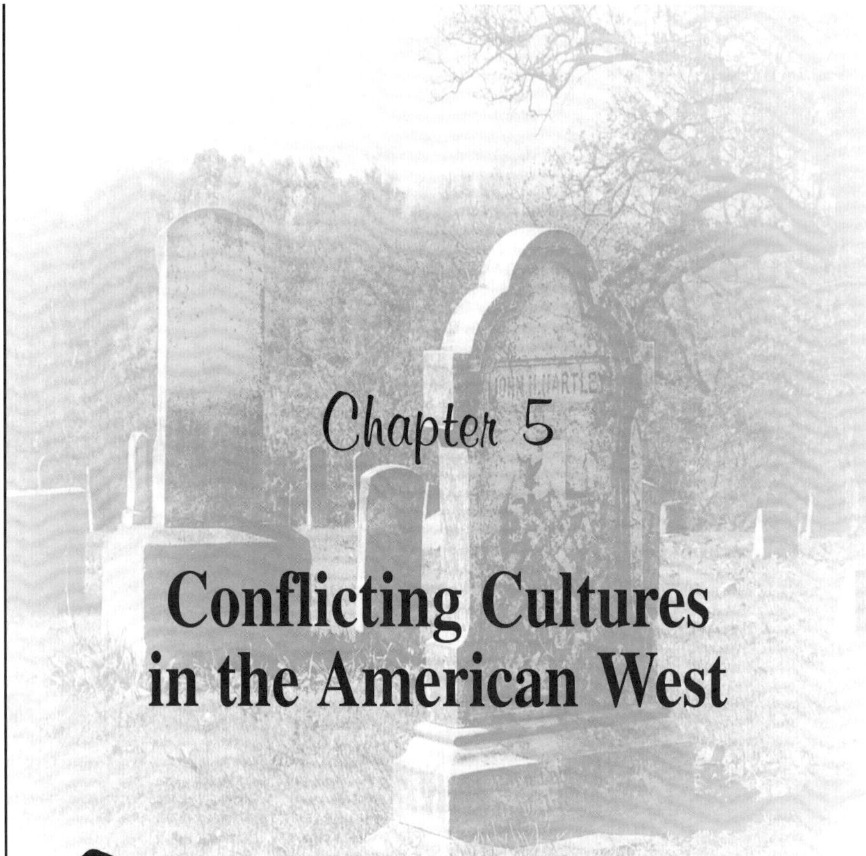

Chapter 5

Conflicting Cultures in the American West

SEVERAL NATIVE AMERICAN tribes lived on the High Plains prior to the arrival of white settlers. These tribes included elements of the Sioux, Pawnee, Cheyenne, Arapahoe, Kiowa, Comanche, and Apache, who were nomadic or semi-nomadic, following the vast herds of buffalo from which they obtained the necessities of life.

Most of the conflicts in Kansas between the settlers and Indians took place in the initial 13 years after statehood in 1861. During this turbulent period, shipping, stagecoach, and railroad lines were being established across the state to the gold-mining areas in present-day Colorado. Settlers, who were farmers and ranchers, followed these lines of transportation, staking out claims on inexpensive railroad holdings or land provided free under the Homestead Act of 1862. These immigrants destroyed huge numbers of buffalo for meat, hides, or sport.

The nomadic tribes of the Plains could see the source of their livelihood being destroyed and responded accordingly. In Kansas, the two most violent years were 1867 and 1868, when 230 immigrants were killed by various Native American tribes (Richmond, 1992).

On the prairie, death was no respecter of race. Native Americans and white and black settlers alike died — often violently — as they began to establish permanent dwellings and villages where heretofore buffalo, antelope, deer, and elk populated the open country by the millions. Although the majority of pioneer contacts with the Plains Indians in Kansas took place prior to 1875, isolated incidents were reported in the sparsely settled western regions of the state as late as 1879.

A Leavenworth (Kansas) letter to the St. Louis Globe-Democrat says: The particulars of a terrible fight by Dr. Tichenour, a white man, single-handed with a band of Sioux Indians, at what is called the Cave, in Ness County, in the western part of the State, have been received, in which he was severely wounded, and four of the red devils killed. An assault was made early in the morning upon the cabin in which the Doctor was asleep, but before they could effect an entrance he securely barred the door and fired through a loophole, instantly killing the chief of the band. A grand rush was then made for the cabin, but the reds were driven back by a well directed fire from the Doctor, who succeeded in killing three others. They then withdrew, and Tichenour, thinking they had gone, sallied out to reach the nearest settlement, when he was fired upon from ambush and severely wounded. Fortunately, a snow-storm was then in progress, and night coming on he succeeded in hiding for that night, and the next day resumed his journey toward the settlements. After being out 16 days, he at last reached them, where his wounds were attended to. — *Inland Tribune*, March 17, 1877.

Periodically, early settlers would happen upon individual grave sites of Native Americans. Rather than treat these burials with reverence, white frontiersmen often excavated the contents, both skeletons and buried memorabilia. In the earliest newspapers, we found no condemnation of Native American grave desecration.

Last Thursday while Mr. Herman was quarrying rock for the new M.E. church, on the bluff north of town, he unearthed a

skeleton of what is supposed to have been an Indian. It was reposing in a sitting posture on the extreme point of the bluff overlooking the bottoms of the Republican river, in fact the most sightly point anywhere in this part of the west. Its hands were locked across its head, and its whole appearance indicated that the body was placed in that position by a supersticious [*sic*] race. It seems the body was set upright, back against the bank, and walled in on the sides and in front, and a flat stone covered over the hole. Mr. Herman, it seems, thought the skeleton in the way, so he dug it out and threw the pieces down the bank, where some of them have been found. We have the skull at this office in a good condition. **— *Scandia Republic*, August 15, 1877.**

Toward the end of the 1870s, a few enlightened editors had the courage to speak out in favor of a proper burial for Native Americans killed on the prairie.

The body of an Indian, who had been killed in the Beaver Creek fight last fall, was brought into town by buffalo-bone pickers on Wednesday. George Griswold we learn, paid five dollars for it. It was badly putrefied. It is our opinion, backed by what little Christianity we can muster, that the body should be put to rest in the ground. **— *Norton County Advance*, July 3, 1879.**

Historically, the relationships between the white settlers and Native American tribes were long and varied. As the Eastern portion of the United States was being settled, many immigrants and politicians wanted to move the tribes onto open lands west of the Mississippi River. There the tribes would be out of the way and their Eastern lands could be settled by "Americans."

President Andrew Jackson enacted the Indian Removal Act of 1830, "clearing several areas of the frontier of Indians" and opening "to settlement large blocks of fresh public lands" (Lamar, 1998, p. 561). Present-day Oklahoma and the greater part of Kansas were designated as "Indian land," where Easterners hoped that the Native Americans would become "civilized" — that is, like white men. But because of pressure from immigrants and the Pacific Railroad, a series of treaties with Kansas tribes led to the loss of most Native American land in Kansas. After 1854, the main reservations were established in the Dakotas and Oklahoma.

Various bands of Native Americans were escorted to the reservations in Indian Territory (now Oklahoma), and during their journey across the Great Plains occasionally had contact with the frontier settlements through which they passed. One such encounter, in Ellis County, resulted in the tragic death of a Pawnee chief.

On Saturday last a Scouting band of Pawnee Indians under the command of Major North arrived here, en route for the Nation and returning from the Black Hills country — where they had been in the service of the Government in the capacity of Scouts. They went into camp on Big Creek, about a half mile from the city, under orders to be mustered out of the service, but were not paid off. All day long the town was full of Indians, and between 9 and 10 o'clock in the evening Sheriff Bardsley's attention was attracted by the sudden crashing of glass at H.P. Wilson's store: he and one or two of his deputies arrived just in in [*sic*] time to see two men running away from the store. He commanded them to halt, but the fleeing parties paid no attention to the order, when the deputies commenced to fire upon the retreating parties — one of which fell, and upon the officers arrival, they found a Pawnee brave stretched out, but who drew out his knife and attempted to show fight, but was too badly wounded to get in any effective work, the ball having entered the small of the back ranging upward, passed clear through his body. He was carried to the jail and Drs. O'Brien and Snyder called. The Interpreter came soon after and sent for the Indian doctor. By this time the news had reached the Indian camp, and as "young" Red Willow — the son of a once chief had been shot by white men — the War Weoop [*sic*] was at once raised, accompanied by the most hideous yells of rage. Major North got up to address them, but they refused to listen and it was not until he got a few of their leaders to talk among them, that he could get their attention. — At midnight quite a numbe [*sic*] of the Indians mounted their ponies and came stringing into town single file, and it was then that light went out, and our citizens went for their side

arms. The wounded Indiau [*sic*] was placed upon a litter about 1 o'clock and taken to the Post hospital where he yet survives, but with no hope of recovery. The next day the Indians were in town trying to find out who shot "Red Willow," but to our citizens it was a counundrum [*sic*]. They said "Pawnee kill white man — Pawnee bad Indian, when made mad by white man — Red Willow die — heaps trouble!" About 4 o'clock, an order came from Gen. Pope for them to move on at once, and they immediately struck camp and started for the Nation. As to the necessity of shooting the Indian we shall not venture an opinion at present as no official inquiry has been made: but our citizens certainly owe Major North a debt of gratitude for holding the revengeful and blood-thi-s-ty [*sic*] red skins in check.

— *Ellis County Star*, May 24, 1877.

The nomadic Native Americans did not adapt well to the restrictions placed upon them by reservation life, and they made excursions outside the encampments. Between 1875 and 1879, two major outbreaks from the Indian Territory resulted in a substantial loss of life in Kansas, both Native American and settler. Both incidents involved members of the Cheyenne tribe who were attempting to return north to their homeland.

A band of 60 to 75 discontented Southern Cheyenne, led by Bull Hump, left the Indian Territory in 1875 and were quickly noted by citizens who alerted the military. Company H of the United States 6th Cavalry, led by Lieutenant Austin Henely, was summoned from Fort Wallace, west of Fort Hays, and followed the Native Americans into northwestern Kansas. There, on the Middle Fork of Sappa Creek, where the Native Americans had constructed lodges and set up tepees, a three-hour battle was joined. Nearly all of the men, women, and children that occupied the camp were killed and the lodges burned (Miner, 1986; Crown, 1950; Webb, 1978).

The following dispatch was received at Fort Leavenworth on Saturday last, by the Assistant Adjutant-General of the Missouri:

Fort Wallace, Kan., April 24.

Attacked at daylight, yesterday morning, on the north fork of Sappa creek, a party of sixty Cheyennes, which I believe to be

some of those who have not been at the Agency. Cut off twenty-seven from their ponies and demanded their surrender. My demand was answered by a volley, when I attacked them. After a desperate resistance, they were all killed. Nineteen warriors, including two chiefs and a medicine man, were among the dead. Captured over one hundred and twenty-five ponies. The remainder of the Indians escaped with a portion of their stock. I burned their camp, consisting of twelve lodges and all their effects. Sergeant Papier and private Fieras, of my command were killed.
"Austin Henley [*sic*],
"Lieut. 6th U.S. Cavalry. — ***Wichita Weekly Beacon*, April 28, 1875.**

Considerable evidence suggests that Lieutenant Henely was less than truthful. A few days after the battle, white hunters visited the scene. They counted 40 Native Americans — men, women, and children — unburned and an additional 27 burned and buried, presumably by the soldiers, in a shallow grave (Webb, 1978). This would bring the total number of Native Americans killed close to the 70 or so that were known to have left the Indian Territory.

The Northern Cheyenne resisted efforts made to integrate them into white man's culture even more than did the Southern Cheyenne. In an effort to force the Northern Cheyenne to become like the white man, the U.S. government withheld rations. Although foodstuffs were restored in about a month, the amount and manner of distribution was not satisfactory to support a nomadic, meat-eating people operating under tribal rule. In addition, the annual buffalo hunt that was permitted on the reservation was a failure in 1878 due to the near-extinction of the animals.

Cultural differences of the white man and the Indian were irreconcilable. And the result could have been predicted — namely an outbreak from the Oklahoma reservation by the Northern Cheyenne (Powers, 1971, 1972). Led by Dull Knife and Little Wolf, the Northern Cheyenne crossed into southern Kansas. Although probably trying to avoid contact with whites, the band of 92 men, 120 women, 69 boys, and 72 girls ranged over a wide area and in doing so, plundered homesteads, slaughtered livestock, and stole horses, guns, and ammunition.

For more than a week it has been known to everybody in this vicinity that a large number of Northern Cheyennes who were

brought from Dakota last summer and located in the Indian Territory, near Ft. Reno [*Oklahoma Territory*], had broken away from the agency and started northward. None, however, could tell . . . what these Indians positively intended doing, or where they intended to go. During the past week it has been learned that when leaving the reservation, they were poorly equipped and provided for a long journey, having few horses, few guns and very little provisions, and under these circumstances it was not expected that they would attempt to move to their former home in the north until they had replenished their stock of provisions and obtained more and better horses then they had when leaving Fort Reno. The circumstances which have transpired during the past week have proven these expectations to be eminently correct, as the Indians have during that time spared no efforts to get possession of all the horses south, southeast and southwest of Dodge [*in Kansas*]. On Monday morning a squad ran into Driskill's camp and captured 55 horses. Dave Driskill, however, had the pleasure of running one of the red devils down and killing him; his scalp now hangs in the Driskill camp.

The same day they ran into Henry Kollar's camp, and captured eleven horses.

On Tuesday they raided all the ranches, and overhauled all the traveling outfits on the Supply road. The ranchmen concentrated at Bluff Creek and Cimarron Stations and gave the Indians a "stand-off."

Near the Cimarron they met Dr. Fowler, of California, who, with his family, was on his road to the Panhandle of Texas for the purpose of engaging largely in the stock business. The attacking party numbered 20. When they first saw them, the doctor and his wife bravely saved their lives by making a ranch near by. His team in the rear, as well as all his goods, were taken in by the red devils, who broke open boxes and trunks, taking with them such articles as they desired and scattering the balance for miles along the road. Mr. G. W. Russel found a large pocket book, containing deeds and mining stock, taken from them, a portion of which he found twelve miles away. Twenty yards of fine silk velvet and 30 yards brown silk, together with a large amount of jewelry

belonging to Mrs. Fowler, was also taken with them. Their loss is over $2,000.

On Wednesday they attempted to get Pat Ryan's horses from his home at the mouth of the Mulberry, 18 miles southeast of Dodge, but Pat foiled them.

They killed a colored man who cooked for Chapman & Tuttle, at their camp on Mulberry, twenty miles south of Dodge; ran off with twenty horses, and chased Sebastian and a man who was with him for several miles. They now live to tell of the "close call" they had.

On the same day they jumped John Frazer's camp, running off 20 horses; also jumped D. Sheedy's camp, shot the cook and ran off 10 horses.

On Thursday they rode into Williamson's flock of sheep, on Crooked creek, and slaughtered 250 of them with bows and arrows, just for the fun of the thing, using but a few pounds of the mutton.

On Friday they jumped Boynton's sheep camp, 32 miles southwest of Dodge, slaughtered the sheep promiscuously.

By Friday morning every farmer within 30 miles of Dodge, south and southwest, had come into town for safety.

On Saturday morning about twenty men arrived in Dodge from Barbour [*sic*] and Commanche [*sic*] counties, southeast of here, and reported six men missing in these counties, the dead bodies of four of them having been found. They started west in search of the redskins, expecting to join the soldiers who were already out after them.

On Tuesday the Driskill boys, with Doc and Tony Day, and about 20 other cattle men and cowboys, fell in with Captain Hemphill's company of cavalry, and the combined followed the trail to the head breaks of Sand creek, one of the feeders of Crooked creek, and there found 200 Indians encamped. A sharp engagement was had which lasted about an hour. One Indian was killed, and one soldier and two cavalry horses were wounded. The captain, deeming it unadvisable to fight any longer against such odds, retreated, the cattle men arriving in Dodge on Wednesday night and the soldiers on Thursday morning. Much comment was had upon the conduct of the Captain in retreating

without at least trying to whip the Indians, some justifying and others condemning his action.

On Thursday night the same company of cavalry, accompanied by twenty-five cow boys and scouts, with provisions and supplies for a several days' march, went west by freight train to Pierceville, forty miles west of Dodge, where they were joined by a company of cavalry from Fort Lyon, Colorado. The whole command, now numbering about 150 men, marched south to find the Indians, who from the accounts brought in by Ervin's outfit the night previous, were still camped on Sand creek [*Clark County, Kansas*].

Wm. Jackson, a scout, arrived at 4 p.m. Sunday from the seat of war with dispatches from Captain Raundebrook to Col. Lewis. Two companies of cavalry and about 80 infantry and citizens were then engaging the Indians, but without much success. A later report says the troops were repulsed and defeated. The scout came in for ammunition and supplies, which were promptly furnished by Col. Lewis.

From cattle men who arrived at 10 o'clock last night we ascertain that an attack was made on the Indians on Sunday, the civilians being in the lead, with one company of dismounted cavalry supporting them. The cattle men under Driskill drove the Indians from the ridge they occupied and were clamorous for a general charge. Captain Raundebrook sent one company to assist them, but retained two companies to guard his camp. A skirmish of half an hour was kept up with Indians, who hid and dodged behind the rocks, after which the troops withdrew. The soldiers were anxious for a general fight, while the officers seemed haunted by the ghost of Custer and were evidently afraid to take the least risk. On Monday the Indians with about 400 captured horses, moved north, while the troops remained all day in camp. Not an officer or soldier was killed or wounded. The troops are now following, using precautions to prevent the track from becoming too fresh.

[*Civilians numbering 52 joined the fight*]. They organized by electing Doc Day captain, C D Nelson, First Lieutenant, and Bud Driskill, Second Lieutenant, after which they proceeded to business, striking about 150 Indians on Sand creek, above A J

Anthony's, cattle camp, where they were entrenched. They fought them from 4 o'clock until dark. The Indians, during the night, moved two miles south and dug 50 rifle pits, from which they fought all the next day (Sunday). They had the Indians entirely surrounded, and the stock men all say that if they had been properly supported the enemy could have been taken in without any trouble, but the officer in command of the troops positively refused to give such support, and the consequence was that during the night the Indians left their stronghold and made for the headwaters of Crooked creek. The stock men followed up the trail three or four miles, so as to satisfy themselves as to the direction they had taken, when they returned to camp and reported to the officer in charge, who, instead of pursuing, pulled up and moved camp about two miles to a place where they had camped Saturday night. When the cattle men saw the action of the officer in command they came home in utter disgust. They speak very highly of the White Horse Cavalry and its captain; so, also, of the infantry troops and officers, who were all anxious to charge the Indians but were held back by an incompetent commanding officer. Thus the troops are left alone to pursue and fight the Indians; but as they are about 36 hours behind them, there is no likelihood of their ever overtaking them. The Indians have with them about 490 head of horses which have been stolen from the cattle men. In this fight it is supposed that four or five Indians bit the dust; no loss of men on the part of the troops or stock men. — ***Ford County Globe*, September 24, 1878.**

A week or so later, additional information concerning the Native American raid was delivered by Colonel Colcord, who ranched, about 30 miles southwest of Sun City (in current Barber County, Kansas).

The Colonel had driven his stock further north, leaving FRED CLARKE and REUBEN BRISTOW in charge of the ranche [*sic*]. On Sunday morning, September 15th, when eight miles south of the house, on the Cimarron road, the Indians came onto the young men and mercilessly murdered them, taking their team. Their bodies were found in the wagon four days later. . . . The red devils went near the Colcord house where Mrs. Colcord

and children were alone, but seeing no stock they passed on west five miles, and called young Dow out of a dugout and shot him dead. . . . A few miles further on, Paine's new ranche [*sic*] was visited, the treacherous fiends walking up to Walter Paine, offering to shake hands and "How," at the same instant shooting him through the neck and leaving him for dead. Mrs. Paine had a shot gun, which was accidentally discharged, frightening the rascals away, after her child had been seriously wounded by a stray shot. At Evans camp and on to Sand Creek, other depredations were committed, which have alreody [*sic*] been made public.

. . . We have on our table a cartridge shell fired from a Winchester, in the hands of an Indian at Sand Creek, which shows that they were armed far better than the soldiers. . . . The Indians had constructed rifle pits and were otherwise well fortified, and the military allowed them to withdraw with their stolen stock and cross the river and road near Cimarron. . . . The cause of the outbreak in part seems to have been caused by the failure of the government to fulfill a promise made more than a year ago to bring the rest of the tribe from the mouth of Tougue [*sic*] river. This separation, the imposition of the agents, and their natural enmity and fiendish nature, started them back to the north.

— *Kinsley Graphic*, October 5, 1878.

Ten immigrants were killed in the region south of Dodge City (Powers, 1972). However some bodies were not found until the following year.

Maj. Kirk came up from his camp Wednesday evening, and brought with him the remains of Frank Dow, who was killed by the Indians during their raid last fall. At the time Dow was killed, he was living in a dugout, holding the range for Mr. Kirk. . . .

— *Kinsley Graphic*, March 15, 1879.

Last Monday in company with other parties we went out on the prairie and found a skeleton of a human being — supposed to be that of one of the Cheyennes that went through here last

fall. We brought the remains to town and gave them a decent burial.
— *New West*, May 17, 1879.

After battling once more at Sand Creek, the Cheyenne headed northwestward (Socolofsky and Self, 1972) and were near Punished Woman's Fork (also called "Ladder Creek" or "Famished Woman") when Colonel Lewis and his men from Fort Dodge attacked.

DODGE CITY, Kas., October 6. — The following details of the battle in which Colonel Lewis was killed are from a participant: The Indians, after crossing the railroad, traveled rapidly to a point, where the fight occurred, at Famished Woman's Fork, 45 miles from Fort Wallace, and there upon sides of the canyon threw up rifle-pits. This plan was laid to draw the soldiers to a point where there could be no retreat and open fire on them from all sides. They led a blind trail, and the troops, suspecting nothing, entered the canyon, and but for a glimpse of danger by scouts would have fallen into the trap. Seeing the failure of their plans, the Indians at once opened fire upon the head of the column. The troops very soon took possession of the adjoining hills and succeeded in driving the Indians from several pits, and while running from pit to pit were shot by soldiers, but their bodies were dragged in by their friends. Colonel Lewis displayed rare courage and remained on his horse, the finest mark on the field. After dismounting, he moved about directing the fire of the troops, until a ball in the right leg severed the main artery and brought him down. [*Colonel Lewis died en route to Fort Wallace.*]
— *Inland Tribune*, October 19, 1878.

The bands led by Dull Knife and Little Wolf then proceeded north until they reached Sappa and Beaver creeks in northwestern Kansas, where extensive damage was inflicted on the settlers.

[Correspondence oi [*sic*] the N.Y. Herald.]

When the news of the massacre in the Beaver and Sappa Valleys of Kansas was first telegraphed to the east it is safe to presume not one in ten of the readers of the Herald knew where these streams were located. The two streams are, at the scene of

the massacre, little more than brooks rising in the extreme western portion of Kansas and flowing northeast into the Republican river. It is a region remote from the highways of travel and has hitherto been but little known except among cattle men as a good grazing range. It is only accessible by a seventy-mile ride from Buffalo station on the Kansas Pacific Railroad or by a still longer ride across the Solomon and Saline valley and thence across the great watershed of Kansas and Colorado. The former trip has just been made by your correspondent, who is, therefore, in a position to testify to the tedium and fatigue of such a journey across the great plains. Some years since Lieutenant Hendley [*sic*] surprised a band of sixty Northern Cheyennes at the head of Sappa vreek [*sic*], and so thorough was the ambitious young officer that very few escaped to tell the fate of their comrades. Some did escape, however, and since that time the Sappa Valley has been set down as an object of the vengeance of the punished tribe. The first stroke of that vengeance has fallen, and fallen so heavily that it will be many years before its effects will cease to be felt. The valley has now been settled about five years and has from fifty to sixty families living along its banks from a distance of forty miles from its head to its mouth. The Beaver Valley is also lined with settlers, and but for the recent raid, last spring would have seen at least two hundred new families settle in the two valleys. But the destruction of property and loss of life will prove a serious backset to the community, which was just emerging from the first struggle for existence in a new country.

THE FIRST DEPREDATION.

The Indians, after crossing the Kansas Pacific Railroad, followed the great Ogallala cattle trail to the north fork of the Solomon. At the crossing of this stream was located Sheridan Post Office, a rude log hut owned and occupied by Mr. Bayles, who supplemented his income from the products of his farm by the pittance of a cross-roads postmaster. This point was reached on the afternoon of September 29th. Mr. Bayles saw them coming over the divide and speedily placed himself and family in a position of comparative safety. When the savages arrived and found the ranch deserted they took the only means of vengeance

possible, and gutted the house. The squaws ripped open the feather beds, and, appropriating the ticks, scattered the feathers to the winds. Everything movable, including blankets and clothing, was speedily transferred to the pack animals, and everything breakable was converted into atoms. While the women were thus employed, the men were busy killing the cattle and hogs, cutting off huge slices of the still quivering flesh and leaving the rest for the coyotes. Having completed the work of destruction they moved about a mile down the creek, to Leatherman's ranch, which they devastated in like manner. Mr. Leatherman also had warning of their approach and escaped.

Before they left Leatherman's two young men, John Young and Charles Leonard, who had been hunting land claims, drove up to the ranch with the intention of stopping over night. As they approached they were met by a party of Indians, who opened fire upon them. Young was mortally wounded, but Leonard succeeded in getting away by driving over the divide toward the settlements on Prairie Dog Creek, a tributary of the Sappa, about ten miles from Leatherman's.

These young men warned the settlers, so that when the Indians reached the Prairie Dog they found the cabins deserted and contented themselves with gutting two or three ranches, the owners of which had the melancholy satisfaction of witnessing the destruction of their properry [*sic*] from their hiding places in the brush. From the Prairie Dog to the Sappa is fifteen miles, and at seven o'clock on the morning of September 30 the savages were on the latter creek. The settlers had not been warned and were pursuing their customary avocations.

The first attack was made upon James G. Smith, his son and John Hudson, who were loading hay in Smith's meadow. Attempting to seize the horses, the elder Smith resisted and was shot seven times with arrows. Still fighting with his only weapon — a-rake he was shot twice with a needle gun [*a rifle with a "needle" or firing pin, propelled by a spring, and activated by the trigger*], receiving wounds from which he di[*e*]d thirty-eight hours later. Their yells frightened Hudson's mules, and while running to catch them he was shot dead. Young Smith ran, followed by a mounted Indian, who fired seven shots at him from a

Winchester rifle, until in very desperation the young man turned on his assaliant [*sic*] with a pitchfork, when, firing a last shot, the Indian fled, leaving Smith to conceal himself in the brush.

The Indians then proceeded to the cabin of Mr. Colvin, but that gentleman and his wife, armed wilh [*sic*] a sortgun [*sic*] and a rifle, resisted the assault until one savage had his arm broken with a ball from Colvin's revolver, when they retired.

HORRIBLE OUTRAGES ON YOUNG LADIES.

From Colvin's they went to the cattle trail, where they met William Laing, his youngest son, aged fourteen, and two young ladies, sisters — one of them the district school teacher. They approached with signs of friendship, and while the old man was shaking hands with one, another sent a ball through his brain. The boy was also shot, and the young ladies were dragged from the wagon, stripped entirely naked and outraged repeatedly. They were then seized by a mounted Indian on each side and dragged through the thick underbrush, the ponies going at a trot, until their bodies were badly lacerated; then again outraged and then released, half dead with fright and the cruelty of their captors.

Within sight of the attack on Laing's wagon was Kiefer's ranch. An Irishman named Lynch was in the cabin, and as the Indians approached he shut the door and waited for them with a needle gun. After dancing around the cabin for several minutes one incautiously exposed himself and received a ball through his body. This satisfied them and they retreated.

OTHER OUTRAGES AND MURDERS.

The column then took the road up the south fork of the Sappa, gutting deserted ranches and killing stock.

A mile above Keiler's [*sic*] they met John Lull and ________ [*sic*] Irwin in a wagon, whom they killed, and taking their horses and cutting the harness to pieces.

At Westphallen's they found Ferdinand Westphallen, his wife and his son John, about getting into their wagon. The two men were killed and Mrs. Westphallen outraged and shot with blunt arrows until she gave up her money, $250.

A short distance further on Moses Abernathy and Marcellus Felt were killed in a wagon as they were driving along the road.

Half a mile beyond Abernathy was E. P. Humphery and his son John, also in a wagon. The old gentleman was killed, but John escaped into the bushes with a broken arm.

A one-legged man named Steadman was then met and also escaped with a broken arm, leaving four fine horses in possession of the savages.

The Indians then crossed over to the north fork of the Sappa Creek, where they met Ed Miskelley, a cattle breeder, riding along the road. He was killed and his horse taken.

HERDERS ATTACKED.

Tuesday they attacked a herd of Texas cattle on the way to the Beaver. Three of the herders were well armed and repelled the attack, but John Foster, who was un.vdarmed [*sic*] was killed, and the ponies of lthe [*sic*] outfit were capturehel [*sic*] Tuesday evenaing [*sic*] they struck the Beter [*sic*]. Near that astream [*sic*] fifteen of them me [*sic*] two herders — Hamper and Rathbun. They saluted them and after passing fired. Hamper was killed, but Rathbun threw himself into a buffalo wallow and kept them off with his revolver until darkness permitted him to effect his escape.

A lame man named Harry Abbott was also killed while working his field.

A Bohemian, name unknown, was met in his wagon and killed, and his body partially burned.

A HEROIC GIRL.

A farmer named Steiver was killed in his bed. His daughter, aged sixteen, ran out of the house with her three little brothers and sisters, and was met by a squad. She fought them so vigorously they whipped her severely, only letting her go when alarmed at something approaching. The lacerated girl pulled grass all night to cover the children.

Another farmer, named Snyder, was killed in his house, and his three little children driven far out on the prairie and left to

the mercy of the coyotes which followed the Indian trail. They were found by a party of herders.

Another young girl, who fought for her honor, so enraged the Indians that they scored her breasts with their knives and then outraged her; and still another was dragged by two mounted Indians a distance of five miles, absolutely naked, and forced to submit to all who chose to embrace her.

Nine others were killed on Beaver Creek, whose names I was unable to get, they being Bohemians, unable to speak the language and only a short time in the settlements.

A party of settlers followed the Indians from the Sappa and engaged the rear guard, killing one. The rest made their escape.

SUMMARY OF THE KILLED.

The total number known to be killed in the two valleys is thirty, and ______ [*sic*] Wright and Fred Walters are missing. From eight to ten more were killed in the Republican valley.

THE MILITARY CENSURED.

Captain Manck, in command of the pursuit, is severely censured by the settlers. On the night of the 1st inst. he encamped at the head of a gulch, directly opposite which and three miles distant was the camp of the Indians, and yet he allowed them to escape. The military authorities had denied mony [*sic*] of these outrages, but I have been on the ground and conversed with eyewitnesses of each of the transactions above noted, and in some instance with the participants themselves. A hundred witnesses can be produced to attest the accuracy of this brief statement.

— *Rice County Gazette*, November 14, 1878.

In addition to the 40 or 41 killed on the Northern Cheyenne trek, 90 claims for property damage and herds lost were accepted and $101,766.83 paid (Miner, 1986; Powers, 1972). Eventually the Cheyenne crossed the South Platte River in Nebraska. Later, in Nebraska's Niobrara Hills, the band divided. Some remained with Dull Knife and others went north into Montana with Little Wolf (Powers, 1972).

Criticism of the military in not bringing Dull Knife and his band of

Northern Cheyenne to justice was widespread. Initial military ineptitude and reluctance can be attributed to their disbelief of an outbreak from the reservation. However, even after being convinced, they failed to pursue the Indians with vigor.

Indian Outbreak.

CAMP SUPPLY, I.T.,

Oct. 17.

ED. GLOBE: The late Indian excitement in this locality having died out, "Field Marshal" Dull Knife outgeneraling the grand pasha of U.S. army, and reaching in safety the goal of his anticipations — being, it is said, snugly ensconced among his old familiar haunts in Wyoming and Dakota, and the little command in a garrison that has been performing extraordinarily hard duty for the past year becoming somewhat settled down to the ordinary routine, your correspondent would sum up as follows:

Without casting the least reflection upon, or detracting a single thing from, the ability, loyalty or bravery of our little army, it must be said that the escape of Dull Knife and his followers from Cheyenne agency and their ultimate success in reaching Dakota territory, is certaily [*sic*] a very remarkable occurrence in the annals of military movements. I have no definite means of giving the exact number of Dull Knife's force, but from the most reliable information (including Indian Agent Miles' statement) it cannot possibly have amounted to more that 130 warriors. Dull Knife's movements immediately after he left the reservation were not unknown to the military authorities. He was pursued and overtaken by two companies of cavalry within 60 miles of the agency he had left. He there gave battle, killing three soldiers, wounding as many more and, if reports of eye-witnesses are to be believed, striking terror into the hearts of the remainder, completely routing them. All the heads of the military in the department of the Missouri were immediately informed of the situation, and yet Dull Knife passed speedily on, passing in close proximity to several military posts and actually marched a

portion of the route along the public highway, robbing emigrant trains, murdering defenceless [*sic*] men, women and children as his fancy seemed to dictate, and at last arrived at his destination unscathed, and is no doubt ere this in conference with his friend and ally, Sitting Bull, as to the most practicable manner of subjugating the Black Hills.

While we look the matter squarely in the face it must be conceded that Dull Knife has achieved one of the most extraordinary coups d'etat of modern times and has made a march before which even Sherman's march to the sea pales. With a force of 130 warriors this untutored but wily savage encounters and defeats, eludes, baffles and outgenerals ten times his number of American soldiers (at one time during his march there were no less than 24 companies of cavalry and infantry in the field against him), and marched almost unmolested a distance of 1,000 miles. Of course most of the country passed through by Dull Knife was sparsely settled; but with the number of military posts — six — lying almost directly in his path, and the great number of cattle men, cowboys, freighters, etc., scattered over the plains that came in contact with his band, it does seem strange that he slipped through the schemes and plans that were so well laid to entrap gim [*sic*]. However, Dull Knife has thoroughly demonstrated the fact that 130 desperate warriors can raid successfully through 1,000 miles of territory, lying partly in Dakota, Nebraska, Kansas and the Indian territory, steal stock and perpetrate outrages too vile and horrible to print, and this in the face of ten times 130 well-equipped U.S. troops. That someone is highly reprehensible in the matter of not capturing or annihilating Dull Knife and his entire band is believed by all, but who the culpable party is will probably never be placed on the pages of history.

— *Ford County Globe*, October 29, 1878.

The cause for the large number of settlers killed in northwestern Kansas is conjectural at best. Some believed that Dull Knife's band was taking revenge for the killing of Southern Cheyenne by the military in this same region in 1875. More evidence seems to point to the general disgust and hatred toward all immigrants. This animosity was worsened by the treatment the Cheyenne received on their reservation in the Indian Territory. In an attempt to make Native Americans function as white settlers, agents were to give provisions if the Cheyenne would pledge to send their children to school. Also a reservation farmer was to instruct them in agricultural practices. Seeds and farming tools were distributed to Cheyenne males. However, most Cheyenne, both men and women, believed that farming was a job for women; men were the hunters and warriors. The government also attempted to get the Cheyenne to raise and herd cattle rather than hunt the buffalo, which were almost gone anyway. This program too failed as the Cheyenne could not accept the ideas of individuals owning cattle and property (Powers, 1963, 1971) — a philosophy contrary to the precepts of a free-roaming tribe of people.

But, essentially, more were killed in the areas of Beaver and Sappa creeks than elsewhere in Kansas because there were more settlers in this region than in the other areas through which the Cheyenne passed.

The cause that led to the outbreak is the same old story — goaded into desperation by starvation at the hands of the Indian agents. There are no buffalo anywhere near Cheyenne agency, and this same band was last fall and winter permitted to go out from their reservation to hunt them in order to supply themselves with meat. They did not find a single buffalo, and came into this post in a starving condition. While here a portion of them killed and ate their ponies, while the remainder feasted on their dogs — an Indian never eats his dog except when served up as a kind of state dinner or when he is driven to the wall by hunger. They applied to commanding officer for food; but the military establishment having no authority to issue rations to Indians, they were refused. Dull Knife appealed so persistently for aid that the commanding officer, seeing their condition and fearing trouble from them, as they were on the eve of an outbreak, ordered a few rations to be issued to them which were eagerly accepted and greedily devoured.

— *Ford County Globe*, October 29, 1878.

When settlement of the Great Plains was in its infancy in the early 1860s, few, if any, on the frontier had any compassion for the Native

Americans; they were viewed as heathen, little better than animals. Native Americans were to be driven from this land either by killing them, eliminating their source of food (the buffalo), removing tribe members to the Indian Territory, or a combination of all three. Sympathy toward the "red devil" did not exist, except from some Easterners who had no direct contact with them. However, as more and more people learned of the poor treatment many tribes were receiving at the hands of the Indian agents and the ill-founded efforts by the federal government to modify the behavior of the Native Americans, a few voices began to speak out in support of policy reformation.

After ten years' soldiering on the plains I am convinced that a majority of the Indian raids have been caused by the vascillating policy of our government, coupled with the avaricious, unscrupulous and dishonest agents. After a century of experiments by our government with the red man in trying to ameliorate his condition — experiments that have cost millions of treasure and thousands of lives — it would seem that the east could introduce some measures by which the Indians and white men could live together on this continent in harmony.

The poor Indian! his complete dependence on the bounty of the white man, his need of spiritual teaching, his unsophisticated manners and his totally uncivilized habits, are advocated by a puritanical class of agents who at the same time rob, steal, plunder, starve and drive him into desperation, causing him to desert his agency and seek the warpath as the only means left him to obtain food to keep the aged andecrepit [*sic*] men, women and little ones of his household from dire starvation. I do not pretend to hold the Indian up as an object of sympathy or charity, but I do folemnly [*sic*] believe that if the cause that led to the mournful murder of Gen. Canby, the deplorable massacre of the gallant Custer and his command, the rascally killing of the beloved Col. Lewis, and the murder of hundreds of other noble officers and soldiers, were thoroughly investigated and understood, the deeds would be somewhat palliated by the circumstances that surrounded the commission of the crimes.

When the present system of governing the Indians is reformed and the field for making fortunes out of what is allowed by the

government for their maintenance, and the miserable, hypocritical, sacrilegious but sanctimonious agents are obliterated — when the Indian is taught to respect the government by the force of arms, and when the government keeps its solemn promises to the Indians — when the Indian has learned to trust and believe the words of the white man instead of looking upon him with disgust — then, and not until then, will the redman be at permanent peace with the pale face. — *Ford County Globe*, October 29, 1878.

During the Northern Cheyenne 1878 trek across Kansas, undoubtedly a number of Native Americans also were killed, but the exact number is unknown. And thus ended the battles with the Native Americans on the High Plains of western Kansas.

This sad episode in the history of the development of the West resulted from a cultural confrontation — one the Native American was certain to lose. People of all races were killed as the nomadic culture of the Native Americans on the Plains met the agricultural pursuit of the settlers.

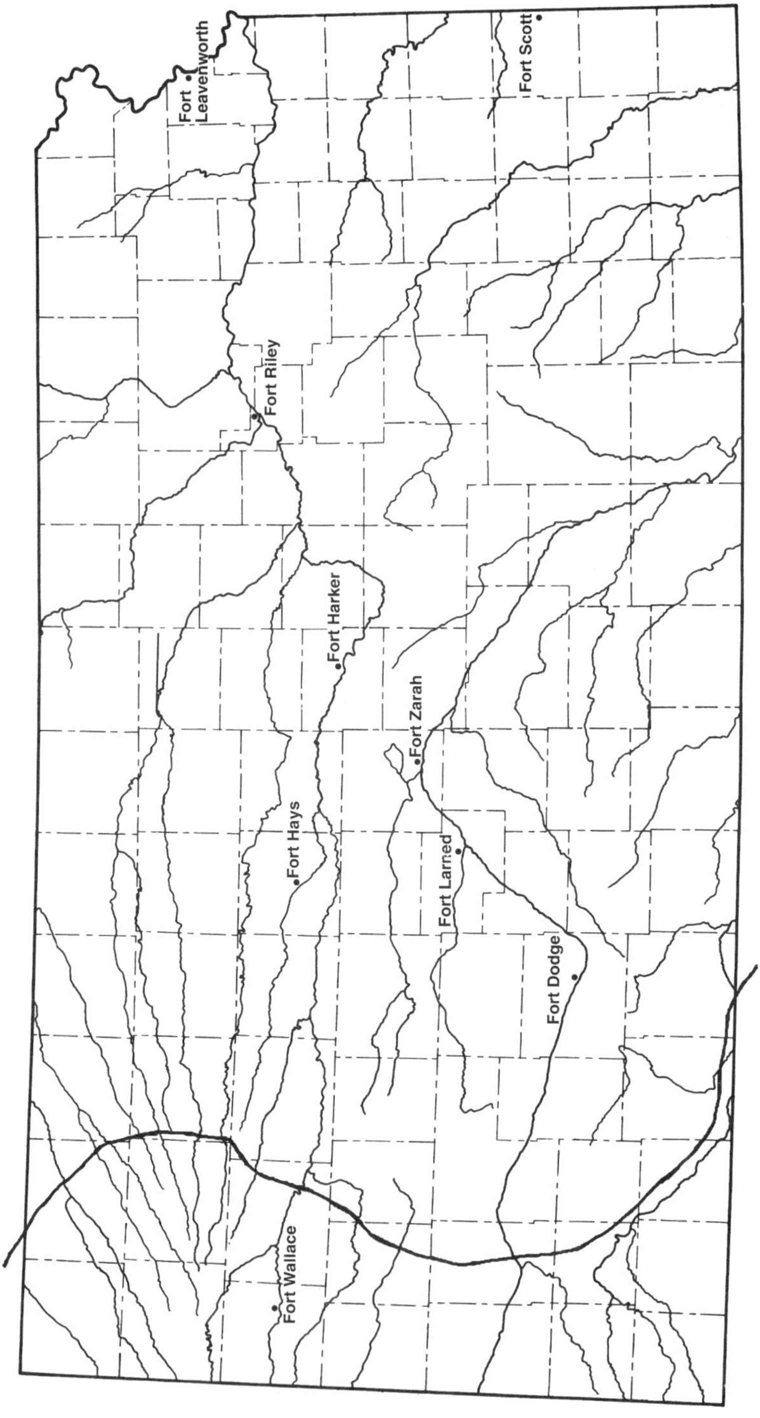

The route of the Northern Cheyenne in their escape from their Oklahoma Reservation, 1878.

Graves on the prairie southwest of Hays, Kansas.
Kansas State Historical Society, Topeka

Railroad accidents were not uncommon in frontier Kansas. Here and opposite, a crowd gathers around a Missouri Pacific wreck near Claflin, *ca.* 1890s.

Kansas State Historical Society, Topeka

Kansas State Historical Society, Topeka

Nowhere was the "wild, Wild West" more typified than in Dodge City, Kansas. Here, the "Shoot Em Up Jake" gravestone is pictured, at Dodge City Boot Hill Cemetery.
Kansas State Historical Society, Topeka

Russell, Kansas, in 1894, was the scene of a lynching, a common experience for frontier justice.
Kansas State Historical Society, Topeka

H. B. Bell's Livery Stable at Dodge City, Kansas, the heart of community activity — often good and bad. *Kansas State Historical Society, Topeka*

An exterior view of the B. F. Zimmerman hardware store at Dodge City, Kansas, *ca.* 1872 or 1873, where guns, pistols, and ammunition were an important part of the retail business along with the hardware and tinware.

Kansas State Historical Society, Topeka

Bank robbers of the "Wild West," who met their fate — Bill Doolin, George Newsome, and Old Yantis — at the town of Spearville, Kansas, just northeast of Dodge City, in Ford County.

Kansas State Historical Society, Topeka

Members of Northern Cheyenne Indian, Dull Knife's band, on the courthouse steps in Dodge City, Kansas, April 30, 1879. Dull Knife and his band broke out of their reservation in Oklahoma and headed northwestward through Kansas, plundering as they went. The Cheyenne pictured were taken prisoner at Dodge City. *Kansas State Historical Society, Topeka*

Privates Sumner and Welsh, soldiers from Fort Hays, dead on the street in front of the saloon, 1873. *Kansas State Historical Society, Topeka*

Above is a re-enactment of the scene of a shooting in 1901, in Lucas, Kansas, northeast of Russell. Andrew Jackson Francis shot his brother-in-law. *Kansas State Historical Society, Topeka*

The first *Hays City Sentinel* building at Hays, Kansas. Owner William P. Montgomery poses in front of the building in 1875. The *Sentinel* was a source for many of the articles about frontier life and death.

Kansas State Historical Society, Topeka

A marker erected in 1938 at Scates Cemetery, three miles south of Buckeye Church, in Ellsworth County, memorializing the people "whose fortitude withstood the perils and hardships of pioneer life." *Kansas State Historical Society, Topeka*

In 1905, the bodies of soldiers who had died of cholera and were buried at the Fort Hays Cemetery were moved to the National Cemetery at Fort Leavenworth, Kansas.

Kansas State Historical Society, Topeka

Chapter 6

Death by Their Own Hand

SUICIDE — THE WORD conjures up fearful images along with feelings of great tragedy and overwhelming sadness. Throughout the millennia, humans have deliberately ended their own lives. The most notable as well as the most ordinary have terminated their existence. People kill themselves either by doing something harmful (commission) or by not doing something helpful (omission), and in most cases they expect the action to be effective in meeting their desired final goal: the cessation of life.

Suicides are not a new aspect of human behavior and certainly were a cause of death in the frontier days. Why does anyone ever consider and sometimes commit suicide? The answers to this puzzling question are varied and often interrelated:

> Because he is psychotic and doesn't know what he is doing. Because he acts on impulse and doesn't think

> about the future. Because his discomfort is so acute that he cares about nothing but escape. Because he believes he is already dying and has no earthly future. Because he believes that the future will be no better, or even worse. Because he feels that what he can gain symbolically through death is more important than anything continued life can offer. Or, most generally, because "life has no meaning." (Kastenbaum and Aisenberg, 1976, p. 210)

The methods for committing suicide were as varied as the reasons for following through with the paramount act. On the frontier, the use of firearms — shotguns, revolvers, and needle-guns; poisons — strychnine and lye; drugs — laudanum and morphine; hanging; knives; razors; and drowning were all reported.

Laudanum, an opium-based drug, was commonly employed to medicate a variety of physical ailments in pioneer days. This opiate, along with alcohol, apparently played a role in the death of a Brookville, Kansas, resident in 1878. It should be noted that his appears to be an "assisted suicide."

A man named Charles Barnes died in Brookville from an overdose of laudanum, on Monday evening. Our Brookville correspondents give the particulars. Dr. Groger, coroner, [*and jury*], found that "Charles Barnes came to his death from an overdose of laudanum administered by the hands of John Godin at the request of the said Charles Barnes, who we believe took the poison with the intent to destroy himself while "insane," from the effects of alcoholic stimulants, etc.

— *Saline County Journal*, June 20, 1878.

On last Sunday night William Coyle committed suicide at Mr. Seltzer's livery stable. He had threatened during the day to kill himself, but his associates believed he was trying to scare them. But just before dinner he went to the drug store of Jacobs & English and purchased an ounce of laudanum, took it to the stable, put some sugar in a tin cup, poured the laudanum on the

sugar and filled the cup up with water. He afterwards poured off the liquid and ate the sugar. At about two o'clock he went to the drug store of Mr. Ross and asked for an ounce of laudanum, said he wanted the strong kind, had a sick horse to which he wished to admininter [*sic*] it. After paying for the medicine, he remarked: "I am the horse. I have been sick for several hours and have taken a bottle or two of laudanum and it had done me no good." Mr. Ross advised him to try smaller doses, about thirty drops at a dose every half hour, saying that they sometimes releive [*sic*] more effectually than large doses. In the evening he asked Mr. Seltzer's boys to go to the hotel and get him a cup of tea. He said he had drank three tin cups of water but water did not answer. On Monday morning one of the boys went into the barn loft to put down some hay for the horses and reported that Coyle was asleep and snoring. Later Mr. Seltzer and his men were in the barn loft and going to Coyle found him about, if not altogether, dead. He was yet warm, and they thought he had still a feeble pulse. Dr. Hodge was called, but on his arrival the man was dead though yet warm.

The above facts were brought out at the inquest held by Coroner Clobridge on Monday. Mr. Coyle left some letters that he had written but never sent. One is dated Valley House, Great Bend, Kansas, March 4, 1879, and addressed to his father. In this he tells of having been sick, and extolls the excellence of his wife and invites his father to come and see them. The letter is unfinished and not signed. Another letter is addressed to his wife, and solicits her to again live with him and promises to go to work in case of compliance. Mr. Coyle told his story to his companions at the stable substantially as follows: His father is a well-to-do physician, Dr. T. P. Coyle, of Baltimore, Maryland. When he left home his father gave him $1100. He married near Great Bend about eight weeks ago. His brothers-in-law burned up his stable and two horses, and defrauded him of all he possessed, and then persuaded his wife away from him. He had tried to make way with himself before but had been prevented.

Another story told by a man who boarded at the Valley House in Great Bend when Mr. Coyle and his wife came there is to the effect that he had been discharged from the employ of the

railroad company for negligence. He never did anything while at the hotel, but finally went to Dodge and engaged a place for his wife to work in a hotel. She refused to go or to have anything to do with him after his return. He left about two weeke [*sic*] ago but his wife remained until last Saturday and worked out the board bill of herself and husband and then went home to her people about twelve miles north-west of Great Bend.

The Stage Driver's Story

The Great Bend and Hays City stage driver overtook Coyle and a girl of about sixteen walking towards Great Bend a few weeks ago, and asked them to get in, they did so and Coyle told the driver that he would pay him for the ride sometime, that he had no money now and was going to Great Bend to get married. The driver told him he was a d——d fool to be marrying when he had nothing with which to support a wife.

Sunday afternoon he took from his pocket a letter and wrote on it two addresses. The first is Dr. T. P. Coyle, Cor. Park and Mulberry St. Baltimore Md. The second is Maggie Rourk, Maherville P. O. Barton county, Kansas.

— *Rice County Gazette*, March 27, 1879.

And teenage suicide is certainly not a 20th, and now 21st, century tragedy.

Yesterday evening a son of J. H. Heldreth, aged about fourteen years, hung himself with a bridle rein, near this place. The circumstances are about these: He and an elder brother were working at a straw shed, where they had set some posts and laid poles upon them, attached to one of which was an old bridle, with rope rein hanging down. About sundown the elder brother went to the house for some purpose, and returning in about ten minutes, found his brother suspended by the aforesaid rope rein, quite dead. The cause of this unfortunate affair is left open for conjecture.

— *Sumner County Press*, December 16, 1875.

Although graphic pictures might be seen today on television or in the movies, such details as those that follow would not be found in a present-day newspaper account of a suicide.

Our orderly and quiet town was thrown into considerable excitement, Monday morning, from the starting [*sic*] fact that a young man in the employ of C. G. Beech, had committed suicide on the previous evening by cutting his throat. It appeares [*sic*] that Meritt Thornton, a young man about 21 years of age, who has been engaged the past summer herding cattle for Mr. Beech, returned home from his usual dutes [*sic*] on Sunday evening, and retired to rest about nine o'clock. Shortly afterwards Mrs. Beech retired to her room, adjoining the sitting-room writting [*sic*]. About thirty or forty minutes after the young man retired, Mr. Beech heard the movement on the bed upstairs, and shortly afterward: heard what sounded like water dropping on the floor. Mrs. Beech also heard the dropping, and called the attention of her husband, when he stepped up stairs to learn the cause. Mr. Beech found Thornton lying upon the bed with a razor in his hand and his throat cut from ear to ear — his head near the side of the bed, and a stream of blood running on the floor. Dr. Freeland was immediately called, and found the man still breathing but past all human aid. — ***Republic County Journal*, October 4, 1879.**

One of the more peculiar and unsubstantiated causes given for a suicide was that religious fervor was somehow responsible. The exact nature of the "religious excitement" is not explained in the following article.

Miss Liona Thurber, a young lady employed as a domestic in the family of H. T. Kramer, in this city, committed suicide on Tuesday evening of last week, by taking strychnine. From remarks made by the unfortunate woman previous to committing the act, and an unfinished note found near her, it would seem that the act was the result of religious excitement. The only relatives of the deceased are a married sister, living about thirteen miles west of Wichita, and a brother, a mere lad, in the employ of Wm. Matthewson. — ***Wichita Weekly Beacon*, April 11, 1877.**

Another suicide that seemed to have religious connotations was equally enigmatic. This preacher seemed to be torn between a fervent aspiration to spread the Word and an equally intense feeling of inadequacy on his competency to do so.

With a heavy heart I seat myself to tell the sad end of Rev. Stephen M. Ernest, who hung himself at his home, on Wednesday morning, the 14th. The cause, we think, was insanity. For the satisfaction of his numerous friends, both in Kansas and Missouri, please insert a short sketch of his life. S. M. Ernest was born August 11th, 1853, in Caldwell county, Missouri. His relatives say that from a child he was affectionate and obedient. His oldest sister said she did not think he ever told a lie. He told his wife that when a little boy he told one lie to a negro woman to get some apples. That lie had caused him a great deal of trouble to his conscience. In February, before he was sixteen years old, he made a profession of religion and joined the M.E. Church. He felt from his profession that he was called to the work of the ministry. His deportment has always been serious and at times he appeared to be of a desponding nature. When fully resigned to God's will, he was cheerful and happy. When he would think of his inability his spirits would sink almost into despair. He said to the writer of this at one time, "I cannot preach. I have tried to get a college education, but Providence has so overruled that I cannot." He, with one brother and two sisters came to Rice county, Kansas, in the spring of 1874. He came here as a licensed exhorter in the church. He and his brother returned to Missouri after the hopper [*grasshopper*] raid. He was sick nearly all winter in Missouri with brain fever [*meningitis or encephalitis*]. He returned to Rice county in the spring of 1875, in poor health, and took a claim. Last winter while Brothers Watt and Vickers were protracting a meeting at the Wildwood School House, he appeared sad and gloomy. One day at his brother-in-law's, Wm. Jones, he went to the stable to pray when he was almost in despair, got a rope and attempted to hang himself in the stable, but the rope broke. He told his intimate friend that he did not know what he had done till he fell. He spoke in church that he had come near taking his own life, but during the meeting he was wonderfully blessed, and his friends had hoped that he would never despond any more. On the 24th of February, 1876, he was licensed to preach, and he succeeded as a preacher to the entire satisfaction of his friends. The Rev. J. W. Fox, P. E. [*Protestant Episcopal*], of the district, imployed [*sic*] him as a supply for three months on the Rush and

Neswork, where I learn he was well received. He was married on the 24th of September, 1876 to Miss Ida J. Monroe.

He was esteemed by all, I think, as a Christian and preacher and good citizen. If he had an enemy anywhere I never heard of it. He was faithful at the weekly prayer meeting; was always faithful at family and social devotion. The last time he prayed with his wife he said, "Oh, Lore [*sic*] I want to live better to-morrow than I have to-day." On the morning referred to, his wife had not, nor had she at any time previously ever seen any thing wrong in his mind. He had always treated her with much affection and tenderness. He got up, started a fire, went back to the bed, kissed his wife, said "now get breakfast, and I will feed the horse and milk the cow." These were the last words she ever heard him say. When the breakfast was ready and he had not returned, she went to the stable. She saw a horse bridled, walking around the stable, she saw the pail of milk setting by the door on the outside of the stable. But when she looked in he was hung by the neck to the ridge-pole of the stable, dead.

— *Rice County Gazette*, February 22, 1877.

Suicides in frontier times seem to reflect the impact of living in an extraordinarily uncharitable environment. However, many remained unexplained and were attributed only to some indefinite mental attitude.

A most sad and unexpected tragedy occurred in Washington township, yesterday morning, by which a human soul was ushered into the presence of its maker.

The particulars as we get them are as follows: James Gardner, one of the most quiet and respected citizens of the county, came into his house about 8 o'clock in the morning and taking his old army musket, went out doors and was gone but a few minutes, when a shot was heard; the wife stepped to the door to see what he had shot at and saw Mr. Gardner lying in the yard but a few rods from the house. She went at once to his side, and what was her feelings of anguish to find that he had shot himself in the head, the charge entering just above the left ear, ranging upwards and came out near the top of his head, tearing a most frightful hole. . . .

We learn that he had been laboring under a fit of insanity for about three weeks, although no once seems to have the least idea of the cause of his affliction. He had never before shown any disposition to do violence to himself, and he had the most gentlemanly disposition and was respected by all his neighbors for his good qualities. His wife and relatives have the smpathy [*sic*] the public in this, their most sad and unnatural bereavement.

— *Republic County Journal*, July 19, 1879.

As in many reported modern suicides, despondency coupled with excessive consumption of alcohol precipitated a self-inflicted demise.

Geo. P. Clark, formerly a resident of Rockford township, and lately a resident of this city, committed suicide by taking strychnine, on last Friday afternoon. He returned to his house, situated just north of the Wichita Elevator, about 4 o'clock p.m., complaining of not being well. He went into the kitchen alone for a few minutes and then went into the bed room, laid down and began to read some newspapers, that he had brought home with him. He soon began to complain of being very sick, and called for the baby, which he fondles for some time. About 5 o'clock he was seized with a fearful spasm, which was succeeded by others until he died about half past six o'clock that evening. He was rational up to within a short time of his death. He did not want a doctor sent for, stating that he could do him no good. His wife sent for Dr. Owens, but he did not arrive until after he died. Dr. Owens, as soon as he saw the body pronounced it a case of strychnine poisoning. . . . On Saturday morning his pocket-book was handed to his wife who opened it and found a small vial containing several grains of strychnine. It appeared . . . that Clark had twice before, some time ago, attempted suicide by taking morphine and laudanum, and has since, while drinking, threatened to destroy himself. The only cause for the rash act that we heard was that he had wasted his substance and run through with his wife's property and poverty stared him and his family in the face. This preyed on his mind, and aided by the demon of strong drink, nerved him up to the commission of the fatal act. When sober he was regarded as a kind husband and father, and a good

citizen. He leaves a wife and four young children, who have the sympathy of the public in their sad bereavement. He was forty-six years of age. . . . — ***Wichita Weekly Beacon*, November 29, 1876.**

A poor financial condition also was cited in frontier accounts of suicide. Although, in one case, unconfirmed bad news apparently drove one man to death.

Our community was on Saturday, the 23d inst. thrown into a state of feeling akin to consternation by the discovery of another "dead man" across the river below the bridge, in the vicinity of that fatal island. The supposition was at first that it was another case of foul play, but the investigation of the Coroner's jury proved it to be a case of suicide, and though melancholy enough in itself, their verdict, which was not rendered until Monday afternoon, was somewhat of a relief to our citizens. There was nothing upon the body by which it could be identified, but by Monday the jury had ascertained that the body was that of Geo. Holtzman, a native of Germany, about 69 years of age, and at the time of his death residing with his son some eleven miles south and west of Wichita on the farm of George Roseberry. The manner of his death was by hanging, for which purpose he used his leather belt attached to the branch of a tree, but which broke loose from its fastenings after serving its terrible purpose, allowing the body to fall upon its face where it lay, as was supposed some three or four days before being discovered. No reason was given by the suicide for his rash act of self destruction, nor can his friends assign any. He is described by them as having been commonly of a cheerful disposition, but of late somewhat depressed by a longing to return to Pennsylvania, and by disappointment in not receiving from parties there, money, with which he expected to return to that state, he having left it for Kansas a year ago. He was last seen by his friends on Sunday, the 17th inst., at which time he left home for the purpose of attending Catholic church at Wichita, which, being a member, he frequently did. He had when he left home about $10 in money, some of which was found on the body. This fact would suggest the idea of a debauch, but on the contrary his friends say he was very

careful and exemplary in his habits, leaving us in a quandary as to where the money went or what figure, if any, it cut in his death. — *Wichita Weekly Beacon*, August 27, 1879.

On Wednesday of last week, a young Bohemian named Frank Kottaer, left his boarding place, at Joseph Bruey's, near Bluff Creek, to go to his claim, about a mile distant. He was seen plowing there with his oxen during the afternoon, but did not return to supper as nsual [*sic*]. Mrs. Bruey and her little girl went to look for him, and as they approached his claim house, were horrified to see his dead body hanging by the neck from the door frame. They hastened to the residence of Mr. Wm. Nelson who with Mr. Cantwell repaired to the claim and examined the body. They found it stiff and cold apparently several hovrs [*sic*] dead. His team had been turned loose and were feeding at a corn shock. He had used the lariat rope, doubling it so as to make a loop, and had wrapped it several times around the cross piece of the door. When found the rope had evidently slipped somewhat so that the body hung inclined forward towards the inside of the house with the toes upon the ground. The frame had not been high enough to suspend the body, and it was for a time a mystery to all who examined it how he could have died in the position he was found in without leaving more indication of a struggle. Messrs. Nelson and Cantwell came immediately in search of the coroner, but not finding him here summoned Col. Zacharias, a Justice of the Peace, to hold an inquest. The evidence was chiefly given by a little girl, Mary Bruey, the only member of the family who can speak English. She said that young Kottaer, who was about 25 years of age, had received a letter a day or two previous which appeared to give him great trouble. He walked the house for hours and "read the Good Book" continuously, but said nothing. Neither this letter nor any other scrap of writing, except his naturalization papers, could be found upon his person, nor in his trunk, which was well supplied with outer and under clothing. Everything was in perfect order and indicated that he was in quite good circumstances, so that it was quite evident that he had

deliberately destroyed his papers and prepared himself for the desperate deed. — ***Sumner County Press*, December 18, 1879.**

In conspicuous contrast to instances in which no notes were left, some individuals went to great lengths to explain the tribulations leading to the deed. However, even when long letters were left behind, sometimes the only conclusion that could be reached, even after an exhaustive inquest, was that frontier life was simply too difficult to bear.

On last Tuesday morning, Mr. J. E. Van Vorhis, the new justice of the peace, came up from Spearville, and informed Coroner Galland that a young man had died on the evening previous, of a violent death, supposed to have been caused by poison. Dr. Gallland [*sic*] being unable to officiate in person, Justice Van Vorhis was authorized to act as coroner. He immediately returned to Spearville, accompanied by the editor of the TIMES. Arriving at the place where the suicide took place, a station of the A. T. & S. F. road, sixteen miles east of here, in this county, a jury was empanneled [*sic*] and the necessary witnesses summoned. After the jury had been sworn, the solemn procession, consisting of coroner, constable, jurymen, witnesses and spectators marched from Mr. Jonas Stafford's house to the railroad water tank, where the body of the deceased lay cold and stiff. It had been placed there the evening before to await examination. The body appeared to be that of a young man near the age of 21 years, not healthy in appearance, and the face bore a sad expression. The coroner and some of the jurymen examined the body, found no marks of violence, except that the lips were eaten as if by acid, and the body was swollen. In the pockets were soine [*sic*] little notions and a letter from an uncle, but nothing to indicate the cause of the suicide. The jury returned to Mr. Stafford's and proceeded to listen to the evidence. A letter written by the unfortunate boy and mailed the day of this death, was first opened and read. We publish it verbatim:

SPEARVILLE, NOV. 26, '77.

DEAR AUNT: After a long time I will try and drop you a few lines. I am not getting along very well at present. I have it pretty

rough. I have a very sore leg; it started from a boil, and I could not take care of it, and catched cold in it, and it has stopped me from doing anything. I dont know how I can get along this winter. I wish you would come out to Kansas and take land. I did not know where you were for a long time. I left the "Rock" a good while ago. I have work now but I cannot do it. I was at Larned to see French. I wanted money to get a team, but could not get it. He will keep me down as long as he can. He has made his brags that I will want to come back to him. His good neighbors told me he would give anything to get me back. If I could have got a team I could have got along very well this winter, but I cannot get it. He has his day now and mine will come some time, and when it does look out, for I will sink him as far as I can. He has no mercy and I will not know what it is when my turn comes. His wife told him he had better come to my terms, for she knew he would not have any more to pay with next summer than he has now. Write soon. From your nephew. WESLEY J. ATKINS

To Bell C. Williams, Altoona, Pa.

French, who is spoken of in the letter, is supposed to be his step-father, with whom he lived from the time he was eight years old until a few years ago, when they disagreed, and young Atkins left. What he means by saying he left the Rock we could not learn.

THE INQUEST

State of Kansas, Ford county.

Testimony of witnesses taken this 27th day of November, 1877, at an inquest. . . .

Mr Samuel Pathemore being duly sworn says: I am stopping at Mr. Winan's: came down to the postoffice last night; as I came by the fence near the lumber yard I heard some one hallowing [*sic*], but paid no attention at first; the sound of the voice came from between the switch and the main track near the lumber pile in Spearville; rode down to the freight car; came back by the lumber yard and still heard hallowing; the voice said "Hello! for God's sake come over here"; rode over toward where the sound came, but could see nothing for the darkness; It was about 7:30

o'clock, P. M.; heard some say "I am poisoned:" I said "how is that, who done it?"; he said "I done it myself. For God's sake go down to Stafford's and get a cup of hot water and some salt"; after I started to Stafford's I heard him groaning; I went on to Stafford's and told Mr. Stafford what I had saw, and then went back; when I got back he was dying. . . .

Mr. Jonas Stafford being duly sworn said: The man who now lies here dead came to me on the 19th day of October, 1877, and went to work for me on the section the same morning. I never noticed anything peculiar about his actions until about eight days ago. About that time he returned from a two day's trip to Larned. He then appeared to be low spirited, sad and dejected. Kept getting more and more dejected, and talked about how he had failed to get some money from his step-father, near Larned, also complained of his sore leg. Yesterday morning he said if his leg did not get better he might as well quit work first as last. Yesterday morning he was unable to go to work. As I came home from work that day I met him near the house and asked him how he felt. He said he felt very badly. This was about two hours before he was found dying. He seemed to have no appetite for supper. Atkins was about 5 feet 8 inches high, had dark hair and eyes, weighed about 140 pounds, had light complexion and was rather good-looking, was about 21 years of age. Since last March I have had a bottle of poison hanging up in the tank in a bucket. I had it for poisoning wolves. It was accidentally knocked down one day last week and Atkins saw it. This was the same bottle found near my house to-day. When I saw the bottle last, before to-day, it was about one-third full of strychnine. When found today it only contained a few grains. It was about a half ounce bottle. . . .

Mr. Parthemore being recalled said: On Nov. 27, I found a small bottle marked "poison" and containing strychnine, near Mr. Stafford's house, about a hundred yards from where the man Atkins was found dying on the day previous; the bottle was afterwards identified by Mr. Stafford as one he had kept in the tank, containing poison. . . .

Mr. C. L. Meacham being duly sworn said: Yesterday Mr. Atkins was talking in my presence and wanted to know how

much strychnine it would take to kill a wolf; said he knew it did not take much to kill a man; he talked considerable about strychnine and how much it would take to kill a wolf; I told him how much I thought it would take to kill a wolf; never heard him say anything about killing himself. . . .

THE VERDICT. . . . That on the evening of the 26th of November the said Atkins came to his death by the means of strychnine administered by his own hand. . . .

—*Dodge City Times*, December 1, 1877.

On the Plains, where life was often uncomfortable, physical infirmities were found to be the cause of severe depression.

A German, named Smith who, with his family, was occupying Judge Fisher's farm east of Chisholm creek, settled the all-important question of "To be or not to be," by shuffling of [*sic*] this mortal coil [*sic*], with a shot gun, on Friday forenoon, of last week. Mr. Smith was an invalid, had been sick for a long while, and became discouraged and apparently hopeless. His family, it seems, had feared that he would kill himself and were very watchful of him. On last Friday, he was left alone with one of his daughters. He complained of the water and told his daughter to take a bottle and go to the spring, fill it, and then cork the bottle up to keep the air from it. When she came back she found the door locked; calling the other members, the door was broken open and Smith was found on the floor dead. He had placed the muzzle of his shot gun in his mouth and pulled the trigger with his foot. His death was instantaneous. . . .

— *Wichita Weekly Beacon*, May 15, 1878.

On Tuesday of last week, Neal Decker, living near Valley Center, attempted to commit suicide by swallowing a large dose of concentrated lye. It seems Mr. Decker had been ill for three or four months, had become discouraged by his sickness and financial troubles and thus sought to put an end to his miseries. He had swallowed the lye some two hours before his family

discovered the rash deed, and too late for the application of proper remedies. Although alive at last accounts, no hopes are entertained of his recovery, as his throat and stomach are terribly eaten with the poison. . . . —*Wichita Weekly Beacon*, June 25, 1879.

Though largely undiagnosed, mental illnesses were surely responsible for some pioneer suicides. Conditions now familiar, such as depression and other mood or personality disorders, cannot always be deduced from suicide accounts. However, where the person was a noted and respected member of the community, the accounts of the suicide were often lengthy and flowery. In these detailed articles, today's readers may glean information that supports the theory of mental illness as the cause of suicide.

It is seldom that a community is called upon so suddenly to mourn the loss of one of their most prominent citizens or a family to grieve for a lost parent in the midst of happiness and enjoyment. Yet such things are destined to be and we little dream of whom the unfortunate victim shall be and every one in the town of Wilson were saddened by the sudden and unexpected departure to the unknown world of Mr. Jacob Fowle, by his own hand, Sunday afternoon about three o'clock. For some time Mr. Fowle has been troubled in regard to his business and has at times been absent minded to that extent that it was peculiarly noticeable, but on Sunday, except on occasions when his mind would wander back to the business of the week, he was unusually cheerful, making remarks that would indicate thoughts of a desired continuance of life. The night before however, after a conversation with his son, on business he remarked to his wife that he was afraid of the boy going crazy. Also two or three days before he had spoke to his son-in-law, saying that he believed his mind was giving way. He had transacted business very strangely for sometime, making purchases that were preposterous and doing other things that were noticeable as strange. In this frame of mind the unhappy thought came to him and as one being led on as if by magnet, not contemplating the deed sufficiently to consider the act or the sorrow that would surround his family, he took a piece of new rope and repaired to the stable in the rear of his store

where after fastening the rope to a joice [*sic*] and placing the noose about his neck he pushed the keg on which he was standing from under him, breaking his neck in the fall, thus rushing from this world of trouble to him to that bourne from which no traveler returns, not a sign of pain in the expression, but a look as if he had fallen asleep. The body was found shortly after, cut down and an attempt made to restore life, but to no purpose, and he is now numbered among the dead, but not forgotten by the hosts of friends who followed his remains to their last resting place, or by his family who mourn the loss of a kind father and affectionate husband and who have the sympathy of the whole community in their sad bereavement. In the inquest held over the body, the coroner's jury returned a verdict of death at his own hands by hanging while temporarily insane. . . . As a business man he was always honorable in his dealings and will be missed in that circle. He was a great worker for the interests of Wilson and left nothing undone that could possibly be of benefit to the place. As a temperance worker he was continually taking steps for the adoption of measures that would raise the fallen from the cups of degration [*sic*]. His good deeds will always live to blot out the memory of his sad decease. The funeral was largely attended. Over four hundred people witnessing the last sad rites in their burial of the poor man's friend and benefactor for such he was in the bestowal of credit and subscribing liberally for anything that would be an individual help or public good, generous to a fault and obliging as honest. Let his untimely end be a warning to men who are so wrapt up in business that nights and Sundays find no rest for their ever toiling brain. What is business success to be compared with health, yet there are many men who, though they may not pass away as did the subject of these comments, they will go down to their grave early and unhappy. . . .

— *Ellsworth Reporter,* September 11, 1879.

Sometimes, however, it was not clear whether the principal died from suicide or from an unknown ailment.

Death is sad enough, when we are called upon to watch by the side of a near and dear friend, and witness the form slowly

wasting away — each hour indicating how surely disease is doing its work; but is made doubly so when it is the work of one's hand. Such a case we will attempt to give to our readers.

Mr. C. C. Cox, who resides about six miles west of Ellis, having business in our city, in company with his wife left home Tuesday morning, leaving their daughter Laura and two other children, with their grandmother to keep house. A man by the name of Charles Insley who was stopping at Mr. Cox's also staid [*sic*] with the family. Mr. Cox and his wife arrived here on Tuesday, finishing their business and returned to Ellis on the passenger train that evening where they remained until after breakfast yesterday morning, when they started for their home in the country. When about half way home, they met their nephew, a boy about fourteen years old, coming hurriedly on horseback; he informed them in an excited manner that Laura had taken strychnine and he was afraid she would die before he could get the doctor; Mr. Cox mounted the horse his nephew was riding, and started in great haste to Ellis for Dr. Watson. Mrs. W and the nephew reached home just in time to see her die. Father and Doctor arrived an hour later — but all was over — the spirit had winged its flight — the casket robbed of its jewel was all that was left him. While suffering in the agonies of death she told Mr. Insley she had taken strychnine that morning in her tea; that she was tired of life and would soon be at rest. She left no written message to tell of her troubles; and the real cause of the rash act will ever remain a mystery. We are informed that the relations of the family were perfectly harmoneous [*sic*], and that her every wish had been gratified. She had just returned from the east, some weeks ago where she had been attending school, and, was admired for her many virtues by all who knew her. The deceased was about sixteen years of age.

"After life's fitfull fever, she sleeps well."

— *Ellis County Star*, April 20, 1876.

Shortly after this account had been published, there was a denial by the father that the act was suicide, which makes the truth of the event even more difficult to confirm. The perceived stigma of having a family member commit suicide may have caused some families to construct fabrications about the death of a loved one.

The reported case of suicide, by Miss Cox, residing near Eliis [*sic*], which has been the topic of conversation for some time past, now turns out, according to her father's statements, to be false.

Below we publish a letter we receiv [*sic*] this morning.

EDITOR SENTINEL: — I wish to correct a statement contained in the Star, pertaining to the death of my daughter.

I and my wife left home on Monday, for Hays. We had to stay in Ellis that night. Mr. Endsly [*sic*] was to come in that night but did not come in till morning, on account of the children coaxing him to stay. On his arrival I asked him if all were well and he said they were. I find from my children that Laura had a fit on Monday — about three hours after I left — and fell in the yard. On Tuesday she was not feeling well. Wednesday she got the breakfast, was taken with a fainting spell, went to her room, laid down on the bed and died. The tea was given to her by her sister, and she drank none of it. I believe she died of the heart disease.

Respectfully,

C. C. Cox.

— *Hays City Sentinel*, May 3, 1876.

Further adding to the confusion in this incident was a subsequent retraction of the suicide comment, but this did not shed any additional understanding of what truly befell Miss Cox.

We are in receipt of a letter from Mr. Charles Endsley [*sic*], who was stopping at Mr. Cox's when Miss Laura Cox committed suicide. In our notice of the suicide we stated that the young lady said to Mr. Endsley that she "was tired of life." Mr. E. informs us that she did not make that remark. We gladly make the correction.

— *Ellis County Star*, May 4, 1876.

Another account of retracted suicide was found in the *Ellsworth Reporter* of 1876. Whether the newspaper was negligent in researching the story or the family felt compelled to rewrite their daughter's history is unclear.

This week Ellsworth county has a story of love, poison, and suicide, the victim of which was a pure young girl, Hannah Wells, daughter of J. F. Wells, of Thompson creek. The circumstances in this sad affair are substantially as follows: Miss Wells had been working out for various families in the county, and at the time of her tragic death was employed by H. Burton, Esq. Sometime during the summer she became acquainted with a young man (whose name we have been unable to get) in the neighborhood, and a mutal [*sic*] attachment sprung up between them. Some time since he left for Ellis and through some means word reached her that he had been making remarks in relation to her, which her too sensitive nature could not brook, and it evidently affected her mind so severely that she determined to end her life. She wrote one of two letters to her mother and other friends, stating that probably when they were received she would be no more. On the day (last Friday) she decided to end her troubles, she procured a bottle of strychnine from some source, it appears in an investigation, and took enough to effect her purpose. While dying she made a statement that the young man referred to had made certain remarks derogatory to her character, and that she could not live under them. — *Ellsworth Reporter*, August 31, 1876.

I wish to correct if possible, the impressions conveyed by your article on the death of Hannah Wells. You have made a statement without any grounds whatever, and by that statement have cruelly wounded the feelings of her family. In the first place, you say she wrote two letters, one to her mother and one to her cousin, stating that when they received them she would be no more. She wrote no letter to her mother and I saw the letter to her cousin. But there was no allusion whatever to death nor any tone of despondency in it. As for any young man going to Ellis and talking about her, there is no truth in it. The only young man who had kept her company with her is here now, and she saw

him the day before she died and he says she was as cheerful as ever. As to her procuring a bottle of Strychnnine [*sic*] she had no opportunity to do it, as she had not been to town for a long time. Mr. and Mrs. Burton both state that they have never had any strychnine on the place. No one has been found who will testify that she procured any or had any opportunity to do so. She never stated before she died that any one had made any remarks deragatory [*sic*] to her character and that she didn't want to live. She cried out to God to spare her life. And kept asking for the doctor, but no doctor came. One of them has given his opinion that strychnine had been used. Is he infallible? or, does he know that strychnine is quicker in its results[*?*]. I have poisoned wolves often and I never have found one a half mile from the place the bait was taken. They run for water as soon as they feel the first symptoms and if they reach water and take a drink, they die immediately. Dr. Fox states that strychnine is very rapid in its work. Miss Wells lived eight hours after her first attack and drank water several times, but showed no more pain after drinking than before. Her mother says that she was subject to such spells. They were brought on by any excitement and also by catching cold at certain periods which are critical to young girls especially. Any woman understands the subject. It affects different ones in different ways. She caught cold, and it resulted in epilepsy, and no remedies being administered it resulted fatal to her. It is a shame to the people of her neighborhood that they should have been so ready to surmise that she poisoned herself. How ready some are to speak evil instead of good — to judge harshly instead of mercifully. Judge not lest ye be judged. If you are, let it be on the side of mercy.

H. T. ANDERSON

We are glad to present this correction to the public, we received our information from parties whom we believed responsible, and how such statements as published should become current we are at loss to determine, except to gratify that love of gossip intended to injure which some of our people delight to indulge in. ED.

— *Ellsworth Reporter*, September 21, 1876.

To compile statistics on suicides of the frontier is made more difficult by conflicting reports.

From our friend, Mr. E. W. Niles, of Dry Creek Post Office, this county, we learn of a terrible accident which occurred in the vicinity of the post office mentioned, last Sunday. Louis Saintpetre, a lad fifteen years old who had been out hunting during the day, arriving home, sat down upon a bed, having his loaded gun with him. While seated there and leaning over the muzzle of his gun, his foot must have come in contact with the trigger. The gun was discharged and its contents passed into his left side, about two inches below the heart, and ranging upward, passed through his heart. His clothing took fire and the greater part of his shirt was consumed, his body being burned in places. If the clothing and bed had been perfectly dry, it is possible that the house and contents might have been destroyed. The boy had been dead an hour or so when found. Some of the neighbors believe that the young gentleman committed suicide, as a tendency to insanity exists in the family. His mother is insane, and has been so for years. She is reported to be at the poor farm.

— *Saline County Journal*, June 19, 1879.

Last Friday, upon trial before the Probate Judge, Mrs. St. Peters [*sic*] and a young son were found to be lunatics, and the report has been sent to the Superintendent of the Asylum at Ossawatomie. It will be remembered by our readers that we gave a few months ago an account of the death by shooting of an older son of Mrs. St. Peters. It was not known at the time whether the shooting was an accident, or whether the young man had committed suicide. In view of late developments the impression is strong that the latter theory is the correct one.

— *Saline County Journal*, July 24, 1879.

Not all romantic despair led to murder, as noted in previous articles. Some lovelorn settlers killed themselves when broken-hearted.

Our community was startled last Wednesday at the announcement that George Skinner, of Ohio township, had killed himself sometime the night before. He was the last man that any one would have picked out as a probable suicide. He was young — only twenty-two years old, full of spirit and ambition. He came to Wichita, Tuesday, with a load of wheat, which he sold, and was to have returned home that day, takin [*sic*] his sister, Ines, who was in the city visiting with him. It was noticed he was drinking more or less during the day, but not enough to excite much comment. Not seeing or hearing from him Miss Skinner started out early in the evening to find him, and did find him in the rear of Ross' furniture store. He refused a [*sic*] take her home, telling her that he was not going home until morning, and that if she would remain in the city he would return Thursday and take her to the Fair. At this interview he told his sister of his troubles, which were connected with his engagement to a young lady in this county. We understand that the engagement had been broken off, and this trouble was praying on his mind and he resorted to the cup to drown his sorrows, and probably while under the influence of a frenzy increased by the stimulants he was led to take his life. It seems that he changed his mind and returned home that night, arriving there about midnight, unhitched his horses and tied them to the wagon. A young brother heard him come into the house, remain a few minutes and then go out. In the morning when it was discovered that he had not slept in his bed the family were alarmed and immediately instituted a search for him. His dead body was soon found, in a sitting posture; leaning up against a dry goods box near the straw stack, yet warm, with a bullet hole in his temple and a pistol in his hand. An empty vial which was full of laudanum the evening before, was found on the table, the contents of which he had evidently taken while in the house at midnight. . . . — ***Wichita Weekly Beacon*, October 2, 1878.**

After reading the following account, one cannot help but wonder what happened to the other players in this tragedy.

The particulars in regard to the death of Valiska Jacobs, the young lady who drowned herself last week are as follows: About

three years ago she resided with her parents in Philadelphia, Pa., who being poor and desirous of bettering their condition removed to Kansas and took a claim, leaving Valiska and two younger children until they should get located. About two years ago they prepared to follow and were accompanied by a young German shoemaker, named Herman Schulke, who was a professed admirer of the young lady. His attention was repulsive to her and she finally dismissed him and refused any conversation with him. It was then the malicious devil in his nature asserted itself and she who before was pure as an angel, was by him characterized as the vilest of the vile. About one year ago Schulke went west and Valiska Jacobs was employed as dining-room girl at the Wilson hotel, where she became acquainted with an estimable young man and in due course of time they were engaged to be married. It was said she had gone home to prepare her wedding out-fit, when the young man received a letter from her former admirer and persistent persecutor, traducing her character in a shameful manner, too proud to offer any explanation or make any defense, the engagement was broken, and likewise the heart of Valiska Jacob's life had no pleasure for her, the whole world looked dark and dreary. On last Wednesday she was in Wilson, returning home about four o'clock p.m., while her mother was milking the cows, she robed herself for death — slipped out the back way — walked a mile and a half to the river and took the fatal plunge. She was found the next morning and buried near her father's residence, where she sleeps the innocent victim of a vile traducer's persecutions.

— *Ellsworth Reporter*, October 30, 1879.

One of the most perplexing suicides is contained in the following articles. Today, these stories would be written into instant novels and movies.

On Wednesday, the 28th ult., Mrs. Seckevic, living near Palacky, this county, committed suicide by cutting her throat. A short time before she committed the act, her husband was giving his horses some strychnine, she asked him to give some to her for other use, but he did not. He went over to a neighbors soon after

and while there his little girl run to him saying that her mother had taken poison, and if he wished to see her alive he must come quickly. He hastened with all his might and just as he got in sight of his wife she cut her throat and expired in a short time. No cause was assigned for the act. Mr. Seckevic and his wife had lived a life of happiness for eleven years together and this sudden change and death of his wife was a severe blow to him and their children. They have the sympathy of the community in which they live. . . . — *Ellsworth Reporter*, June 12, 1879.

Monday morning a case of suicide near Palacky, about eighteen miles south of town, was reported to us, and on inquiry we gleaned the following facts:

Sunday afternoon between the hours of one and three o'clock, in her fathers house, Miss Anna Sayiz a young lady of twenty summers, good-looking and smart, of Bohemian descent, took her own life by taking poison. Last Thursday she was in town and was noticed by parties to have been unusually happy and high spirited, and on that day bought the strychnine she used in self-destruction. Coroner Seiber was summoned and held an inquest over the body, but nothing was developed, except that she left two letters, one to her parents and the other to her betrothed, Frank Seckavic [*sic*], whom it is said she was to marry in six months. In her letter to her parents she said, "You must excuse me, as the troubles of this world are too much; My sister knows all." She put the strychnine in some alcohol and took it in the presence of her sister, dying in the presence of all her folks.

It will be remembered that not long since the wife of Frank Seckavic [*sic*] committed suicide the same way. She was a sister of the one whose death is herein chronicled. Nothing further can be learned as to the cause that led her to commit this death blow, but that it was premeditated is evident in every action, and that the fear of death was not comparable to her troubles in this world. One more unfortunate. — *Ellsworth Reporter*, July 17, 1879.

Under present-day law, the following victim might have been saved if her lover had been prosecuted for statutory rape, taking a child for illicit purposes across state lines, or some other related crime.

At 12 o'clock on Monday last, Sarah Trueblood committed suicide in the house owned by B. F. Whitlock, on Topeka avenue near Douglas, by taking a dose of strychnine, at least that is the supposition. We believe no remains of the poison were found on the premises. Gus Melander prescription clerk in Charley Lawrence's drug store remembers selling the poison in the forenoon of that day to a young woman but didn't fully identify the corpse. The coroner was notified and proceeded to the scene of the tragedy. After empaneling a jury it was decided to have a post-mortem examination. Drs. Whitehorn, Leonard, Oakley, Jones, and McKinney being sworn in began the dissection and the jurors adjourned until three and a half o'clock p.m. The post mortem not being finished at that time, the coroner adjourned the inquest until Tuesday, at 9 a.m. From parties who have known her for years, we learn that Sarah Trueblood belonged to a respectable family living in the town of Anderson, Ind., and up to two years ago she bore a good character. She came to Wichita on the 10th day of last January, in company of B. F. Whitlock and since that time they have lived together as man and wife. Whitlock has a wife and family living in Anderson, and it seems the wife has heard of his living with his girl, and was raising a rumpus about it. We hear that for some time past, Whitlock has been trying to get her off his hand in view of the arrival of his family, but she refused to leave him. Perhaps anticipating an inevitable separation, she resolved to die as the last alternative. At the time of her death, she was just seventeen, and is represented to have been [*a*] good-hearted, simple-minded, childish kind of girl. She is one more victim to the ruthless and cruel lust of degraded humanity, and is, perhaps, more sinned against than sinning. The following letter was found in the room shortly after her decease. . . .

DARLING FRANK: — I will write you my last letter. Pet, don't grieve for me. I don't want to live. I hope you will enjoy your life with the one you love better. You are a man that I

trusted and all the man that I loved. Write to my father and tell him that I died for you. Tell Nan that she can take all my things. My new suit will be done Wednesday. She has been so good to me. She knows my trouble. Darling, you went away this morning without giving me even good day. Telegraph to Pa, and he will send for my remains; if he don't, throw me in the river. This shall be the last time I shall write my name.

On the back of the letter was found the following: "Miss Sarah Trueblood to her lover, B. F. Whitlock, Wichita, Kansas. The examination of witnesses began at 9 o'clock, Tuesday morning and was continued all day. An analysis of the contents of the stomach was made on Monday night, at the office of Dr. Whitehorn, by the latter, aided by Drs. Leonard and Oatley [*sic*] and strychnia was found. Upon the convening of the inquest on Tuesday morning, a bottle labeled STRYCHNIA, POISON, was handed to the jury, by some of the ladies living near, who said she [*sic*] found it in one of her dresses. Gus. Melander testified that though he could not positively identify her, yet to the best of his knowledge and belief, she was the same person who came into the store between 10 and 11 o'clock Monday morning, and asked for a quarters worth of strychnine, saying that she intended to poison all the dogs in her part of the city. There was no one in the house when she took poison, but soon after her screams attracted the attention of the neighbors, and Mrs. Price, Mrs. Moyer, and Mr. and Mrs. Hervey went in. They found her lying on the bed and evidently suffering intensely. She told them to take off her shoes and stockings and open her clothing. She would utter piercing screams and go into spasms of several seconds duration with short intervals of a second or two between the attacks. She said she had not taken anything and when the question was repeated several times, she would shake her head. When first approached, she asked them to send for Frank, (Whitlock). He came in a few seconds before she died. From the circumstances surrounding the case and from the testimony, so far as we heard it, she evidently poisoned herself. Her reasons for the dreadful act are perhaps to be found in her unfortunate and unhaypy [*sic*] relations with the man she was living with.

— *Wichita Weekly Beacon*, November 28, 1877.

Sarah's uncle in Indiana, upon hearing of his niece's death, penned the following letter to the mayor of Wichita.

DEAR SIR: My object in writing to you is to ascertain the particulars of one Sarah Trueblood's death. I received a telegram a few days ago, from one B. F. Whitlock, of your place, announcing her death from poison. Sir, if such be the case, he is her murderer, as he stole her from her parents and took her out there and I supposed deserted her, which led to the rash act. Sir, Mr. Whitlock left a good woman and two small children in Anderson, to grub for themselves, and since has written letters here for her to come out to Wichita, telling her that Sarah had left and had come back to Indiana, which was false, according to his dispatch. If you are a father, think what your wrath would be if some scoundrel would steal your child from you and cause her death. The girl was only sixteen years old; she is not my daughter, but is my niece. Sir, the murderer has served one term in the state prison and should swing to a lamp post for his offence. Just send him back to Indiana, and his hide won't hold shucks in twenty minutes after he lands here. If you wish to know whether my statement is correct, I will refer you to some of your own citizens; one Richard Faucet, one Oliver Smith and one James Dickson, and others I could mention, but this is enough. Sir, I will say no more till I hear from you and I hope will not be long. Yours

H. L. TRUEBLOOD

The above letter was handed to us by Mayor Hope with the request to publish it. It speaks for itself. We understand that B. F. Whitlock is making his boasts of having killed seven men during his career. He states that he told the editor of this paper that he had killed seven men and that he, the editor, would be the eighth to bite the dust, if he did not retract. There is no truth in this. He has not been in our office. We met him on the street and we must say that he behaved in a gentlemanly manner. He said we had done him some injuustice [*sic*] in our account of the death of Sarah Trueblood. We told him we had no desire at all to do him injustice and would willingly publish his vindication and told him to write it out. We still say we have no wish in the world

do him a wrong. We, however, have nothing to retract. According to his own statement he is a man that needs the attention of the law. — ***Wichita Weekly Beacon*, December 5, 1877.**

The most frequently reported cause of suicide in the frontier period involved some facet of domestic unhappiness. In many instances, the precise nature of the familial dissension was never identified, but marital discord often appeared to be the provocation that ultimately resulted in a voluntary death.

The following suicides were only ascribed to "family troubles" and "domestic infelicity." Many of these heartbreaking situations involved suicides by women, and young children often were left behind.

The community three miles north of Glasco, was shocked and horrified on Friday afternoon, March 15th, by the suicide of Mrs. Gray, wife of Charles Gray, of this (Solomon) township.

For some time past Mr. Gray and his wife had not lived as pleasantly together as people ought, and many angry words had at times passed between them; and about two weeks ago they had concluded to separate. But by the persuasion of friends they went to living together again, but old feuds were renewed, and on last Friday she expressed to a friend that she could not stand this much longer, and in the afternoon about 3 o'clock, she took down a double barreled shot gun that was heavily loaded and placed the muzzle against her side and resting the breech upon the floor, discharged the gun by placing the ramrod against the trigger, killing her instantly. She leaves a family of several children, and was a woman of about 30 or 35 years of age.

— ***Concordia Expositor*, March 21, 1878.**

Children were not only left behind, but, in the following account, subjected to unparalleled cruelty at witnessing the suicide.

Last Wednesday afternoon the town of Ellis was thrown into great excitement by the report that John Gyer, an old resident, had committed suicide. Investigation proved this report only too

true. Tired with this life, lying very low with consumption, and worried, it is said by domestic troubles, he killed himself and in a manner most horrible to contemplate. He was left alone in his house and bed Wednesday afternoon in company with his five-year old daughter, and there in the silence of his chamber devised a scheme for ridding himself of a material existence. Calling his little daughter to his side he bade her wheel up a baby carriage, standing near, and with her assistance succeeded in taking down a double barrelled shot-gun hanging over his bed. Placing his feet and the stock of the gun in the baby carriage, he cocked it, placed the muzzle in his mouth and with an iron poker succeeded in reaching the trigger and sending a charge of shot crashing into his brain. (Perhaps the baby stood by the bedside clapping its hands in innocent glee at the prospect for a frolic; perhaps she devined his intention and stood by in silent horror. We condemn John Gyer more for making his child a witness than for committing the deed itself.) Death followed instantly. Neighbors were called in and listened to the child's story, and decided that a coroner's inquest would be unnecessary. . . .

— *Hays City Sentinel*, February 16, 1878.

The following account illustrates that one of the major domestic problems prevalent on the frontier was related to the separation of some couples by great distances for prolonged periods. Often the husband left the Eastern U.S. first, and his wife and children later followed him to the prairie. One can speculate about whether the isolation drove Mr. Wilcox to suicide.

About three o'clock a.m. this morning L. J. Atkins and Samuel DePoy, of Carr Creek township, arrived in this city and reported to the Coroner that Simon Wilcox had, Tuesday evening sometime between sun-down and dark, committed suicide by blowing the top of his head off with a shot gun. In the early part of the day a neighbor, Mr. Isaac Skinner, had reported to Mr. Atkins that the said Wilcox was out of his head, or in other words crazy. Mr. Atkins went to Wilcox's house just after dinner and found him out of his head and talking incoherently about being hung and all that sort of thing.

Atkins talked to him and, to some extent, pacified him then went out and watered and fed stock about the premises. He then left Wilcox seemingly all right, and went to see Hon. Samuel DePoy, one of our County Commissioners, and consult with him as to what was best to do. It being two and a half miles to Mr. DePoy's they did not get back until dark. Then in company with Mr. DePoy and Mr. Skinner they went down to see Wilcox and make him comfortable for the night, taking with them some provisions that Mrs. Atkins had prepared.

On arriving at the house Mr. Atkins rapped, and receiving no response, opened the door and spoke again. Receiving no reply struck a match and as it blazed up a sight met his eyes that sent A THRILL OF TERROR through the hearts of all present. Wilcox sat upon the side of his bed propped up with pillows, his feet resting on the floor, a double barrelled shot gun between his feet, the muzzle near his face, the ramrod grasped firmly in his hand, the top of his head from the eyes up blown entirely off, the bed and walls of the room covered with his blood and brains. Two men who were hauling straw in a field about one fourth of a mile distant, heard the report of a gun about dark, but thought nothing of it, supposing some one to be shooting rabbits along the river, but from the fact that the suicides body was yet warm, when discovered there is no doubt but that the report they heard was the discharge of the gun that sent Wilcox out of this world.

Wilcox had lived in that neighborhood about seven years, all alone, having parted with his wife in Illinois sometime previous to his coming to Kansas, the wife and children remaining there. He has often spoken to his neighbors concerning them and particularly the children. He has been considered rather a recluse, in the neighborhood, but has always been in his right mind, and a good worker, having opened up and been farming about fifty acres of land. He had about him personal property worth from three to five hundred dollars. No one knows how many days his mind has been wandering, nor the cause of it. All that is known at this writing is that he killed himself. . . .

— *Beloit Weekly Record*, December 12, 1878.

Spouse abuse, particularly husbands abusing wives, also created a domestic atmosphere that forced some women to take the final step and end their existences. The trauma endured by these unfortunates was undoubtedly worsened by their isolation on the frontier and the lack of legal recourse and financial opportunities.

We received, last Saturday, the following particulars relative to the dreadful "taking off" of a Cloud county mother by suicide:

The deed was done on Friday afternoon, 15th inst., by Mrs. Charles Gray, who with her family resided about three miles north of Glasco. Our reporter informed us that for some years her life had been made miserable by family difficulties, her husband being cruelly abusive in his conduct toward her, which had produced a desponding state of mind and ultimate self-destruction.

On the morning of the day above-mentioned, she remarked to a neighbor upon whom she was calling that she had endured this state of things as long as she could — she wasn't going to stand it any longer; having previously come to the decision, doubtless, to send her soul, by her own hand, into the presence of her Maker.

At about three o'clock in the afternoon she took a shot gun, and withdrawing from view, put the muzzle to her heart, the butt of the weapon resting on the ground, and with the ramrod moved the trigger and fired. She was of course killed instantly, the charge tearing a hole in her body that would admit a hand.

The poor woman was about 30 years of age, and left five children to mourn her untimely death.

The community is much shocked and saddened by the event, and our reporter says the husband "takes it hard." We should think he would! — ***Concordia Empire*, March 22, 1878.**

Last week we published at the request of Mr. T. R. Sprague, of Center township, a short account of the desertion by his daughter, Mrs. Eugene Sawdy, of her home under very distressing circumstances on Thursday the 11th inst. The sequel has developed a sad case of domestic cruelty and suffering, followed by the

desperate resolve to commit suicide by drowning — leaving little children motherless and filling with woe parental hearts. We would the story might be left untold for lack of existent facts; but there can be little doubt of the death of the lady, or of the facts leading thereto, and it is our duty, though painful, to give the facts, as we have obtained them, to the public.

On the Saturday evening following Mrs. Sawdy's disappearance, we understand that a lady who belonged to a party of campers who had pitched their tent just above the bridge, found in the brush the woolen sack carried by Mrs. S. when she left home. Rolled up therein were two letters — one to her mother and one to her husband — which we publish below by request of her parents. The bundle and the information were conveyed to town at once, and word sent to Mr. Sprague of the discovery. On Sunday morning a large number of our citizens gathered at the river near the mill, and during most of the day the most earnest endeavors were made to recover the body of the poor woman, who evidently drowned her sorrows with her body in the Republican. But without success. We will state here that we are informed a something was seen floating down the river a few miles from town a few days ago, which was not particularly noticed at the time, but which, since the facts of the case have been made public, the person who saw it is inclined to think was the body of the deceased.

The letters spoken of above reveal the reasons why the poor subject of this article left home and ended her existence. Reading them, one can scarcely wonder that life was a burden to which death was preferable. They are as follows:

Dear Mother: — I will write this so you will know what has become of me. I am tired of living and being tormented to death, and prefer a water grave to such a life. I cannot endure the thought of bringing another child in this world by one that treats them and me so cruel. You do not know the talk he uses to me. I would rather die by my own hand than die by his. If he will let you, you see the children are cared for, and not let to suffer. If his mother had them I know they would be well cared for.

All I went back to him for, when we lived on our place, was to

save pa's life, for he had sworn to kill him and would have done it. And now, rather than raise another such fuss, will end my life; but treat him as well as you can, for the children's sake. I have been thinking of this for a long time. I did not know which was best, but had rather trust to you the care of the children than slave and try to have them brought up right. It is no use trying to live right with him — it is impossible. I have tried and could not for he will provoke one to anything. He has always accused me of being mean with other men, and God knows I never was guilty of such a deed. It makes no difference what he gets mad at, that is always thrown at me and I well endure it no longer.

It is no use to leave him for he would not let me have the children, and there would be no comfort left for me without them, and I can not bear to live and see them be so poorly provided for.

Ma, I always have caused you more trouble than the other children. I ask you to forgive me all, and this shall be the last. I have seen enough to make it all back. Do not blame me, for I have been driven almost wild by the man that swore to protect and provide for me, and he cares nothing for me but to slave for him, and then I get curses in return. No, I will die before I will live such a miserable life. I am in the brush waiting for night to come to let me out of this awful misery. Get him to either go where his mother is, or have her come out here to take care of the children; I know she will be kind to them. You have raised enough children, and I don't want you to trouble with them. See that he gets them some good clothes, so they can go to Sunday school — it will please them and learn them. They are the only thing I hate to die for; if it was not for them I would welcome death; but I trust them in God's care. Do all you can to have them brought up right. If he only would do better! but it is no use to think of it, he has promised so many times. Do not grieve for me, for I am better off when you read this. If there was only another way! It will not do to live any longer for I am getting cross and irritable like him, and what would the children be? I ask all the neighbors to forget any wrong inflicted on them by me. I have no hard feelings toward any one. This from ELLEN SAWDY.

GENE: — I care not how soon you get married again, but for the children's sake let your mother have them. And never be guilty of accusing your wife of having to do with other men; you have tormented me to death about that one thing. I will endure it no longer. Clothe yourself and children after you harvest, and try to pay your debts. Stand square with the world, and try to be a man. After this I will hinder you no longer. Treat the children the best you know how; do not cuss and swear at them as you have done. I will die now before there is another for you to take care of.

Have those piece blocks finished and divide them between the children. Have them quilted and lay them away for them, so they will have something left from me. Have ma finish Myrtle's clothes that are in the basket.

This is from your wife that has always been true to you.

At the top of the first page of the letter to her mother she had written: "Any one finding this, take it to T. R. Sprague's on Oak Creek or leave it at the Post Office, and give ma my coat and bonnet."

Report came to town last week, that the neighbors of Mr. Sawdy had been threatening to lynch him, and that he had disappeared. Mr. Sprague, his father-in-law, hearing of these threats, endeavored to get him to leave the country. It was thought he had left; but he returned, and on Tuesday an effort was made to arrest him by Mr. Lon. Wood, who had been deputized by Sheriff Wilson for the purpose. The attempt was not a success, however. Sawdy stood on the defense, and several shots passed between him and the officer, Sawdy firing first. Wood received several small shots in his right limb, we understand from Dr. Hewitt, who was sent to attend him but was not seriously wounded. And Sawdy escaped.

On Wednesday Sheriff Wilson and others went out to Oak Creek to arrest the desperate man, (who has, we are informed, threatened to kill his father-in-law Mr. Sprague). At the hour of going to press the Sheriff has not returned to town, and we conclude that the arrest has not been made.

— *Concordia Empire*, July 26, 1878.

What ultimately happened in this unfortunate case? Was the husband ever apprehended? Was there ever any action taken against him? Did someone take care of the children? Were the facts really as reported in the newspaper account? No further reports of Mr. Sawdy's legal standing or the status of his children were reported.

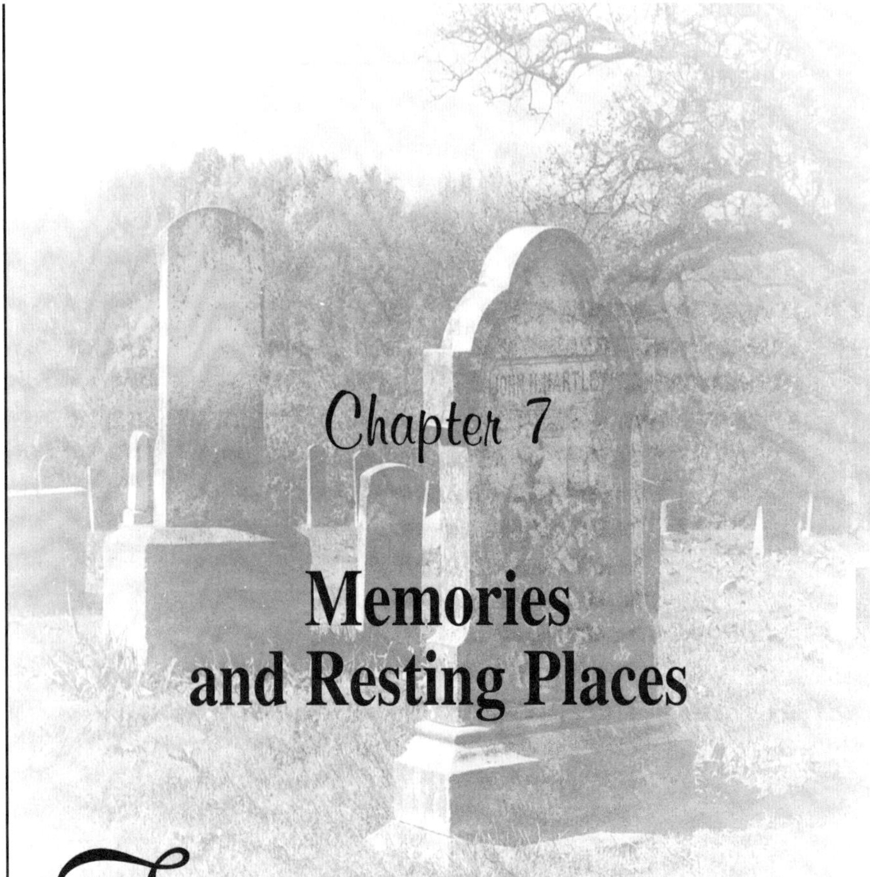

Chapter 7

Memories and Resting Places

THOUSANDS OF CEMETERIES can be found on the Great Plains. Sometimes they are fenced with the grass mowed, neatly kept by some unseen caretaker. More often the fence is broken-down or absent, head markers fallen, unreadable, or gone — graves overgrown. Occasionally, only a single grave marker or two remain to mark a dozen graves, the tombstones protruding above the grass as if to hail some passerby. Sometimes only a pile of headstones carelessly stacked in the corner of a field or propped against a lone cedar tree marks the location of an old cemetery.

In his three-volume work, *Abandoned and Semi-active Cemeteries of Kansas* (1983, 1985), Don L. Ford lists 1,120 such cemeteries. However, he also states

> . . . I know there are many more old ones out there and more being destroyed each year from lack of concern or care.

If cemeteries are to remain as lasting tributes, they need a settled community. Many of the burial grounds listed by Ford were never established — that is, no governing body had the responsibility to plat the ground, sell burial plots, keep records of the interred, and provide general maintenance.

Burial of early settlers was usually a simple affair. Unless death came when alone on the broad expanse of the prairies, they were either buried where they perished or their remains were shipped by rail "back home" to the East. For those immigrants who homesteaded, the dead were commonly buried in a plot on the family's land. Frontier townspeople usually ended up in some sort of communal graveyard. Although occasionally a citizen made a formal donation of land for a graveyard, early cemeteries simply sprung up as the need arose, usually on private property. Once burial customs were established, additional graves were added. At least initially, the cemetery was not under the jurisdiction of any governing body, and unless individual tombs were cared for by loved ones, graveyards rapidly fell into disrepair.

Formal cemeteries were seldom established during the early development of a new community. Settlers were often strangers, and setting aside land for a cemetery required planning and cooperation. In addition, for new settlers, water wells had to be dug, buildings and dwellings constructed, corrals laid out, the prairie broken, and crops planted. Cemeteries could wait.

Newspaper editors of the Plains, however, continued to urge their readers to develop a proper place to inter the dead.

It is a shameful fact that our city has no cemetery. Our dead are buried in the prairie, and there is nothing to protect their graves from the trampling of stock, and the ground is at any time liable to be converted into a hog pen. This last has even been done with a portion of land which had been used as a burying ground, and now some of our citizens connot [*sic*] find the resting place of their children. Our eastern readers, when they see this last sentence, will think us a set of heartless heathen. But we shall not on this account cease to tell of these things while they are allowed to continue. **— *Rice County Gazette*, December 28, 1876.**

Our citizens show either a wonderful lack of energy in their absence of an effort to locate and enclose a cemetery, or else perhaps a lofty supposition that death will not enter into our midst. Whatever may heretofore have been the reason, or more properly excuse, for there is no reason for delay, it is now time to act, so that if death should claim one among us, we will have a proper place to inter his remains. It is not at all to our credit that with a population of nearly three thousand persons in our county, we have no ground set apart for the last resting place of the bodies of our departed friends. We have numerous societies here, some of whom it would seem might move in this improvement. We are sure that the matter would move right along if it only had a start, for none will doubt the need. The delay heretofore is doubtless to be accounted for in the fact that each one comes here a stranger to the other, and in starting in a new country all who have had experience know that it takes about all of one's time to get fixed up around home. But admitting all that, we must take hold of this matter as one of imperative necessity, for none know how soon occupants will be in waiting for reserved places. Let some of our societies take charge of the subject, and the object will soon be obtained. — ***Valley Republican*, March 16, 1878.**

Many citizens believed that the presence of a well-kept cemetery was proof that a town had attained a level of refinement and respectability. The best cemetery was fenced and landscaped with shrubs and trees that provided a picturesque setting of white marble against a background of green. Such a place imparted tranquility and peacefulness, where one could meditate and reflect on the meaning of life and death.

One of the best proofs of refinement and true affection in a community is a beautiful cemetery. White marbles emblem the purity of the departed, the green foliage emblem their immortal freshness. We have in Ellsworth but recently established a place for those who shall die in our midst, it is plainly but neatly fenced, and is an evidence, a strong one too, of our social advancement. There are as yet happily but two or three graves; one — the most recent, that of a beloved wife, has already had reared above it, a simple but beautiful stone, this is the only one that

graces our new city of the dead, but we trust that the affection which prompted him to mark the last resting place of his life partner, may be emulated by those who have had to leave loved ones there, and that not only fair stone, but beautiful trees will be set out thickly. Do not let us leave our cemetery, as many are often left, forsaken wastes, so dreary somber cold, that no visitor turns in thither to meditate. How sad is a grave in a desert place! Some think it matters but little where we repose our earthly ashes, but to some it does. And nearly all in the silence of their own hearts surely prefer a beautiful spot where the fresh earth shall be their winding sheet, and where willows and roses shall give evidence that they are beloved in memory. The certain knowledge of this to some, robs the grave of its terrors if it is to be where love and beauty delights to linger. Let our people this fall, turn out en masse as they did in the spring at the School House grounds, and beautify the new cemetery.

— *Ellsworth Reporter*, August 17, 1876.

Despite an abundance of prairie, some graveyards were deliberately reused for other purposes. Cemeteries were sometimes moved to clear the land for its new purpose.

The old burying ground west of the city, known as Boot Hill, has been sold by the Town Company to Messrs. Fringer and Marshall, who will probably cut the land into lots and place it on the market. And thus in a short time what was once Boot Hill will be dotted with handsome residences, and the last vestige of memory of those who rest beneath the sod will fade away into oblivion. There are now about twenty of these graves, mostly the graves of persons who met death by violent means. There were a few who died from natural causes, but who possessed no money or friends to give them a more aristocratic burial place. When Gabriel blows his horn, verily it will be a motley crowd of sinners that the graves on Boot Hill send forth to attend the final judgment.

— *Dodge City Times*, May 4, 1878.

The skeletons removed from the graves on Boot Hill were found to be in a fine state of preservation, and, even the rude box coffins were as sound as when placed in the ground. The reason of their keeping so well was because they were buried on the side of the hill were the water ran off instead of soaking into the earth. Col. Straughn, the Coroner, who removed them, says they were as fine a collection of the extinct human race as he ever handled. Some were resting quietly with their boots on, while others made more pretensions to style, having had their boots taken off and placed under their heads for a pillow. Only a few of them could be recognized, as all the head-boards, if there ever were any, had long since wasted away, and nothing remained to denote where their bodies lay but little mounds of clay. They are now all resting side by side, like one happy family, at the lower end of Prairie Grove Cemetery, northwest of the city. The enchanting click of the festive revolver they no longer hear. The sighs of the Kansas zephyrs are unheeded, and the sportive grasshopper, perched on a head-board, chews his cud and chants his harvest songs without the fear of God in his heart.

— *Ford County Globe*, February 4, 1879.

In 1868, laws were passed to structure cemetery corporations, which helped alleviate the problems caused by private-property graveyards. Cemetery corporations had the power to divide the land into lots and to tax property for the purpose of general improvement. It also was mandated by statute to:

> . . . convey, by deed, or otherwise, any lot or lots of the cemetery for the purposes of sepulture. When such lots shall have been surveyed and platted, the survey and plat shall be recorded in the office of register of deeds of the county wherein the same are situated, and shall not be afterwards changed or altered. No lots shall be sold or disposed of, until such plat shall have been recorded. All the ground held by such corporation for burial purposes, while so held, shall be exempt from public taxation. Every lot sold and conveyed in such cemetery shall be

held by the proprietor, for the purposes of burial only, and shall not be subject of attachment or execution.

All such owners of lots, purchased of any such corporation, shall become members thereof, and be entitled to vote in the election of its officers, and upon any other matters, to the same extent as stockholders in other corporations. (*The General Statutes of the State of Kansas*, 1868)

That hereafter all private burying grounds, not otherwise expressly provided for by will, deed, or in the actual possession of the owner in life, shall be under the exclusive control of the probate judge of the county in which said burying ground may be situated, and it is hereby made the duty of said probate judge to commence and conduct a civil suit or suits for any damages that any other person may do or cause to be done to said burying ground, or to the fence, gates or bars enclosing the same, or any of the graves or monuments therein.

All damages collected by said suit or suits shall be used by said probate judge applied to the repairing of said burying grounds. . . . (*The Laws — State of Kansas*, 1870)

At a meeting held at the school house in District No. 31, Wm. P. Hyter was chosen chairman and Michael Moorhead Secretary. The object of the meeting was stated to be for the purpose of associating a number of persons into a corporate body, under the Statute Laws of Kansas, in order to secure and maintain a public Cemetery on the south-east corner of Section 18, Township 21, Range 13. Eden Valley Cemetery was adopted as the name for said place of burial. Motion made that the school house in Dist. No. 51 be called Eden Valley School House and be the place of business for the corporation; adopted. A constitution and bylaws for the corporation was presented, read and unanimously adopted.

— *Inland Tribune*, March 2, 1878.

Cemetery associations usually purchased land from a private individual to improve and maintain as a cemetery.

The Cemetery Association have bought ten acres of land from the Lang farm, about half a mile north of town, and will use the same for a city burying ground. The Association intend to plant a hedge around the Cemetery, and will ornament the grounds with trees, shrubs, and vines. We are pleased to learn this.

— *Cawker City Free Press*, March 15, 1879.

Lots were marked off by cemetery associations and offered for sale. In some cases, it was evident that the lots were not considered equally desirable.

The Sego cemetery association is now completed, the lots marked off and for sale. Those coming first had first choice.

— *Hutchinson News*, December 26, 1878.

At a meeting of the Board of Directors of the Prairie Grove Cemetery, held in Dodge City, Kansas, on the 28th day of August, the following resolution was adopted:

Resolved, That hereafter single graves in the Prairie Grove Cemetery will be sold at $5 each, and family lots 20x20 feet, $25 each. . . .

— *Ford County Globe*, September 3, 1878.

Some cemetery associations established committees to make recommendations about the operation and maintenance of the local cemetery.

We understand that the officers of Gypsum Hill Cemetery Association have or are about to establish the rule that they will no longer permit wooden pailings to be constructed around the graves. The recent prairie fire has certainly proved that wooden enclosures are not very serviceable.

— *Saline County Journal*, April 27, 1876.

To the Hon. Mayor and City Council of the city of Ellsworth.

GENTLEMEN: — Your committee appointed at the last meeting of the council, to examine and report on the condition of the cemetery, have attended to the duty assigned them, and beg leave to submit the following report:

With but a very few exceptions, the graves are in a sadly neglected condition, being sunken, levelled and in some cases almost invisible.

The grave of Mrs. Cadle is directly on the pathway between lots Nos. 5 and 6, there is also a grave in the pathway between lots 109 and 110.

The fence over the grave of the late sheriff Whitney, projects some three feet into the pathway and should be removed. The gateway opens directly opposite lots 79 and 91 inclusive, or thirteen lots in all, and your committee recommend that these lots be cancalled [*sic*], and the same be opened for a roadway.

Your committee further reccommend [*sic*] that the pathways on each side of the above lots and extending from No. 66 to No. 78 inclusive, and from lots No. 92 to 104 inclusive, be added to the above roadway, which would give a roadway from east to west of about 20 feet in width.

Your committe would further recommend that some suitable person be appointed to dig and take care of the graves and lots, and that lot owners should pay a small sum per annum for the maintainance of their lots.

Your committee further reccommend [*sic*] the erection of suitable hitching posts for horses, believing the cost will be more than saved in a few years by the preservation of the fence.

We also recommend that pathways be laid out at suitable distances, and also a roadway running north and south.

Your committee also reccommend [*sic*] that a committee of not less than two or more than three members of the council be appointed to take charge of the cemetery.

We also recommend that no interments be allowed unless the lot is paid for, unless the Clerk is satisfied that the party is responsible and willing to pay.

As near as your committee could ascertain, there are graves in

lots nos. 1 2 and 3 between lots 5 and 6, an appearance of one in no. 8, two in no. 13 three in no. 14, one in each of nos. 21 and 22, both of which graves are in the center of the lot, nos. 24, 25, 26, (L.A. Littlefield lot unpaid for), 66, 74, 75, between lots 107 and 110—128, 130, 131, 145, 150, 151, 152, two in 154, and one in no. 156, making 29 in all, but your committee are satisfied that there are others now invisible through neglect.

In drawing this report to a close, we cannot refrain from adding that in our opinion the site is poorly situated, and the citizens who take pride in the welfare and beauty of our city, should take action in securing a more suitable place on higher ground, ere it is too late, as in wet weather the road leading to the cemetery is nearly or quite impassable.

If, however, the citizens should decide to retain it in its present location, the relatives and friends of those now buried there, should take immediate action in the beautifying and adornments of their lots, by the setting out of trees and shubbery, and take care of the graves of the departed ones; and your committee feel that under the present circumstances, most any expenditure would be justifiable in beautifying the last resting place of our dead, one that would be an ornament to our city and a source of pride to our citizens, instead of the present sadly neglected condition of the one which we have this day inspected, and which we are unanimous in saying is a disgrace to our city.

The thanks of your committee are due to Mr. Hertzig for the free use of his team, thereby saving the city perhaps, one dollar, as one of our number was too rheumatic to walk that distance.

COMMITTEE — John G. Wiggin, George Seitz and W. H. Bradshaw.

— *Ellsworth Reporter*, December 13, 1877.

Material for grave markers was limited. Wood, although relatively scarce, was most frequently used by the early settlers. However, wooden head boards deteriorated rapidly. Limestone was also used, and although longer lasting, is soft and erodes rapidly, removing any present engraving.

Marble was the best rock to use in constructing headstones. It erodes slowly, lasting for decades and even centuries. However, marble had to be imported from the East and required considerable skill in dressing and carving. Nevertheless some of the early settlers were able to afford and use marble grave markers, which were greatly admired.

We saw a grave-stone last week which had just been cut by Fred. LaRocque. He had dressed off a block of limestone to a fine degree of smoothness, and had cut the lettering of the inscription in elegant style. Mr. LaRocque is an old and skillful marble cutter, and he has developed the fact that in the white limestone, to be found in such abundance near here, there is splendid material, if properly handled and worked, for tombstones and monuments, in the absence of financial ability to procure the costly marbles of the east. — ***Concordia Empire*, July 21, 1876.**

We were one of a party last Monday which went out to view some of the monumental work which has recently been done in our Cemeteries by Mr. Geraughty, the well-known marble man of Leavenworth. Our attention was first called to the tomb-stone which has been erected in the Catholic Cemetery in memory of the late A.J. Schwartz. The lot itself has been surrounded by a handsome, substantial stone coping, which is an innovation in cemetery fences that can be most heartily recommended. At the head of the grave stands a beautiful stone which tapers into a cross, and about the cross clings the vine which reaches out from a sheaf. The design, the work, the finish, and all connected therewith, shows that the sculptor was the right man in the right place. At the Gypsum Hill Cemetery was the elegant little monument erected at the head of the grave of little Adolf Seitz. Its sculptures are all emblematical of the little life which went out so quickly, of the purity of the childish character, of the affection of the grieving parents, of all that is intended to be illustrated by the garniture of the tomb. Mr. Geraughty could not have placed before the public finer advertisements of his skill in marble work than these two elegant monuments.

— ***Saline County Journal*, November 27, 1879.**

The cost of dying was a national concern at the time. Funeral costs varied greatly, depending on the type of coffin purchased. Although a respectable funeral could be had for $50, many burials on the frontier cost much less, and few would have been in the stylish category. The following article was published by the *Cincinnati Times* and was reprinted by various newspapers, including some in Kansas.

In these days of hard times and general financial stringency, when, to many, the problem of where to look for tomorrow's bread is almost beyond their divination; while others more affluent are chipping off the corners of expense, seeking to economize wherever opportunity offers the cost of living so occupies the mind of the average man that he has no time to think of what it costs to die. There are but few reflecting and economic people, who, if they would look over prices and figures in this line of business previous to their departure for the land of wooden overcoats, would not postpone their trip, until they could get a discount, so heavy is the burden of taxation upon those who would die after the most modern style. Of course one can be returned to mother earth in the pauper style, but few care to wrap the drapery of their couches around them and lie down to pleasant dreams if the drapery is to be cheap and thin, the couch poor and uncomfortable, and the pleasant dreams, nightmares in which one can see his friends going to their last resting place, followed by a whole string of carriages and borne in a hearse with two horses and ten plumes.

But to the philosophic mind the formal pageant of the modern "swell" funeral seems of a relic of the barbaric ages, and even the extravagant expense attending the burial of those less affluent ought to be curtailed. Now-a-days more money is spent in respectability interring a dead body than would suffice to feed a dozen live ones for months.

With such thoughts as these occupying all his surplus brain a reporter for this paper put on a new suit of sackcloth and ashes and getting his visage down to regulation funerality and standard solemnity, started out on his undertaking of pre-

senting undertaking in all its presentable phases to those who will sooner or later have to accept the disagreeable duty of dying.

Undertakers and Undertaking.

The chief thing in an undertaker's business is what is commonly called a coffin, but a coffin is a generic term, and is divided into three classes — caskets, cases and coffins. Caskets are made of iron, handsomely finished inside with silk or satin, and splendidly finished on their exterior with silver mountings and beautiful japaning. They range in price from $90 to $1,000, and are simply long iron boxes, with an iron and glass top. Cases come next, and are of light metal or the finest woods; they have the traditional coffin shape, and vary in price from $30 to $300. Last come coffins. These are of plain, common woods, and cost from $3 to $30, and are only in demand by the poorer people. Undertakers make the distinction in their talk as we have given above, but we shall not do so, simply calling the receptacles for the dead by their common name — coffin.

Generally speaking, coffins vary in price from $3 to $1,000, and the thousand-dollar variety is as handsome as the three-dollar kind is ordinary. These expensive coffins are not kept in stock by undertakers, but the manufacturer is called on when an order comes in for this quality. They are, of course, elegant and artistic, beautifully painted on the outside, with rich silver bar handles, a plate of the finest French glass for a top, and the softest white silk for internal decoration, making them as nearly comfortable as the appreciation of the contents can comprehend. The cheap coffin, on the other hand, is cheap, very cheap. Plain common wood, stained on the outside to make the Final Resurrectionist believe it is cherry or rosewood; muslin lining, no glass lid for the friends of the dead to look in upon the face, no nothing that will infringe upon the meagre profits of the generous undertaker. The material used in coffins is wood, iron, and occasionally, as in the "Oriental" casket, a light metal like zinc; the lead coffin is no more used except in rare instances. Of woods there are cherry, rosewood, walnut and poplar, the poplar stained in imitation of all the others. Rosewood is the favorite,

while cherry and walnut come in for a share of the patronage. Mohogany [*sic*] is completely out of style, and no one of taste now ever starts over the river in a mohogany [*sic*] outside. In size, coffins range from two feet, the smallest, to six feet three inches, the largest, and these are always kept in stock, anything larger or smaller being made to order.

In the trimming of coffins much is left to the taste of the undertaker, and he has almost as wide a field for the display of genius as the painter in the mixture and application of his colors. There are fifteen or eighteen varieties of coffin tacks and a great number of plates, which are in order if any one has a desire to have his coffin so ornamented. Coffin plates are stylish and are made to suit all tastes, and are usually plated, genuine silver ones only being made as ordered. Solid silver, however, is not desirable as it adds another incentive to the business of body snatching.

With coffins we naturally associate shrouds, hearses, and carriages in a line. Shrouds are popular, the majority of remains being clothed in that fashion in preference to the more rational idea of wearing the ordinary worldly clothing. Shrouds are as varied in quality and price as coffins, and range from $5 to $50, as kept for sale by the manufacturer. Hearses come in next, and are furnished, however, for one occasion only at from $7 to $10, according to the style of the vehicle. White hearses are fashionable, and are considered comme il faut at childrens' funerals. Hearse plumes are used in the same way as crape, black for the old, and white for the young.

What it costs to die.

When a corpse becomes a corpse, the first thing to do is to notify the undertaker. He comes, at once, and takes complete control of the whole matter, and does not surrender his full charge until he receipts the bill. Of course he furnishes everything, and the bill of an undertaker for a first-class funeral will read about as follows:

Coffin $300
Shroud 40

Crape	**5**
Gloves	**2**
Flowers	**50**
Hearse	**10**
Carriages (20)	**100**
Grave	**20**
Incidentals	**10**
Total	**$577 [*sic*]**

A cheaper funeral than this, of course, is procurable, and the majority of funerals are cheaper than this. A very respectable pageant may be gotten up for from fifty to seventy-five dollars, and the poor man can have the satisfaction, on that amount of outlay, to go to his grave followed by three or four carriages, in addition to those of his friends which may be in attendance.

These are only funerals, and if we should put the figures at the high notch, it would be not less that $1,000 more, or about $1,500 to die stylishly, and $600 to fade away in an ordinarily respectable quiet manner. This is in painful contrast with the friendless poor, who have a grave in Potter's Field; a plain wood box and a horse and wagon to convey them to the shore of the dark river. **— *Arkansas Valley Democrat*, December 21, 1878.**

Part of the funeral practice was the use of burial shrouds, sheet-like material that was wrapped around the body or enclosed it within the folds. Many settlers were no doubt buried in their "Sunday best" rather than the shroud.

"Death is the enemy of all." Sooner or later his icy hand will close our eyes to the world and our friends will bury us beneath the sod. — To such friends we would say that Mr. J. H. Roberts has what is kdown [*sic*] as "Ready made burial robes." These robes are neater and far more adapted as a burial suit than any that can be made for double the money. Those which he has for infants and children are so neat and pretty. He has them also for ladies and gentlemens. When you order a coffin do not fail to

order also a burial roke [*sic*] of him. Now remember this. Go now and see them. — ***Beloit Gazette*, November 10, 1877.**

Many of the settlers who died desired to be sent "back home" to the Eastern U.S. However, lack of proper preparations prior to shipping sometimes prohibited transport. Bodies either had to be encased within an airtight coffin or packed in ice.

The body of a man by the name of Burnett, who had died at Lincoln Centre, was brought here Friday to be sent by express to his former home in Ohio, but was not permitted to be shipped on account of not being encased properly, it being necessary to have a metalic coffin or packed in ice, in such a manner as would answer the same purpose. Time would not permit them to carry him back to Lincoln Centre, so the friends were compelled to bury him here, away from them. The deceased was a young man, married less than two years, with a loving wife and a beautiful little girl. He was a druggist in Lincoln Centre and was doing well in business when the fell destroyer, death, removed him from his pleasant surroundings, leaving a wife and child in sorrow. — ***Ellsworth Reporter*, November 27, 1879.**

And funerals varied from simple services attended by the immediate family and the local preacher to elaborate processionals.

The funeral of Mr. Price was very largely attended. Although his residence in this community had been of short duration, many of our best citizens had formed his acquaintance and were much pleased with his appearance and gentlemanly demeanor. The fact of his being an intimate friend and at the time of his death the guest of our esteemed fellow citizen, Mr. J. C. Connor, with the family of Hon. R. M. Wright, at Fort Dodge, was of itself sufficient to guarantee a high regard for him from the citizens of this community. A few weeks before his death Mr. Price was elected an honorary member of the Dodge City Fire Company and the members of this organization, comprising more than

fifty of the leading men in Dodge City, did everything in their power to make the sad rites which it was their lot to perform, expressive in actions, as well as in words, of the high respect and esteem in which they held the deceased. The company was called together and dressed in their uniform, each wearing a badge of black crape on the left arm. Six of their number, Messrs. C. M. Beeson, Lloyd Smith, C. S. Hungerford, S. A. Hall, Charles Roman and Charles Campbell were selected as pall bearers. They proceeded to Fort Dodge where the friends of the deceased awaited them. After a short time spent in preparation the procession moved out toward the city bearing their mortal charge. About a mile east of the city they were joined by the balance of the company on foot. This swelled the procession to a larger size than was ever before witnessed in Dodge City. First came the Fire Company, marching in double file, their flag decked in mourning weeds and the music playing a solemn dirge, then the carriage upon which rested a square platform or frame-work, and draped all around with black muslin. On the center of this platform rested the beautiful metallic coffin, partially covered by the stars and stripes. The two black horses attached to the vehicle were lead by two firemen and the pall-bearers walked on either side. Then came the carriage bearing Mr. J. C. Connor and Mrs. R. M. Wright, the chief mourners, followed by carriages and vehicles crowded with people. The procession marched up Locust street and down Bridge street to the depot building. The casket was carrid [*sic*] to the broad platform near the building and there in the presence of several hundred people, who listened with uncovered heads, Rev. O. W. Wright performed the last ceremony previous to sending the remains to New York, where the grief-stricken parents mourn the loss of an only son. The ceremony was very impressive and many sad faces turned away after the casket was placed in its box to be ready for the evening express train. . . . —*Dodge City Times*, April 7, 1877.

Cemeteries, adjacent and within the cities and towns of the Kansas Great Plains, remain a witness to remind the living of those who have perished. So, too, the many small, abandoned graveyards remain as quiet vestiges of a bygone time. As we pass those silent gravemarkers let us reflect and ponder the dreams that were held for this prairie land by those who have gone before, remembering that we, in a short time, will add our dreams to theirs.

Chapter 8

The More Things Change . . .

NEWSPAPERS PUBLISHED DURING 1875 through 1879 provide indisputable evidence that premature death was a commonplace, albeit painful, part of everyday life on the prairie frontier. During this time, one danger — that from the native Indians — was removed, and we are no longer confronted with the aspect of death from the peoples whose land we took. Yet, as ever, the unanticipated death continues to be an unsettling part of our lives.

Interestingly, the list of contemporary causes for premature death, as reported by local and national news media, is nearly identical to the litany of violent deaths that plagued those formative years of the frontier: suicides, murders, manslaughters, accidents, and deaths from drownings, tornadoes, lightning, and fires. The methods may be somewhat more sophisticated, but the type of death remains the same. We have made some progress in holding down the toll for certain categories of deaths — such as those due to violent storms, but we have been woefully deficient in reducing the rates of others. Some, in fact, may be increasing — such as accidental deaths, particularly from motorized vehicles, suicides, and homicides.

Little progress has been made in the control of natural phenomena — the so-called "Acts of God." And thus, of necessity, people must learn to function within the constraints placed on them by the environment. Whether in 1875, or today, the vagaries of nature must be recognized and dealt with. We have modified some areas of the environment, as with air conditioning, and we have learned how to alleviate the ups and downs of agriculture through the use of irrigation and herbicides and pesticides. But we can control only to a limited extent such natural disasters as floods, tornadoes, and lightning strikes, all of which still take vast tolls of human life and property.

In meeting any new environment, an element of stress is involved. As settlers came Westward to an open prairie where the "damned wind" blew unceasingly for days on end, drought and grasshoppers could financially ruin a family in one season. Frequently one had to live underground in a dugout. Loss of hope and resultant suicides were commonplace. Yet, even today suicide rates remain formidable. Americans have overcome many of the frontier problems that led to suicide by the settler, but have replaced them with other stresses — daily pressures to succeed financially, sickness, starvation, and overpopulation.

And humans are still careless. Many of the deaths in the 1875 to 1879 period could have been prevented if the people had been more cautious or had heeded the advice of their neighbors — if they had not been in such a hurry to get somewhere or complete some task. This was particularly true in deaths caused by accidents and to a lesser extent in those from natural causes. Yet, today we are no less careless — no more careful — than those who lived on those frontier prairies. For even though most states require that young people take courses in driver training and all of us have to take examinations to obtain license renewal to operate motor vehicles, most of the vehicular accidents that lead to death are caused by inattentiveness, or carelessness, rather than mechanical failure. Likewise, most other accidents are caused by lack of foresight. It seems that regardless how we attempt to circumvent these tragedies through education, humans continue to hurry or to believe that accidents always happen to someone else.

In the frontier days, newspaper editors described deaths and the circumstances leading to them in a straightforward manner. Writing in graphic detail, the reporters left little to the reader's imagination, noting how blood dripped onto the floor or how one's anatomy was rearranged by an accident. Today, newspapers tend to edit the accounts of death and events leading thereto — perhaps because the details no longer shock and affect us, or perhaps because modern society is less inclined to openly recognize the reality and finality of death. Most of us certainly do not want some newspaper writer telling us explicitly how utterly awful some deaths are. If editors of modern papers attempted to use the linguistic style of the 1870s, exploring each step as death progressed to claim a loved one, they would probably at the very least be flooded by letters decrying such tastelessness and invasion of privacy, and often might eventually find themselves answering suit in a court of law. Yet, this aversion to graphic detail does not appear to be true for other modern media, such as television and film.

No matter how much education is provided, no matter how many support groups exist, no matter how many stress seminars are conducted, no matter how much science and technology become a part of our lives, there will always be unexpected and, frequently, violent death. Some people will not head advice, some will always be careless, and some will never master control of their personalities to conduct productive inter-personal relations with their fellow humans.

And so, perhaps, the more things change, the more they *do* stay the same.

Bibliography

Books and Articles

4th Annual Report of the State Board of Agriculture to the Legislature of the State of Kansas, for the year ending November 30, 1875 (Topeka: George W. Martin, State Printer, 1875).

Aitken, William. *The Science and Practice of Medicine*. Vol. 1 (Philadelphia, PA: Lindsay and Blakiston, 1866).

Coffin, M. M. *Death in Early America* (Nashville, TN: Thomas Nelson Inc., 1976).

Collins, Joseph T. *Amphibians and Reptiles in Kansas*, University of Kansas, Museum of Natural History, Public Education Series No. 13 (Lawrence: University Press of Kansas, 1993).

Crown, Winton L. "A Study of Indian Raids in Northwest Kansas, 1864-1878" (Fort Hays, KS: Fort Hays State University, M.S. Thesis, 1950).

Eakle, Arlene and John Cerney, eds. *The Source: A Guidebook of American Genealogy* (Salt Lake City, UT: Ancestry Publishing Co., 1984).

First Biennial Report of the State Board of Agriculture to the Legislature of the State of Kansas, for the Years 1877-1887 (Chicago, IL: Rand, McNally, 1878).

Fleharty, Eugene D. "Apply Salt, Gunpowder, and the Yellow of an Egg: The Treatment of Rattlesnake Bites by the Western Kansas Settler." *Kansas History* 21(1) (1998): 18-29.

Ford, Don L. *Abandoned and Semi-active Cemeteries in Kansas*, Vol. 1 (Dechora, IA: Anunden Publishing Co., 1983).

_____. *Abandoned and Semi-active Cemeteries in Kansas*, Vol. 2 (Salem, MA: Higginson Books, 1985).

_____. *Abandoned and Semi-active Cemeteries in Kansas*, Vol. 3 (Salem, MA: Higginson Books, 1985).

The General Statutes of the State of Kansas. 1868. Cemetery Corporations. Chapter 23, Article 15, 224. (Topeka: Printed for the State, by John Speer, Public Printer).

Guide to Public Vital Statistics. 1942 Records in Kansas. Kansas Historical Records Survey, Division of Community Service Programs, Work Projects Administration, sponsored by the Kansas State Historical Society, Topeka.

Kastenbaum, Robert, and Ruth Aisenberg. *The Psychology of Death* (New York: Springer Publishing Company, 1976).

Lamar, Howard R. *The New Encyclopedia of the American West* (New Haven, CT: Yale University Press, 1998).

The Laws — State of Kansas. 1870. Private Burying Grounds. Chapter 44, 93-94 (Topeka: S. S. Prouty, Public Printer, Printed at the "Commonwealth" State Printing House).

Miner, Craig. *West of Wichita: Settling the High Plains of Kansas, 1865-1890* (Lawrence: University Press of Kansas, 1986).

_____. *The Wichita Reader* (Wichita, KS: The Wichita Eagle and Beacon Publishing Co., 1992).

Powers, Ramon. "The Dull Knife Raid of 1878: A Study of the Frontier" (Fort Hays, KS: Fort Hays State University, M.A. Thesis, 1963).

_____. "Why the Northern Cheyenne left Indian Territory in 1878: A Cultural Analysis." *Kansas Quarterly*, 3(4) (1971): 72-81.

_____. "The Northern Cheyenne Trek Through Western Kansas in 1878: Frontiersmen, Indians and Cultural Conflict." *The Trail Guide*, XVII (3-4) (1972): 1-35.

Richmond, Robert W. *Kansas: A Pictorial History* (Lawrence: University Press of Kansas, 1992).

Socolofsky, Homer E., and Huber Self. *Historical Atlas of Kansas* (Norman: University of Oklahoma Press, 1972, 1988).

Webb, Bernice Larson. "First Homesteader and the Battle of Sappa Creek." *Kansas Quarterly*, 10 (1978): 52-57.

Kansas Newspapers

Arkansas Valley Democrat (Great Bend)
Barbour [*Barber*] *County Mail* (Medicine Lodge)
Beloit Gazette
Beloit Weekly Record
Cawker City Free Press
Clyde Herald
Concordia Empire
Concordia Expositor
Chronoscope (Larned)
Dodge City Times
Edwards County Leader (Kinsley)
Ellinwood Express
Ellis County Star (Hays)
Ellsworth Reporter
Ford County Globe (Dodge City)
Garden City Paper
Great Bend Register
Hays City Sentinel
Hutchinson Herald
Hutchinson News
Inland Tribune (Great Bend)
Jewell County Monitor (Mankato)
Jewell County Monitor-Diamond (Jewell)
Kirwin Chief
Kirwin Progress
Kinsley Graphic
Larned Optic
Larned Press
Logan Enterprise
Medicine Lodge Cresset

New West (Cimarron)
Newton Kansan
Norton County Advance (Norton)
Phillips County Herald (Phillipsburg)
Republic County Journal (Scandia)
Rice County Gazette (Sterling)
Russell County Record (Russell)
Saline County Journal (Salina)
Saline Valley Register (Lincoln)
Scandia Republic
Smith County Kansas Pioneer (Smith Center)
Smith County Pioneer (Smith Center)
Solomon City Newspaper
Spearville Enterprise
Sumner County Press (Wellington)
Valley Republican (Kinsley)
WaKeeney Weekly World
Wichita Weekly Beacon
Wichita City Eagle

Index

by Angela L. Dawdy